THE MEDIA AND THE FALKLANDS CAMPAIGN

The Media and the Falklands Campaign

Valerie Adams

MACMILLAN

First published 1986

Published by
THE MACMILLAN PRESS LTD
Houndmills, Basingstoke, Hampshire RG21 2XS
and London
Companies and representatives
throughout the world

Typeset by Wessex Typesetters
(Division of The Eastern Press Ltd)
Frome, Somerset

Printed and bound in Great Britain
by Anchor Brendon Ltd,
Tiptree, Essex

British Library Cataloguing in Publication Data
Adams, Valerie
The media and the Falklands campaign.
1. Falkland Islands war, 1982—Journalists
2. Mass media—Great Britain—History—20th
century
I. Title
997'.11   F3031.5
ISBN 0-333-40904-3 hardback
ISBN 0-333-42774-2 paperback

Contents

Author's Note

I should like to thank the Ministry of Defence for making the study possible, and the many people who have helped me. I am particularly grateful to Professor Lawrie Freedman for his invaluable advice and guidance, to Dr Mike Dockrill for access to his research material on the British participation in the Korean War, and to Eileen Bell, Joanna Connell, Jean Murphy and Margaret Long for their typing and secretarial assistance. Thanks are also due to the staff of the libraries of King's College and the Ministry of Defence, to those at the BBC and ITN who helped me find relevant material, to David Jones of the Ministry of Defence Naval Historical Branch for his assistance with the chronology, and to the many people listed in Annex A who gave freely of their time and knowledge on the subject.

Finally, special thanks to Derek Adams, who listened to (and criticised) my arguments, found material for me and gave me both practical and moral encouragement.

V. A.

Foreword

Professor Lawrence Freedman

For a military commander, information is a weapon of war. He seeks to gather as much information as possible about the capabilities, dispositions and plans of his adversary. The more he knows about the enemy's strengths and weaknesses, the more effectively he is able to plan his operations. For the same reasons the more the enemy can find out about the commander's own capabilities, dispositions and plans, the more difficult and dangerous his task. Unless, of course, the enemy can be persuaded to accept inaccurate information. Deception plays an important role in military strategy.

For this reason a military commander has an interest in accurate information being withheld and, on occasion, inaccurate information being disseminated. The media have another interest. They live off information, and scavenge for it wherever it might be found. Their reputation depends, in part, on the accuracy of the information they can obtain.

This inevitably leads to a degree of tension between the commanders and the media, especially at times of armed conflict. In practice both recognise that a line has to be drawn somewhere. It would do little for the reputation of a television programme or a newspaper if it could be accused of losing a war, or the lives of servicemen. Equally military commanders recognise that their operations, at least in a democracy, have to be justified to a sceptical Parliament and public and that in war, no news is often taken to mean bad news.

More seriously, many limited conflicts in the modern world take place against the backdrop of intense diplomatic activity in which the impressions made on allies or influential neutrals might be crucial. Assessments of relative military capabilities and performance in battle help shape the policies of other nations. In this sense information is an important instrument in the campaign for international support. The United States has now identified a branch of the diplomatic art described as 'public diplomacy', which some might think of as just a nicer word for propaganda. Part of the challenge of public diplomacy stems from the difficulty of controlling information. Strict censorship might be imposed on the media at home. But not on other nations. Military commanders and their political masters have to cope with a world in which communications are becoming easier and the expectations of a steady flow of high-quality information higher.

The Falklands Campaign of 1982 was unusual in that it was fought in one of the least accessible parts of the world. Enterprising newsmen could not just move in and out of the combat zone and then send back an instant report. News from the combat zone could be, and was, subjected to close control by the military authorities. Many of the journalists who travelled to the South Atlantic with the British task force bridled against the resulting constraints. Yet they were also in a better position to understand the risks that they too would face if the wrong information let slip.

The control exercised by the Ministry of Defence over the dissemination of information from the South Atlantic led to immense frustration in London. The supply coming through was not sufficient to satisfy the appetite of the media, which grew with the size of the 'story'. As the media became desperate for more information to fill the new slots being created in recognition of the importance of the crisis, the military wanted to talk even less. As a result, the slots became filled with speculative material, as a variety of experts sought to make sense of the information that was available. One might add that even if much more information had been available, the media would still have looked to their own and outside specialists to interpret it for their audience.

The appearance of a variety of retired military gentlemen as media experts infuriated many of their colleagues still in service and busy fighting the war. All an Argentine agent had to do was to tune in and there in front of him was an exhibition of the workings of the British military mind, carefully analysing all the options actually facing the task force commanders. This was all probably of far greater irritation to the commanders than it was of use to the Argentine. Nevertheless many military officers consider the behaviour of those who indulged themselves as commentators to be scandalous and something of a myth has developed to the effect that the speculation seriously jeopardised the British campaign. Nevertheless, the controversy itself raised a very important issue concerning the manner in which the public can be kept informed of the course of a hazardous military campaign being conducted in its name, without making that campaign even more hazardous.

In July 1982, just a month after the conclusion of the Falkland Islands conflict, the Ministry of Defence invited a number of universities to submit proposals for studies on 'the relationship in time of armed conflict between newspapers and other media and the Ministry of Defence, including the armed forces'. The Department of War Studies at King's College, London, submitted a proposal based on its areas of competence. Rather than attempt to compete with the specialist students of the media and look at the collection and dissemination of hard news during the Falklands Campaign, we proposed to examine the speculation over the course of the conflict and the future options open to the task force commanders. We were especially interested in the role played by academic specialists and retired military officers in giving substance to this speculation. At the end of the year the Ministry of Defence announced two contracts based on the bids that they had received: one to the School of Journalism at the University of Cardiff and the other to the Department of War Studies at King's College.

In designing the study, two questions connected with the media speculation were of interest. First, how well informed was it possible to be about military operations without reliance on 'leaks' from official sources? Many of those concerned about the release of sensitive information of great value to the enemy appeared unaware of just how much was available in specialist journals and works of reference. The second question concerned the accuracy of this commentary. Was it sufficient to provide a reasonable grasp of the course of the campaign for the 'interested and intelligent layman' that specialists claim to have in mind when they address the public? The answers to both of these questions would enable us to offer judgements on how commentary might be conducted in the media in future conflicts and whether there was much that the Ministry of

Defence could do about those aspects of this commentary that were considered prejudicial to national security.

Valerie Adams was the natural person to undertake this research. She had worked in the Ministry of Defence and understood how it operated, as well as having a wide-ranging knowledge of defence issues. In addition she had done some work for the House of Commons Select Committee on Defence during the course of its inquiry on the Falklands and the media and was thus familiar with the particular questions central to this study. What perhaps we had not appreciated is that she also has a capacity to achieve part-time what most people would be happy to achieve working flat out full-time. As the following pages fully illustrate, this is combined with a capacity for rigorous argument and independent judgement. The result of her work is a book that will give many of those who have been involved in the controversy over the Falklands and the media cause for thought. As Valerie Adams makes clear in her conclusion, there are no simple answers to the tensions generated by the different requirements of military commanders, political leaders, programme or newspaper editors and independent specialists. At least at the end of this lucid and balanced book they might begin to appreciate each others' problems!

Part I
The Context

1   A Freak of History

The Falklands campaign was, to say the least, an unexpected
type of war for Britain to fight in 1982. It was militarily self-
contained, limited in time, location and objective, and conducted
at an enormous distance from the UK – Port Stanley is further
away than Calcutta from London. The campaign has been
described as 'a freak of history'[1] and an 'atavistic interlude':[2] it
is certainly easy to see it as an anachronism, left over from the
colonial past. But the colonial past refuses to be dismissed from
contemporary politics – and not only those of Britain and
Argentina. Even as the fighting in the Falklands was drawing
to a close, its predominant position in the British media was
being overtaken by the conflagration in the Lebanon. Elsewhere
on the African continent – Ethiopia, Chad, Zimbabwe, Southern
Africa – the uneasy heritage of both colonial and tribal divisions
continues to make itself felt. In the Caribbean, the American
invasion of Grenada, impelled in part by the collapse of the
post-colonial government there, led to one of the most serious –
if temporary – rifts experienced in relations between Britain
and America in post-war years. Thus the Anglo-Argentine
conflict over the Falkland Islands was typical of the 'increasing
tendency towards regional disorders which cut across East–
West lines'.[3]

In other respects too, the war was not entirely unrepresentative
of what might happen in the future. Although the terrain
prohibited armoured warfare, and although the full range of
available equipment was not deployed, the weapons and kit
used in the Falklands came largely from the standard inventory.
The land forces sailed to the Falklands with materiel from their
established war maintenance reserves. The Royal Navy operated
the same ships and weapons which usually form part of NATO's
defences. The experience gained in the fighting would be valid
in other conflicts – including one in Europe. In terms of crisis
management too, the lessons of the Falklands would be

applicable to other limited wars and have implications more generally for theories of decision-making and escalation control.

In information terms – at least initially – the conflict was seen by many both within and outside the media as unique.[4] The military and the Ministry of Defence were able to exercise almost complete control over the limited number of journalists with the task force, whilst the government had a monopoly in the dissemination of authoritative news about events in the South Atlantic. Despite the advances in technology which have made the instant reporting of news from the other side of the world an everyday event, dispatches from the South Atlantic were slow to reach editors and news desks and film had to be physically transported back to the UK rather than being electronically transmitted.

In fact, the problems which led to the 'media war' were far from unique to the Falklands – such issues as the difficulty of transmitting copy, or censorship, or the alleged manipulation of the news, or the risks of speculation, all had historical precedents. Moreover, in the short time that has elapsed since 1982, a number of the same problems have already arisen elsewhere: notably in relation to the US operation in Grenada, where the media were initially debarred from the island and so from observing any part of the military action.

Many of the difficulties experienced in the Falklands were due to oversights or failures in planning, but others were not isolated episodes. Rather, they reflected a broader set of relationships within society – between MoD and the media, between the government and the governed, and between journalists and the public. In a recent book, Robert Harris, himself a journalist, claimed of the Falklands crisis that 'It *exposed* habitual abuses by the armed forces, Government, Whitehall and the media; it did not *create* them.'[5] This both oversimplifies and overstates the situation but none the less it contains an element of truth. The Falklands campaign can tell us a lot about the attitudes of the Ministry of Defence and the media and it raises issues of wider application concerning the use and abuse of information.

*   *   *

The last major mobilisation of British forces to fight a war overseas prior to 1982 had been the Suez expedition of 1956.

The Falklands War was thus Britain's first taste of a campaign fought in the full glare of modern media attention. Press interest in the various overseas undertakings by British forces in the previous decade or so had been sporadic: Oman and Borneo, for example, had received only limited coverage. The early part of the 1970s had certainly seen quite intense interest in the Army's operations in Northern Ireland, but reporting those operations was not fundamentally different from covering other domestic events potentially sensitive in political or security terms. Northern Ireland is not geographically remote from the UK; it is accessible to modern media technology and there is no machinery for censorship, although 'D' Notices could be issued if necessary.[6] There have been claims that either the military or the journalists are abusing their respective positions, but these complaints have in general referred to isolated instances rather than to an institutionalised approach.

The short three months of the Falklands War, by comparison, gave rise to severe criticism of the media by politicians, soldiers and the public. At the same time, the media's complaints about the treatment they received from the government (particularly the MoD) and the task force were so bitter that the Defence Committee of the House of Commons (the HCDC) decided even before the fall of Port Stanley to investigate the subject.[7] Peter Fiddick, writing in the *Guardian* on 20 May 1982, summed up the mood of the moment when he said of the Falklands crisis that it 'has stripped bare the relationship between the mass media, the politicians and the public in ways not seen since Suez or the Second World War'.

THE ARRANGEMENTS FOR THE MEDIA

The involvement of the media in the Falklands campaign was contentious from the start. MoD had no contingency plans for dealing with an Argentine invasion of the Falkland Islands, much less for handling the media in that event.[8] Ian MacDonald, then the MoD's acting Chief of Public Relations, caused wry smiles at an HCDC hearing when he said he remembered locking himself in his office and trying 'to think it out for 5 minutes'.[9] Clearly few listeners thought he had taken long enough. That so short a time was allowed to devise a policy illustrates better than any argument the MoD's initial failure to grasp the importance of their arrangements for disseminating information about the conflict.

At first the Royal Navy were reluctant to take any correspondents at all on board the task force ships. Fleet headquarters then allocated six places with the task force to journalists; this was subsequently raised to twelve and then, after what has been described as 'the most violent media lobbying of No. 10 [Downing Street] in recent history',[10] the number of places for reporters, technicians and cameramen was raised to twenty-nine. Task force commanders were instructed by MoD on 8 April 1982 on a list of subjects to be avoided with the correspondents, including speculation about operational plans; operational capabilities of individual units and of all types of equipment; particulars of current tactics and techniques; logistics; intelligence about Argentine forces; communications; defects in equipment.[11]

The correspondents sent their written copy back to London over the ships' military communications systems to the Defence Communications Centre in MoD. Oral reports were transmitted from ships fitted with a commercial satellite communications system (known as INMARSAT or MARISAT) directly back to the correspondents' parent organisation. At first, pictures could also be relayed back by satellite, but once the task force moved into the South Atlantic, film had to be transported back to Ascension Island (usually by ship), then either fed back by cable or flown to the UK. Once correspondents went ashore with the land forces in the Falklands their reports had physically to be transported back to the ships for transmission.[12] All copy had to be cleared with the authorities at first either in the Falklands or in London. Later MoD set up a further vetting system back in London to act as a long-stop, in case unacceptable material got past the task force censors and everything coming from the task force correspondents had to go through this second censorship.

There was, however, no formal general censorship applied to material written in the UK. The arrangements made in Whitehall for handling the press were improvised. Normally, a great deal of information is given to the media at 'unattributable briefings'. These are off-the-record sessions when officials give information to the press and answer questions relatively informally, on the understanding that the spokesmen will not be identified. (They are normally described as 'senior defence sources' or some similarly vague term.) Unattributable briefings of this kind are not to be confused with more routine background briefings at which journalists (and sometimes academics) are given a detailed briefing on a specific subject – one that may not necessarily be in the news at the time. On Ian MacDonald's advice, all non-attributable briefings ceased.

Only formal on-the-record statements were to be made, with limited question-and-answer sessions following. This was the pattern until 11 May, when some non-attributable briefings were restored. The formal statements tended to be short and factual and they frequently gave little information. They were often couched in a peculiarly cryptic and bureaucratic style. For example: when Ian MacDonald first announced the bombing of Stanley airfield on 1 May, in a raid undertaken by a Vulcan B2 aircraft from Ascension Island and by Harriers from the task force, what he actually said was that British forces had 'taken action designed to enforce the total exclusion zone and deny the Argentines the use of the airstrip at Port Stanley'.[13] It is hard to see what secrets would have been given away by a more direct statement that the airfield had been bombed. As it was, announcements like this made the media feel that MoD was being uninformative, to say the least.

The correspondents with the task force were even more unhappy about the arrangements made for them. Their evidence to the HCDC is by and large a catalogue of complaints about inadequate facilities, inconsistent censorship and downright obstruction by the Royal Navy and the MoD public relations officers accompanying the task force and although most found the land forces more cooperative they did not escape criticism. However, it was not until the campaign was drawing to a close that the correspondents with the task force were able to tell their story. The controversy over information began back in London.

There, the media made up for the lack of official information by drawing on their own sources. Alan Hooper, a serving officer in the Royal Marines, described the common perception when he wrote

The failure to brief the media off the record led to all sorts of difficulties. Unable to check on a number of facts and lacking any form of in-confidence briefing, the media reported all they saw and heard. Worse still they speculated. The result was a mass of information about ships' movements, the composition of the task force, weapon capabilities and continuous comment about the various options open to the task force.[14]

THE WAR OF WORDS

In the early stages of the conflict, the government seemed reluctant to be drawn into criticism of the media and indeed had some praise – albeit faint – for the Falklands coverage. On 18 April, when asked by Michael Marshall MP whether HMG was concerned about the 'generous' information being given away on television, Francis Pym, the Foreign Secretary, replied that he wished film extracts had a caption indicating their source (this was to identify Argentine film intended as a vehicle for propaganda rather than fact), but he went on to say, 'It is also fair to say that the correspondents who are with the task force are reporting in a way that people find acceptable.'[15]

This relative harmony was short-lived. By the end of April, serious dissatisfaction was being voiced both within and outside Parliament, by members of the government as well as backbench MPs, the military and the public. Criticism was levelled on two particular scores. The most impassioned complaints were on the grounds that some commentators were taking objectivity too far, when they appeared to be placing the same credibility in Argentine government statements as in those made by the British government. The other main cause for concern was the extent of the commentary on military matters such as equipment, capabilities and possible tactics by so-called 'armchair strategists'. These were mainly retired Service officers and defence correspondents with a few academics and professional defence analysts – the unofficial commentators. Their prominent place in the media was forecast as early as 7 April when Michael Mates MP pointed out that 'Armchair strategists and those with the wisdom of hindsight proliferate daily in an atmosphere such as this.'[16] At first, it was this unofficial commentary which bore the brunt of government complaints. On 28 April, the Prime Minister said of the commentators

'Everything they say may put someone's life in jeopardy.'[17] A few days later, John Nott, the Defence Secretary, told Parliament:

> it would be of assistance to us if retired Service officers and others would not speculate so widely on all the military options that are open to us. It would also naturally be of help to us if the BBC and other media could have rather fewer programmes of this kind because we are talking about lives, and the lives of our own Servicemen, and at the moment some of these programmes go rather too far.[18]

The intensity of attacks on the media, especially the BBC, was soon to increase. On 2 May, in the BBC2 *Newsnight* programme, the presenter Peter Snow gave an assessment of the information available from British and Argentine sources. He pointed out that so far the British sources had been proved the more accurate, and went on, 'Until the British are demonstrated either to be deceiving us or to be concealing losses from us, we can only tend to give a lot more credence to their version of events.' In retrospect, his choice of words, meant only to emphasise the credibility of the British government, can be seen to be infelicitous: at the time it provoked an outrage.

On 6 May, the *Daily Telegraph* reported complaints made by Mr John Page MP to the BBC that this programme was 'totally offensive and almost treasonable . . .' The same day, Mr Page asked the Prime Minister, Mrs Margaret Thatcher,

> to judge for herself whether she feels that the British case on the Falkland Islands is being presented in a way that is likely to give due confidence to our friends overseas and support and encouragement to our Servicemen and their devoted families.

The Prime Minister's reply was in temperate language, but it reflected widespread concern:

> Judging by many of the comments that I have heard . . . many people are very concerned indeed that the case for our British forces is not being put over fully and effectively. I

understand that there are times when it seems that we and the Argentines are being treated almost as equals and almost on a neutral basis . . . I can only say that if this is so it gives offence and causes great concern among many people.[19]

A letter from Admiral Sir Louis le Bailly appeared in *The Times* criticising the BBC for being taken in by Argentine propaganda, referring to 'the lies the BBC so naively put out in the early days of the crisis, culled from Argentine TV' and went on to describe as an 'obscenity' a BBC news report of a ship sailing to the Falklands with a hundred coffins aboard.[20] The controversy over reporting continued in the letters column of *The Times* for several weeks, fuelled by a BBC1 *Panorama* programme broadcast on 10 May which its critics claimed gave too much exposure to those who disapproved of military action in the South Atlantic. Mrs Sally Oppenheimer, for example, described the programme as 'an odious subversive travesty'.[21]

Meanwhile, the tabloid newspapers had engaged in their own conflict – a campaign of mutual vilification. An editorial in the *Sun* declared the *Daily Mirror*, the BBC (especially Peter Snow) and the *Guardian* guilty of treason;[22] in reply, a *Mirror* editorial called the *Sun* 'a coarse and demented newspaper . . . the harlot of Fleet Street'.[23]

As the campaign in the Falklands intensified, so did speculation about the likely course of military operations, and criticism of that speculation. Not even MPs were exempt: on 13 May, the Prime Minister clashed with the Leader of the official Opposition, Michael Foot, when the latter proposed that the House should have the chance to vote on whether to maintain a continued blockade of the islands, before there was any escalation of the conflict. Mrs Thatcher replied, 'We really cannot have a full debate on military options with the House making a decision. Nothing would be more helpful to the enemy or more damaging to our boys.'[24] She took up the theme again a fortnight later:

I know that my hon Friend and many hon Members are very much aware that too much discussion about the timing and details of operations can only help the enemy and hinder and make things more difficult for our Forces. In wartime, there used to be a phrase 'Careless talk costs lives.' It still holds.[25]

Media debate about the military options open to the task force was also criticised by serving officers. Vice Admiral Robert Squires RN, Flag Officer, Scotland and Northern Ireland, said,

> We have given far too much information to the enemy, particularly in terms of details of men and kinds of equipment ... When the crisis is over, I hope someone will study the question of media coverage in depth because one thing of which I am certain is that we have not got it right.

He went on to argue that the public was 'saturated' with debates, information and speculation by 'armchair experts' and added,

> I believe we have given too much information to the enemy. I hear the psychological argument for demonstrating your strength, but I am a sceptic and I believe that by this continual publicity of names and numbers and types, we are giving away far too much.[26]

The Chiefs of Staff were apparently alarmed, even to the point of questioning whether there was some way of damming up the flood of material – although they accepted the advice they received that there was not.[27]

This concern on the part of the military was aired in the evidence to the HCDC, by the former Chief of Defence Staff, Lord Lewin, and other senior officers. The then First Sea Lord, Sir Henry Leach, confirmed, in reply to a question, that he had been concerned about the media's use of recently retired officers in speculating on military intelligence and plans. He elaborated on his answer:

> ... to take for example the actual landing on islands, there were strictly limited operations and so (as indeed was done) if you say to the media 'Now they could land to the north, or to the east or to the south or to the west', then you have really covered all the options and one of them was almost certain to be the right one. The trouble is you come back to security and endangering your forces. If you allow widespread speculation like that by people who are intelligent and more or less informed on the broad circumstances that confront

you, it is inevitable that they will hit on a fairly accurate bit of speculation. It is then a matter of debate as to whether you judge the enemy has thought that through in similar vein or not, but it is open to him to obtain that information because it will emerge in, say, the next day's press and just in case he had not thought it out, he then undoubtedly would, and that sort of thing, I believe, is potentially, if not actually, highly prejudicial to the success of the operation, and it certainly occurred over this one.[28]

The media did not remain silent. Some, as already noted, tried to align themselves with the side of the angels by joining the critics, occasionally in highly abusive terms. Others sprang to their own defence or that of their colleagues. The BBC was particularly robust in defending what it saw as not merely a right, but a duty, to be as objective as possible in its reporting of the conflict. Mr Richard Francis, Managing Editor of BBC Radio, spoke of the BBC's objectivity in speeches on 11 May and 26 May.[29] Mr George Howard, Chairman of the BBC, stoutly defended that organisation in a speech on 6 May:

> Coupled with that is a determination that in war, truth shall not be the first casualty ... The public is very rightly anxious about the future, and deserves in this democracy to be given as much information as possible. Our reports are used around the world precisely because of our reputation for telling the truth.[30]

Mr Alisdair Milne, Director General designate of the BBC, gave an interview to the *Standard* on 12 May in which he roundly denounced the *Sun*'s 'treason' charge and reaffirmed the BBC's 'broad policy'. That evening, he and Mr Howard attended a meeting of the Conservative Party's backbench Media Committee where they were fiercely criticised by MPs, but refused to climb down. This appeared to be the climax of the attacks on the BBC's loyalty.

The force was taken out of many of the claims of widespread public outrage by two opinion polls. One was conducted on 13 May by Audience Selection for the BBC. It found that 81 per cent of the 1049 people questioned thought that the BBC had behaved in a responsible manner in its coverage of the Falklands crisis.[31] The second poll, conducted by Gallup for the *Daily Telegraph* on 16 May, found that overall 62 per cent of those questioned thought the BBC had reported fairly and only 22 per cent thought the BBC had been unfair. ITV fared even better.[32] Perhaps the most unexpected champion of the BBC was the Prince of Wales who, in a speech to members of the Open University on 14 May, 'contrasting the BBC coverage with that of totalitarian regimes . . . said it was made of independent personalities who were not the servants of the state machine. . .'[33] There was thus support for the view put by George Howard to the *Observer*:

> . . . I definitely take the view that the British public is sufficiently sophisticated to detect Argentine lies quite easily. I think it is also important that we should understand what is happening on the other side . . . When we speak the truth because we are the BBC, this actually helps the Government. Why are our figures about Harrier losses believed? It's because Brian Hanrahan said 'I saw them take off and I saw the same number land' – that's what went round the world and everybody believed it.[34]

Not only did the media defend the BBC, they also counterattacked, criticising the arrangements made by the MoD and the task force for disseminating information and accusing the government of attempting to manage or even manipulate the news. This criticism, boosted by the accounts of the task force correspondents, covered every aspect of MoD's handling of the press.

Christopher Wain, the BBC television defence correspondent, wrote to *The Times* pointing out that 'HMS Sheffield was sunk by a missile, not a journalist', and claiming that speculation had, if anything, been encouraged by the MoD.[35] A spate of letters and articles attacked MoD's handling of the media and defended the coverage of the crisis;[36] these culminated in a *Times* leader on 27 May which stated that 'The first, indeed the paramount interest in a democracy must be to inform the public as soon as possible about what is happening on its behalf.'

On 11 June, the HCDC's decision to enquire into 'the handling of press and public information' during the Falklands conflict was announced in the House of Commons.[37] The MoD, editors, journalists and others were invited to give evidence, and the enquiry began in July.

THE HCDC ENQUIRY: PRACTICALITIES AND PRINCIPLES

In the evidence, much acrimony was directed at individual public relations officers (PROs) – described by Max Hastings in an article he wrote in the Falklands (and which the PROs cleared) as 'mere flotsam drifting meaninglessly from ship to ship'.[38] It became clear as the enquiry progressed that the PROs had faced an impossible task. Their role was to reconcile the military penchant for secrecy with the journalists' demand for exposure. Moreover, they were concerned, as PR has consistently been in MoD, with avoiding political embarrassment to their masters. Tact and expertise might have enabled them to muddle through, but they were relatively junior people, lacking the authority, the experience, or perhaps the ability to negotiate successfully with either party – hard-bitten journalists or even harder-bitten military. For example, when the HCDC asked why no photographs had been taken of the Argentine surrender at Port Stanley, it emerged that the PRO on the spot had been too junior to gain access to General Moore to request them.

A number of problems stemmed from MoD's failure to think in advance about how the media should be handled. The urgency with which the task force set sail compounded the difficulties, as did the distances involved and the technical problems encountered. The evidence to the HCDC revealed, however, that the MoD were not solely to blame. Correspondents had frequently failed to understand the good operational reasons for the restrictions imposed on them. For example, when facilities for essential naval communications were limited, then it was inevitable that journalists' copy would also have to be restricted. It is reported that at one point about 30 per cent of the daily work load of HMS *Invincible*'s communications centre was devoted to press reports.[39] This led the Captain to insist that the reports should be transmitted at night – the slackest working period – which meant that copy missed deadlines and stories frequently appeared two days after being written. Eventually the journalists on *Invincible* were limited to 700 words each per day.

As the HCDC's enquiry progressed, much of the evidence from the media became less heated and more philosophical. In the end the HCDC's report recognised that many of the issues in dispute were trivial and, in effect, it found for the government on many of the charges. It concluded that the basic goals of information policy during wartime had been met: the campaign was successful and no serious breaches of security had occurred. The campaign had been reported and the public thirst for information met. British credibility had by and large been sustained.[40]

There was, however, a much more fundamental aspect to the HCDC's enquiry than simply looking into journalists' allegations about ineffectual public relations officers. The Committee recognised this and devoted most of a chapter of its report to the issues of principle involved. It identified two main principles: the public's right to information and the government's duty to withhold information for reasons of operational security.

The right to information is an essential feature of a democracy: in the US it is regarded as being enshrined in the Constitution in the First Amendment – the provision for freedom of speech: attempts to muzzle the press are regarded as violations of the Constitution. In the context of the Falklands, David Fairhall, the *Guardian*'s defence correspondent, summarised the requirement: 'it is vital that the public at home should not be dependent on a military view of the campaign, should not be dependent on a political view, that they should hear an independent description of what is going on . . .'[41]

The Committee was unambiguous: 'It would have been quite unacceptable if information from the South Atlantic had been withheld simply because it might have provided opposition to the Government's actions',[42] but they recognised that this could conflict with the requirements of operational security. It is in judging those requirements that the complexity of the issue becomes apparent. The HCDC identified two levels of requirement for operational security: at the minimal level, the denial of vital intelligence to the enemy; but at a more sophisticated level, they found that '

there is another view ... according to which ... there is a
more positive function: the furtherance of the war effort
through public relations if practicable. Propaganda in itself is
not objectionable and it certainly need not involve lying or
deception.[43]

The Committee found that in practice, the public were ready
'to tolerate being misled to some extent if the enemy is also
misled, thus contributing to the success of the campaign',
although it recognised the dangers for 'democratic accountability'
in such an approach.

As far as news management was concerned, the Committee's
comments were nicely balanced:

Although there may be human wisdom, as well as cynicism
in doubting the absolute integrity of the Ministry of Defence
in their timing of announcements we can only conclude that
the factual evidence against them on this count is flimsy.[44]

On the issue of misinformation, the Committee was again
generous to the MoD, although it did query the exaggerated
impression given of the damage done to Stanley airfield in the
'Black Buck' Vulcan bombing raids.[45]

THE MINISTRY, THE MILITARY AND THE MEDIA

The MoD thus emerged relatively unscathed from the HCDC's
enquiry; it stood accused of nothing more sinister than a degree
of muddle and some failures in foresight. No subsequent
evidence has emerged to suggest that the HCDC's report
glossed over any specific and serious failings on the part of
MoD: the report and the passage of time served to damp down
the last flickers of public debate over this particular issue. None
the less, the material examined in the following chapters gives
credence to the view that the difficulties encountered during the
Falklands campaign reflect a more sustained, although not
necessarily coherent, manipulation of public information.

The natural instincts of the leading players in the interaction
between military, government and media are almost inevitably
at variance. Journalists and their editors wish to publish. The

military understandably err on the side of caution in giving out information: on the other hand, each service has vested interests to protect, and publicity can be useful. Politicians wish to present themselves and the consequences of their decisions to the public in the best possible light. Civil servants on the whole prefer not to present themselves to the public at all and, in the Ministry of Defence, the sensitivity on political or security grounds of so much of the information handled reinforces a natural tendency to reticence. The result is that however it may nod in the right direction, the MoD does not by its actions acknowledge what the HCDC described as the public's 'absolute' right to know.

The problem of protecting ministers and officials while satisfying the press's curiosity is resolved in two ways: by 'approved' unattributable briefings, and by leaking material. Much leaking is intended to be helpful, but much is undoubtedly inspired by inter-service rivalry or anxiety about government plans: advance publication of planned cuts, for instance, can lead to effective lobbying and so preempt decisions, or at least make them much more difficult.[46] Thus a great deal more information may be available than is officially made public, but the means of its dissemination may be questionable. The public generally does not know its source and has no means of judging its authenticity, and neither in some cases do those publishing it. Moreover, it can and does get out of hand: stories fed to the media can get out of control and take on a life of their own.

News management can take many forms; it may serve overtly political ends, or it may have other objectives. Military and official reactions to material published during the Falklands campaign were inevitably coloured by the traditional practice of news management to 'promote' the services and the department's activities. At its most elementary level, this involves open days, charitable efforts, pushing 'local boy makes good' stories at the provincial press and so on: such activities are clearly innocuous. The problem is that 'promotion' has become endemic to the institutions concerned. A booklet prepared and published by MoD Public Relations for internal use in the Ministry of Defence states

The function of the Defence Public Relations Staff (DPRS) is to keep the public informed of Defence policy and events and of the activities of the Armed Forces by means of the press, television and radio. *At the same time the DPRS has to create a favourable climate in support of these activities by the use of the news media*, films, exhibitions and literature [emphasis added].[47]

The final sentence suggests something akin to manipulation of the news: the creation of 'a favourable climate' comes close to propaganda – not directed at an enemy in wartime, or even to maintain the morale of an embattled population, but propaganda aimed at the general public in peacetime for no clearly identified purpose.

As the HCDC pointed out, propaganda need not necessarily involve lying:[48] the MoD booklet referred to above stresses that MoD press officers do not deliberately 'mislead or misinform journalists'. But it can and does involve attempts to deflect critical comment even when the latter is merited, and to divert attention from shortcomings. It also involves presenting an 'image'. In the case of a function of state such as defence, that in itself is a political act, and one not obviously paralled by other government departments. The Inland Revenue, for example, does not seek by promoting itself 'to create a favourable climate' in support of its activities.[49] The attitude of the Ministry of Defence can be seen as developing in part from the relationship between the armed forces and the public within a democracy. The armed forces in the United Kingdom are in no sense in rebellion against democracy and indeed see their role as its preservation. At the same time, the very fact that defence of the nation is identified as the prime function of the state leads those responsible for defence to believe that its claims rise above the seemingly more trivial demands of party politics. The closely integrated structure of the armed forces means too that there is a tendency for servicemen to see themselves as a group set apart from and not properly understood by society as a whole.[50] In these circumstances it is not surprising that the forces should be both hypersensitive to criticism and eager to promote an image that will win public support and sympathy.

Leaks and unattributable briefings can provide an ideal vehicle for attempts to massage the news in this way. Moreover, the failure to identify sources means that a government line or the views of officials can be presented informally. The media are drawn into collusion with their sources; the public are outsiders to be fed appropriate information.

The system is not, however, risk free. There is clear evidence that during the Falklands campaign both official statements and leaks from government sources directly fuelled speculation in potentially damaging areas. The clearest case involved speculation about the retaking of Goose Green: official statements made on 23 May warning that British forces would advance soon led to widespread speculation about their target, which was generally agreed by the media to be the Argentine garrison at Goose Green. When the British land forces moving towards Goose Green heard reports on the BBC World Service which accurately identified their location and objective, they were outraged. This incident did much to sour relations between the military and the media.

The problems surrounding the reporting of the Falklands campaign – the practical difficulties, the mutual suspicion between MoD and media, the speculation and the management of news – were greeted at the time as if they were a new phenomenon. They prompted outraged articles and letters, even television programmes. In fact, there was nothing new about them. A brief survey of war reporting in the past forty years, and of relations between officials and media, shows that the Falklands can be set firmly within an historical context.

NOTES

Full details of books cited are given in the Bibliography.

1. Max Hastings and Simon Jenkins, *Battle for the Falklands*, p. vii.
2. Professor L. Freedman, 'The War of the Falklands, 1982', *Foreign Affairs* (Fall 82).
3. Professor L. Freedman, 'The Falklands War: Exception or Rule', paper presented to the British International Defence Studies Association, Southampton, December 1982.
4. See for example Alan Protheroe's evidence to the HCDC: *House of Commons Defence Committee First Report: The Handling of the Press and Public Information during the Falklands Conflict* (subsequently referred to as the HCDC *Report*) vol. II, Q166: 'It is very difficult to draw comparisons between the Falklands conflict and anything else that we have covered in recent years.'
5. Robert Harris, *Gotcha!*, p. 152 (emphasis in the original).

6. 'D' Notices are issued by the British government to inform the media that a given item is regarded as secret and to request that it should not be published. Compliance is voluntary, but publishing classified information would carry the risk of prosecution under the Official Secrets Act.

7. HCDC *Report*, vol. I, para 9.

8. HCDC *Report*, vol. II, Q920.

9. Ibid., Q955.

10. Michael Cockerill, *The Listener* (21 October 1982). For details of the Navy's initial plans and the way in which these changed, see the HCDC *Report*, vol. I, Chapter III.

11. HCDC *Report*, vol. I, para 54.

12. There was one exception to this when Max Hastings transmitted some copy back directly to the UK using the SAS network link to Hereford. This caused some ill-feeling among those correspondents who thought that Hastings was being given preferential treatment. It also led to some embarrassment for the MoD when Sir Frank Cooper first denied to the HCDC that the incident had occurred and had subsequently to retract his denial.

13. Reported on *The World at One* (1 May 1982).

14. Alan Hooper, *The Military and The Media*, p. 161.

15. House of Commons, 19 April, quoted in K. S. Morgan (ed.), *The Falklands Campaign: A Digest of Debates in the House of Commons 2 April to 5 June, 1982*, p. 109.

16. House of Commons, 7 April, quoted in ibid., p. 47.

17. House of Commons, 29 April, quoted in ibid., p. 144.

18. House of Commons, 4 May, quoted in ibid., p. 189.

19. House of Commons, 6 May, quoted in ibid., p. 218.

20. *The Times*, 10 May 1982.

21. House of Commons, 11 May 1982, quoted in Morgan, *The Falklands Campaign*, p. 231.

22. *Sun*, 7 May.

23. *Daily Mirror*, 8 May.

24. House of Commons, 13 May, quoted in Morgan, *The Falklands Campaign*, p. 236.

25. House of Commons, 27 May, quoted in ibid., p. 326.

26. Speech to the British Legion, reported in *The Times*, 29 May 1982.

27. Reported by Neville Taylor in interview with the author, 25 February 1983.

28. HCDC *Report*, vol. II, Q1425.

29. Speeches to the International Press Institute in Madrid on 11 May and to the Broadcasting Press Guild in London on 26 May respectively.

30. Speech to the Chartered Building Societies Institute, London, 6 May 1982.

31. Harris, *Gotcha!*, p. 89.

32. Reported in the *Daily Telegraph*, 17 May 1982.

33. Reported in the *Guardian*, 15 May 1982.

34. *Observer*, 16 May 1982.

35. *The Times*, 17 May 1982.

36. For example, in the *Financial Times* on 12 May, the *Guardian* on 14 May and 15 May, the *Observer* on 30 May 1982.
37. House of Commons Official Report (Hansard), 11 June, col. 168W.
38. Quoted in Harris, *Gotcha!*, p. 137.
39. Ibid., p. 35.
40. HCDC *Report*, vol. i, para 117.
41. Ibid., vol. ii, Q1344.
42. Ibid., vol. i, para 21.
43. Ibid., vol. i, para 25.
44. Ibid., vol. i, para 96.
45. Ibid., vol. i, para 100.
46. An interesting sidelight was thrown on the attitudes of senior officials to leaks by a *World in Action* programme on 26 March 1984. The programme dealt with the controversy surrounding the prosecution of a junior Foreign Office official, Miss Sarah Tisdall, under Section 2 of the Official Secrets Act, following her leaking of classified documents to the *Guardian*. When asked 'Is the unauthorized leaking of official material acceptable?', Sir Frank Cooper replied, 'Never!' He went on, however, to deny that the disclosure by senior officers of government plans or intentions constituted a leak, which he defined as 'a deliberate betrayal of a specific piece of information'. Elaborating on this, Sir Frank distinguished between the theft of documents and the disclosure of 'concern' about government intentions where no such theft occurred. He did however admit that the line between the two was 'very fine'.
47. *MOD and the Media: A Brief Guide to Defence Public Relations* (MOD Public Relations, 1983).
48. HCDC *Report*, vol. i, para 25.
49. Veteran journalist Chapman Pincher does not however single MoD out for criticism in his book *Inside Story*, where he states that 'Despite the common belief that Britain is free from censorship, from state control over newspapers and political tyranny over journalists, attempts are repeatedly made by politicians and civil servants acting on their behalf to suppress news or present it in a warped manner favourable to them. News management is regularly exercised through the large public relations and press departments operated by Whitehall' (p. 208).
50. These arguments are fully developed by a number of commentators, for example, Professor S. E. Finer's *Man on Horseback*; Shelford Bidwell, *Modern Warfare*; John Ellis, *The Sharp End of War*.

2   Reporting the Wars

A former colonel in the Royal Marines tells of an incident which occurred in Tanganyika in 1964. His men had just taken up their positions along the coastal road when he received a radio call from an obviously worried junior officer: 'Sir, a journalist has arrived. Shall I arrest him?'[1] On this occasion the pressman escaped being clapped in irons, but the lieutenant's reaction to the media's presence at a sensitive operational time was far from untypical. Kitchener, both in the Sudan and subsequently, rarely disguised his suspicion and dislike of newspaper men.[2] During the First World War, reporters were not allowed to the front until June 1915; and then were kept firmly under the control of the military with strict censorship being applied.[3] The Royal Navy refused to embark journalists on warships – Winston Churchill, at the time First Lord of the Admiralty, is quoted as saying 'A warship in action has no place for a journalist.'[4] Similarly in the Second World War, the Royal Navy decided against taking reporters to sea on operations, although this ruling was later relaxed a little.[5]

SECOND WORLD WAR

The HCDC report in 1982 distinguished between the requirements for control of the media in a limited campaign and in a total war such as the Second World War when, it acknowledged, the threat to the security of the nation limited the public's basic right to information.[6] It is clear that during the Second World War the government was actually far from happy that the media were being effectively controlled. This unease was expressed at the highest levels. In his memoirs Lord Reith records a number of occasions when ministers, especially Lord Halifax, criticised the BBC and reports that in Cabinet, in November 1940, 'Churchill spoke [of the BBC] with great bitterness: an enemy within the gates; continually causing trouble; doing more harm than good.'[7] Lord Reith also recalled criticism by Churchill of the press: in March 1940, he told Reith that the country was not taking the war seriously. He blamed the Service Departments for their failure to release news but 'it was abominable, he added, how some newspapers behaved'.[8]

The government's criticism of the press and radio was particularly directed at the interpretative and speculative commentary; thus on 1 January 1941, Sir Winston Churchill called for 'a new intensive drive' to secure secrecy including 'Renewal of the cautions issued a year ago against gossip and talk about Service matters' and complained that 'The newspapers repeatedly publish – with innocent intentions – facts about the war and policy which are detrimental. Where these have not been censored beforehand, a complaint should be made in every case.'[9] Fifteen months later, problems of this kind were continuing to exercise both Churchill and Roosevelt. The latter wrote to Churchill: '. . . we are both menaced by the so-called interpretative comment by a handful of gentlemen who cannot get politics out of their heads . . .'[10] A few days later, Churchill wrote to the Minister of Information:

> It should surely be possible to point out to the newspaper proprietors or to the editors that before articles are printed advocating specific operations or drawing attention to dangers attaching to particular places, the Military Adviser to the Ministry of Information should be consulted . . . For instance, supposing that it were desirable for us to occupy Bear Island or Spitzbergen, articles advocating this would make the operation far more dangerous to our troops . . . When operations are intended or in progress, surmise is just as bad as leakage. The enemy does not know that it is not leakage . . . I get little comfort from the theory that so much is written that the significance cancels itself out. The enemy is very intelligent . . . All is carefully sifted and worth collating at some length.[11]

It is claimed that some at least of the speculation was originally inspired by the government and that the risks of doing this were dramatically exposed in Operation 'Overthrow', launched in 1942, in which the Germans were to be convinced by a deception campaign that France was going to be invaded. This was intended, in part at least, to distract attention from the invasion of North West Africa. The BBC warned that the coastal regions of occupied France were likely to become a theatre of operations and repeatedly instructed the French to await instructions before rising to support an invasion. Speculation began to mount in the British press and radio, and in other countries. Consequently, German troops at Dieppe were in a high state of readiness when the Allied forces – mainly Canadians – landed there on 19 August 1942, and were repelled having suffered enormous losses.[12]

A year later, in July–August 1943, the media were allegedly again being encouraged to speculate that an invasion of Europe was imminent.

> ... stimulated by calculated leakages from PWE [Political Warfare Executive] correspondents and broadcasters did more than speculate about an imminent invasion. The United Press told the word: 'An unofficial source states that the Allies will move against Germany by the autumn and the race for Berlin is on with Anglo–American forces poised to beat the Russians. Signs multiply that the Allies may land in Italy and in France within the next month.'[13]

The BBC announced that liberation was about to begin. Their broadcast and other reports of this kind were reported worldwide, with the result that the resistance movements in Europe embarked prematurely on a series of attacks on the occupying forces and Nazi supporters. Eventually the PWE were forced to take editors into their confidence, explaining to them the need to keep the Germans in a state of uncertainty without leading to a premature rising in occupied Europe. Once this explanation had been given, apparently the comment and speculation stopped.[14]

Later, in 1944 as D-Day approached, security was tightened up even further, with censorship of the press, monitoring of letters and phone calls by servicemen and officials, and restrictions on travel. Churchill was in part persuaded to these draconian measures by Captain Basil Liddell Hart, the military writer, who 'showed him that it was possible to have made reasonably accurate deductions about Allied intentions between June 1943 and February 1944 simply by reading the main British and American newspapers'.[15] Not only speculation, but also actual reporting continued to be a cause of contention: there was apparently continuing tension between the BBC and the military over the reporting of operations in North Africa in 1942 and 1943, and in Normandy in 1944 and 1945.[16] Thus even in total war, where the government had ostensibly the means of controlling the media, that control was not entirely effective.

KOREA

At the outbreak of the Korean War in 1950 there were five newspaper reporters in Korea and one radio reporter. The numbers were soon to increase: by late August 1950, there were 271 correspondents from 19 countries covering the war.[17] The Army had done little to provide for communications, transportation or accommodation for the war correspondents. Initially only one line from Korea to Tokyo was made available to the press by the military. Rather than queue for hours to use this line, which was apparently of poor quality, newsmen would fly to Tokyo to deliver their material and then return to Korea. At one stage Rutherford Poats, a United Press correspondent, tried using carrier pigeons to get his material to Tokyo: one pigeon apparently took eleven days to make the journey. By late August, however, the situation had improved, with telephone and sometimes teletype lines available at Divisional Headquarters, so that 'On good days Korea copy reached Tokyo anywhere from one to six hours after it was filed.'[18] Even so, radio reporters lacked the personnel and equipment to report fully, while television film had to be flown back physically to the United States and normally took several days to get there.

In addition to all these problems, General MacArthur's press chief, Colonel Marion P. Echols, was hostile to the media. Echols ordered two correspondents, Tom Lambert of Associated Press and Peter Kalischer of United Press, to keep out of Korea, on the grounds that they had filed dispatches giving 'aid and comfort to the enemy'. When challenged to give his reasons,

Echols referred to a Lambert report quoting a GI who criticised the inadequate equipment given to the soldiers and said that some dispatches by Kalischer also 'made the Army look bad'. When approached, MacArthur denied knowledge of the decision, and revoked it.[19] A few days later he had to reverse a decision by another subordinate Commander, Lieutenant General Walton H. Walker, when the latter banned veteran war correspondent Marguerite Higgins from Korea on the grounds that he feared for her safety on the front line.[20]

At first there was no formal system of censorship operating in Korea. The British government was less than happy about this; on 4 July 1950 the Prime Minister Clement Atlee minuted the Foreign Secretary Ernest Bevin expressing concern about possible publicity relating to the movements of British troops; he suggested asking editors to exercise discretion and that the possibility of censorship should be raised with General MacArthur.[21] A few days later, Sir Avery Gascoigne, head of the UK Liaison Mission in Korea, reported back to London that Colonel Echols had sent a telegram to Washington urging the War Department 'to impress on senior press representatives in Washington the vital need for exercising the utmost discretion in publishing Korean war news'.[22] In fact, the UK issued a 'D' Notice covering the composition of the United Kingdom forces to be sent to Korea, and this was complied with by the British press. None the less, the Chiefs of Staff were reported to remain concerned at the failure of the US press to be 'equally discreet'.[23]

The American military were also unhappy about the open comment in the press. General Walker 'complained bitterly' about the lack of security in Tokyo: 'he was hard put to it to discover the strength and disposition of the enemy forces whereas those of his own were published to all and sundry . . .'[24] MacArthur did not want censorship, which he described as 'abhorrent'. He believed it was the journalist's responsibility to ensure that reports were balanced and gave nothing away.[25] The press, however, were not pleased at having this role thrust upon them, particularly since it was becoming increasingly apparent that the US military objected to any articles which criticised the conduct of the war, or reported on the sometimes poor morale of the US forces. *Time* commented that 'What particularly irked the correspondents was that MacArthur's aides seemed to make no distinction between military security

and military prestige.'[26] Moreover, the press were concerned
that while they could quite rightly be criticised for exaggerating
American losses in Korea, this had happened because
MacArthur's staff had refused repeatedly to provide regular
briefings which would enable the media to assess the reports
they got from the front.[27] In July the magazine *Broadcasting*
reported that the issue of censorship

> . . . arose into sharper focus last week among broadcasters,
> press association correspondents . . . and legislators on
> Capitol Hill, some of whom 'erupted' over public disclosures
> involving American troop movements.[28]

Apparently the correspondents began to demand censorship so
that they would have 'uniform guidance'.[29] It seemed, not
surprisingly, unfair that they should be required to exercise
their own judgement and then be criticised when it differed
from that of the military. Moreover, even the military were
inconsistent in publishing details of troop movements and
equipment.[30]

By August, the situation was beginning seriously to concern
both senators and the Army. UP's Robert Miller had already
been reprimanded for stories from the front line giving details
of operational plans. In the first week of August, Bill Costello, a
CBS News presenter, reported the landing of the 2nd Infantry
Division at Pusan while it was still in progress. He had picked
the story up from a UP dispatch, but beat the afternoon
editions of the newspapers. The dispatch originated with the
International News Service's Bureau Chief in Tokyo, Howard
Handleman, who defended his violation of an agreement to
await an official release on the grounds that since there were
two bands waiting at the dock to meet the division, its arrival
was hardly secret. The next day, again following INS reports,
Associated Press announced the arrival of the 1st Marine
Division in Korea nearly twenty-four hours before it actually
happened.[31] Speculative commentary about the conduct of the
war ranged wider than troop movements. By September 1950,
widespread conjecture about (and indeed advocacy of) a
possible preemptive nuclear strike against the Soviet Union
reached such a pitch that President Truman found it necessary
to speak out publicly against this idea – a situation that was to
be repeated in the Vietnam War.[32]

During the autumn of 1950, friction between the authorities and the media increased. Correspondents at the front continued to be outspoken in their criticism of the conduct of the campaign and in their emphasis on the shortcomings of the US forces. In the UK, the Chiefs of Staff were worried about the publicity given to details of military operations,[33] while they and the Foreign Office were less than happy about General MacArthur's predilection for talking to the press. The Foreign Office drew attention to 'the undesirability of the UN Commander letting himself go in political communiques and interviews' and the subject was to be raised by the Prime Minister when he visited Washington.[34]

By mid-December, the British liaison headquarters in Tokyo were reporting the persistent uneasiness felt by UN Command and by 'responsible correspondents' about coverage of the war.[35] General Robertson, the Australian Commander-in-Chief, urged that censorship be introduced. On 11 December, Colonel Echols issued a directive containing four rules: there should be no stories about planned or current movements; correspondents should not relate enemy movements to UN military boundaries or weaknesses in UN positions; there should be no reports about the effectiveness of specific items of equipment; and the operations of friendly troops should not be reported, except in general terms and then only when they were in continued contact with the enemy.

On 18 December, a meeting between the US Defense Secretary, George Marshall, and twelve senior media representatives agreed that 'The security of information from the combat area is the responsibility of the military'[36] – a sharp reversal of MacArthur's earlier approach. This resolution was interpreted by MacArthur as permitting the establishment of a strict regime of censorship which came into effect on 20 December 1950 when the Public Information Section of the UN Command established a Press Advisory Division to 'assist correspondents in [news] matters relating to the Korean situation'. All reports on Korean operations originating in Tokyo or Korea were to be submitted for screening.[37]

On 9 January 1951, more detailed rules covering reporting were promulgated. All news stories originating in Korea had to be cleared by HQ Eighth US Army Korea (EUSAK). Military officers were not to be quoted except where specifically authorised.

The presence of American troops at a particular location was not to be referred to unless it was known that 'the enemy has established this as a fact'. Movements, plans and the effects of enemy bombardment were not to be revealed. Censorship was applied not only to factual military information which might help an enemy, but also to that which might injure morale or embarrass allies.[38]

These rules, however, covered only material written in Korea. No restrictions were imposed on reports written in the United States or the UK and for some time there continued to be a fair volume of material which was either speculative or critical of operations and, in the UK press, of MacArthur. Some speculation was prompted, albeit unintentionally, by official statements. For example, at a press conference on 15 February 1951, President Truman let himself be drawn to comment on the 38th parallel, that the question as to whether the UN forces would cross it remained an open one.[39] Other articles and editorials concerned the long-term prospects for the war; some of these posed not only security but also political and diplomatic problems in South Korea and in negotiations with the Chinese.[40] None the less, by the middle of 1951, after MacArthur had been removed from command, relations between the military and the media seem to have improved and the stringent regulations imposed at the beginning of the year were gradually relaxed. Subsequently, the two parties came to a better understanding of each other's requirements and the conflicts between them lessened. Senior officers talked to the press more freely about the progress of the war; censors explained the reasons for their decisions.[41] Moreover, the war was ceasing to be a front page story: by the autumn of 1951,

> As casualty lists became shorter the Korean conflict tended to fade from the public consciousness, events in Korea lost their place on the front page of daily newspapers; and in weekly news magazines those events sometimes received less than a single column . . .[42]

In these circumstances, the scope for animosity between soldier and correspondent was much reduced.

The early part of the Korean War offers a number of parallels to the arrangements for covering the Falklands campaign. In

Korea, lack of preparation and foresight led to inadequate provision for the media, who were in consequence hostile to the military. Failure to draw up an overall concept for censorship led to subsequent recriminations as material was published which the correspondents believed was acceptable in security terms, but which the military saw as dangerous. Moreover, because adequate official briefings were not available, the media broadcast inaccurate reports and they failed to observe agreements about withholding information. The Korean War was, however, more sensitive politically, in both domestic and international terms. It also went on for much longer than did the Falklands campaign, allowing the UN Command to revise and develop its policy for handling the media. The reports emanating from the front led rapidly to a growing sense of unease, and eventually to the imposition of strict censorship. MacArthur's view that the press should be their own censors is one that few of his military counterparts shared then or would now. In their report on censorship, the study group set up by the British government after the Falklands campaign commented:

> We do not doubt that most journalists would exercise self-censorship when lives and the interests of their own country were at stake ... But in our view, and in that of some journalists themselves, they cannot always identify precisely the information that would be of use to an enemy ...[43]

The introduction of a formal system of censorship with clearly-defined rules seems to have provided a framework within which the press and the military could learn to work with each other.

SUEZ

The close relationship which had made Britain one of America's staunchest allies in Korea was to be put to its most severe test by the Suez crisis. At the time of Suez, no formal system of censorship was introduced in the United Kingdom but 'informal guidance was given to editors by means of what was termed a "pseudo D Notice" requesting them not to publish certain types of information which might compromise "D-Day".'[44] In military terms, the Suez campaign was so brief that there was only the most limited time available for comment and speculation. In any case, the controversy over the political and diplomatic aspects of the crisis dominated all reporting and discussion. None the less, during the two and a half months leading up to the ceasefire on 9 November, there was a steady stream of reports about troop movements and unit strengths accompanied by speculation about operational plans. On 4 September, for instance, *The Times* reported that two French merchant vessels with 2000 troops aboard had left Marseilles the previous day and went on: 'This and similar news gives strength to reports here that 5,000 French troops will be in Cyprus by the end of the week.' On 30 October, *The Times* reported that several hundred parachute troops had been brought back to Nicosia from anti-terrorist operations in the Cypriot countryside, that naval vessels had sailed 'to take part in "a communications exercise" in the [Eastern Mediterranean]' and that the Royal Marine Commandos had been placed on twenty-four hours' stand-by. Clearer warning of impending events could hardly have been given. On 1 November, the *Daily Express* reported current operations: 'Substantial allied forces were at sea last night but cannot be expected to reach Egypt until early this morning . . .'

There was a black-out on news, but even this prompted speculation. The *Daily Express* published an article by Air Marshal Sir Philip Joubert, who had been a radio commentator during the Second World War. He suggested that one reason for the official silence was that an attempt might be underway to win local air superiority by air attacks on Egyptian airfields.[45]

Sure enough, the next day's *Times* reported that the Egyptian air force had been nearly destroyed and that if it was out of action the main prerequisite for a seaborne invasion had been fulfilled. Landing operations, it was suggested, would be 'militarily feasible' at the weekend.

These reports appeared when operations were at their most vulnerable. The land forces were embarked at sea; despite the military commanders' misgivings, an airborne assault was planned to go ahead even though it would be twenty-four hours before the seaborne landings could take place to support the initial attack.[46] Yet the Egyptians were given clear warnings of what was to come, without any obvious and public signs of concern on the part of the British government or the commanders in the field.[47] One reason for this may well have been that it served precisely to support political endeavours – no one actually wanted to fight over Suez. Nasser was perceived to be engaging in a kind of brinkmanship; the threatened use of force was intended to call his bluff.[48] Once the RAF had bombed Egypt, however, this argument must have been weakened, unless it was assumed that Egyptian casualties would undermine, rather than strengthen, Nasser's resolve.

Perhaps the clue lies in the *political* controversy surrounding the operation: so intent was the government in dealing with the opposition to its overall policy that relations with the press were a side issue. Whatever the reasons, the Suez affair forms an interesting comparison with relations between the media and Whitehall in the Falklands. Speculation at the time of Suez was accurate, timely, widespread and detailed; there is a prima facie case for thinking it could have put lives and operations in jeopardy to a far greater extent than in the Falklands and yet it appears to have aroused little or no public anxiety.

BORNEO

Suez was a very public affair by contrast with the Borneo campaign, which appears amost unique in the annals of modern war reporting: it is one of the rare occasions when the troops involved complained that they were receiving insufficient media coverage.[49]

The British involvement in military operations in Borneo lasted from December 1962, when 2000 British troops put down an uprising in Brunei, until 1966 when, following the overthrow of President Sukarno, Indonesia finally relinquished her claim to North Borneo, and began to mend fences with Malaysia. By October 1963, there were some 4000 British forces in Borneo, while at the height of the campaign British and Commonwealth troops operating in Sarawak, Brunei and Sabah numbered some 17 000.[50]

Clearly this represented a quite major military commitment: for example, although some 25 000 servicemen and civilians were directly involved in Operation Corporate, only 10 000 British troops actually landed on the Falklands. Moreover, Borneo was not a short-term operation: by autumn 1963, it was clear to journalists and to military commentators that insurgency could continue for some time.[51] It might therefore have been expected that there would be sustained reporting and detailed analysis of the objectives and progress of the British campaign. This was not the case. This was probably due in part at least to official reticence: the Beach Report on censorship gives a general description of the kind of measures applied by the British government in 'low intensity' operations, including Borneo:

> The military authorities have attempted to withhold as much sensitive information as possible by controlling access to information and activities ('security at source'); whenever the operation was particularly sensitive, cover stories have been invented to mislead the opponent; and occasional appeals have been made to the media not to disclose operationally damaging information.[52]

To take one example, *The Times*, like other newspapers, seems to have relied very largely on official statements for its reporting of the campaign. The great majority of its reports were written either by journalists based in London or by *The Times'* correspondents in Kuala Lumpur and Singapore. Occasionally special correspondents made visits to Borneo and produced more detailed reports, but these were rare. There is no evidence of a greater public demand for material on the military aspects of the campaign. Judging by letters to *The Times*, and indeed by the reporting and editorials in that newspaper, such interest as there was focused on the political background to the campaign, and on relations between the new federation of Malaysia and her neighbours.

There are a number of possible reasons for this. First, Borneo followed the Malaysian campaign and was just one of a number of other similar, more dramatic conflicts. British, or even European, civilians were barely affected by it. There was terrorism in Cyprus, Algeria and Aden, decolonisation and the Rhodesian unilateral declaration of independence in Africa, while a number of countries elsewhere also gained independence. The various negotiations which followed the Cuba crisis were underway; nuclear weapon tests and the possibility of a test ban were recurring topics. The US and Soviet space programmes were burgeoning; so was the American commitment to Vietnam. There were plenty of exciting domestic events to fill the newspapers as well – the Profumo affair, the election of a Labour government in 1964, the 1960s 'pop culture'. Borneo had much to compete with in news terms.

Neither was Borneo an easy campaign to report. Operations took place in the dense jungle, often out of radio contact even with the local headquarters for days at a time. The only ways to move were on foot, by water or by helicopter. Reports of operations could only be filed once the reporter had access to reasonable communications – in Kuching, for example. The jungle was hot, wet and uncomfortable, and waiting for an operation to start could involve standing waist deep in muddy water for hours at a stretch. Moreover, most operations took place at section and platoon level – involving well under 100 men, and often well under fifty. They were thus very small-scale; the large numbers of troops involved reflected the frequency rather than the size of operation: for example, in one period of eight weeks, 45 Commando Royal Marines made 305 major night patrols,[53] but none of these involved set battles. So, to report the campaign from the Borneo hinterland would have been physically difficult, time-consuming and, in media terms, relatively unproductive. The kind of account a reporter might give a patrol could have differed little from the short official statements regularly issued by Far Eastern Command – all the reporter could have added was 'colour'.

There are also grounds for thinking the British authorities might have been content with a low-key media approach, for several reasons. First, the soldiers themselves, when on patrol, would probably have been reluctant to have the responsibility of looking after a civilian on any but the odd occasion. Jungle warfare requires training and skill; reporters would have been a liability. Second, the British assistance to Brunei and then Malaysia was not enthusiastically endorsed by the world community as a whole. Indonesia's claim that Britain was conducting a colonial war received a sympathetic reception in some quarters, and the British were clearly sensitive to this – hence, for example, their pressure on the Sultan of Brunei to introduce a greater degree of democracy. Finally, the British were concerned that the publicity given to their operations should be discreet: there was some domestic political controversy over the British presence – and over the delicate 'hearts and minds' campaign which was proceeding steadily, with good results; operations were being kept low-key; the cross-border operations (of dubious legality under international law) were not arousing public controversy.[54]

In their evidence to the HCDC on the Falklands, the BBC suggested that the government deliberately suppressed information.[55] This may have been the case, but even so, it seems extraordinary that there should not have been more sustained analysis of, for example, the tactics employed on both sides, or the relationship between Indonesian terrorist and political activity in the light of theories of guerrilla warfare. Some British measures were indeed quite innovative and vital to the success of the campaign – for example, the decentralised forward deployment of helicopters in support of the 'front line' troops and the use of guerrilla-style ambushes to defeat the enemy using his own tactics.[56] Others – such as the 'hearts and minds' campaign – reflected the years of experience gained in Malysia. The whole concept of small-scale operations and ambushes, paralleling the terrorists' own tactics, should have been of immense interest at a time when the United States was taking very different measures in Vietnam. Yet there was little analysis or interpretation of the British operations in Borneo.

By January 1964 a (short-lived) ceasefire had been declared, but when despite this the Secretary of State for Defence announced plans to strengthen British forces in South East Asia[57] this seems to have given rise to no particular comment. By that summer, the campaign had intensified: the reporting of it had not. The media continued to report operations as they were announced in official statements. A report in *The Times* that some of the British troops involved doubted the value of what they were fighting for gave rise to no passionate correspondence – nor even mild controversy, so far as can be judged from the letters column. The same edition of *The Times* was able to print photographs from Borneo with the caption 'Indonesian military operations against the Borneo territories of Malaysia have moved into a new and potentially dangerous phase', with no further explanation of what this phase entailed.

Given the limited coverage accorded to the Borneo campaign, it is interesting to note how much concerned the Special Air Services Regiment – the SAS. The SAS of the 1980s is almost notoriously shy of publicity. Members of the regiment are not generally photographed or identified in the media, and relatively little publicity is given to its operations. This secrecy adds to the political impact of SAS counter-terrorist operations.

During the Borneo campaign at least, the SAS seem to have been much more relaxed about publicity. Reports described organisation, training plans, roles and operations.[58]

The reporting of the Borneo campaign seems to have been controlled by the military but in such a way as to be broadly acceptable to the media. There was no censorship, and when journalists were given facilities to visit the commanders and troops in the field, they were talked to freely. On the other hand, the media were dependent on the military to get to the scene of operations and to interpret the questions for them. There was no great pressure for detailed or intensive reporting and analysis of the campaign, nor did the press question the rationale and effectiveness of operations. Such commentary as there was appears to have been accurate, sympathetic to the military and not much inclined to speculate about tactics. Controversy centred rather on the British involvement in general, on some of the political aspects of the campaign and on such things as the enforced movement of the Chinese population out to new homes, in order to deprive the clandestine communist organisation of shelter and support.[59] So while the government attitude to speculation and comment on the military aspects of Suez appears to contrast sharply with its concerns in the Falklands campaign, in the case of Borneo it is the media which seem to have stepped out of character.

VIETNAM

Borneo, with its British residents, its police stations, head-hunters and long-houses, seems light-years away from Vietnam. Yet a number of commentators pointed to the confrontation in Borneo as a potential Vietnam;[60] the low-key British tactics and eventually the internal troubles which beset Indonesia prevented the conflict from escalating in the way that was to devastate so much of neighbouring South East Asia. A detailed analysis of the media coverage of the Vietnam War is not within the scope of this study, but Vietnam deserves a brief glance because of its importance, in the context of the Falklands, as a source of military perceptions about the effects of war reporting on both military and public. There is a widely held view that the media lost the Vietnam War for the United States. 'For the first time in modern history the outcome of a war was determined not on the battlefield, but on the printed page and, above all, on the television screen . . .'[61] Depicting the horror of war on television, runs the argument, exposed the civilian population to material from which it is normally protected and, in so doing, 'it was crucial in shifting the emphasis from fact to emotion'[62] and leading to public pressure to end the war. There is evidence that the commanders of the British task force were at least conscious of this argument.[63] It is, however, open to challenge. If the war is unpopular anyway, then detailed reports on losses may well reinforce public dissatisfaction. But what if the public believes the war is worth fighting? News of casualties, and even pictures of them, may actually strengthen the public's determination to fight on, so that lives shall not have been lost in vain. Two American academics have established that those who watched TV news regularly during certain periods of the Vietnam War 'frequently express a higher regard for the military and a greater support for defence spending . . . than those who watch TV news infrequently'.[64] This would seem to bear out the adage that there's no such thing as bad publicity. None the less, the common perception of the media's role in Vietnam remains that it let the United States down.

The arrangements made for the media in Vietnam were mentioned several times in the evidence to the HCDC. Vietnam was held up as an example of a war where reporting was assisted rather than hindered by official and military attitudes.[65] In fact, relations between the military and the media were often far from smooth. In 1963, when relations between the American press and the Executive were already at a low ebb following the Cuba crisis, American newsmen were described by the US Mission in Vietnam as 'handmaidens of the foe' for their failure to endorse US support for the Diem regime.[66] General Westmoreland considered imposing censorship and decided against it only on grounds of practicality. The Joint US Public Affairs Office (JUSPAO) was charged with arranging press accreditation, trips to theatres of operations and so on, and by 1968 this was 'an extremely helpful even luxurious center for newsmen'.[67] None the less, official briefings were unhelpful and often misleading; the description by one correspondent of their 'guarded obscure prose' could equally well have applied to the Falklands.[68] Communications inside Vietnam were slow and difficult and, even with military transport, getting to the combat zone could take time and stamina.[69] Although there was no official censorship, a set of fifteen rules was laid down for journalists to prevent the enemy from learning about tactics, troop movements, casualties or other useful information.[70]

The absence of censorship and the provision of facilities for correspondents to get a story did nothing to damp down comment and speculation. Peter Braestrup records that Ambassador Bunker and General Westmoreland were instructed on the need to put into perspective 'the dire prognostications of the commentators'.[71] Braestrup's account reveals the way in which speculation can become a newsworthy event in itself – first it is reported, and then debated, until it becomes confused with reality. For example, speculation about the use of tactical nuclear weapons to relieve the besieged American troops at Khe Sanh (which seems to have had some substance to it) apparently originated with an anonymous phone call to a Senate committee. Official refusal to speculate on the subject or to deny the rumour was taken as confirmation that it was planned. Debate on the issue became so intense that President Johnson had to call a press conference, specifically to deny that any recommendation for the use of nuclear weapons had been put to him.[72]

There was widespread comment on the detailed conduct of the war – the US networks presented eighteen film reports from Hue during the fighting for that city in February 1968, each with detailed commentary on the action shown on film.[73] There seems little doubt that some of the comment and speculation at least risked inhibiting or damaging US operations.[74] An analysis provided for the US Army states:

> . . . we run into a fundamental problem in the conduct of US military-strategy options. That is the inherent conflict between a free and democratic American society and the need for security in the conduct of US military operations . . . Our experiences in Vietnam indicate what a serious problem this can become. Although there was no instance where the news

media jeopardized *tactical* security and surprise, the very nature of their craft makes it almost impossible for them to preserve *strategic* security and surprise.[75]

At least one journalist had his accreditation temporarily suspended for failing to preserve secrecy: John Carroll of the *Baltimore Sun* was banned from reporting from Vietnam for sixty days, following publication of the information that the US was planning to abandon Khé Sanh. Carroll claimed that the Vietcong and North Vietnamese were well aware of the move long before his article appeared.[76]

The widespread comment and interpretation came under fire not only from officialdom, but also from some of the more seasoned war reporters. In 1966, Hanson Baldwin of the *New York Times*, wrote in *The Reporter*:

> Some of the correspondents in Saigon simply are not capable of adequately reporting military operations and some of the TV reporters have delivered generalized editorial judgments that they have neither the competence nor the knowledge to sustain.[77]

Peter Braestrup concluded that the press had failed to convey to the American public an accurate understanding of what had happened. Thus the commentary which should have fulfilled a useful purpose failed in its objective because it was inaccurate. So despite the provision of lavish facilities and despite the freedom of access allowed to correspondents, relations between the military and the media in Vietnam were not without friction.

NOTES

1. Private conversation with the author.
2. Rupert Furneaux, *News of War*. There is more than one parallel between the arrangements for handling the press in Kitchener's campaigns and those in the Falklands. The correspondents who accompanied him when he was Sirdar of the Egyptian Army had to send their reports by the military telegraph; they were limited to 200 words daily. At the start of the campaign in the Sudan, Kitchener tried to limit press representation to one man who would only be allowed to report official information.

3. HCDC *Report*, vol. I, para 19. In his article 'Getting the Story: Some Facts about War Correspondents', A. E. Sullivan wrote that in 1914 'the Government had realized that trustworthy information was simply not practicable. What was far more important was not to let the public get depressed by learning the truth . . . War correspondents were allowed to see little and say less about operations. They were under the constant supervision of press officers and their source of information was the Intelligence Department at GHC. Any editor who attempted to penetrate the "fog of war" ran the risk of prosecution . . . Thus in May 1915, *The Times* was cleared of a charge of publishing a letter about the number of young men obviously *not* in the Army only because it was proved that the German Press was already aware of it.' *Army Quarterly* (January 1961) pp. 204–11.

4. Knightley, *First Casualty*, p. 87. Despite (or perhaps because of) his own experiences as a war correspondent, Churchill seems to have been generally unsympathetic to the freedom of the press. According to A. E. Sullivan he proposed early in the First World War that *The Times* should be 'commandeered' because of its indiscretions. Asa Briggs records that 'At many moments during the war relations between the BBC and Admiralty had been far from cooperative, especially when Churchill was First Sea Lord'. *History of Broadcasting in the UK*, vol. III, p. 43.

5. Knightley, *First Casualty*, p. 223. According to Knightley, the censorship applied by the Royal Navy was tougher than that of the Army and RAF. The same appears to have been true of the US Navy: see Benson P. Fraser, *The Broadcast Coverage of the Korean War*, p. 17.

6. HCDC *Report*, vol. I, para 21.

7. J. C. W. Reith, *Into the Wind*, pp. 437–8.

8. Ibid., p. 373.

9. Winston Churchill, *The Second World War*, vol. III, Appendix C, p. 635.

10. Letter from Roosevelt to Churchill, 18 March 1942 in ibid., vol. IV, p. 177.

11. Ibid., vol. IV, Appendix C, p. 757. Reith had tried to give some sort of steer to editors the previous year; he records in his memoirs an instance when he gave one editor twelve guidance points on covering the Norwegian evacuation.

12. For a detailed account of Operation Jubilee, see Anthony Cave Brown, *Bodyguard of Lies*, pp. 80–90 passim.

13. Ibid., p. 322.

14. Ibid., pp. 323–4. According to Briggs, the 'V-Campaign' which was inspired by Douglas Ritchie of the BBC as a form of morale-boosting propaganda for the occupied countries of Europe, had to be brought under control by the government because its success was leading to the risk of clashes with Special Operations Executive plans for occupied Europe. *History of Broadcasting*, vol. III, pp. 365–76.

15. Cave Brown, *Bodyguard of Lies*, p. 529.

16. Briggs, *History of Broadcasting*, vol. III, p. 42.

17. 'Covering Korea', *Time*, 21 August 1950.

18. Ibid.

19. 'Needed: A Rule Book', *Time*, 24 July 1950.

20. Ibid., also 'Last Word', *Time*, 31 July 1950. This was one argument advanced for the exclusion of the media from the US invasion of Grenada in 1983: it was received with contempt by correspondents who recalled the many occasions in the Second World War, Korea and Vietnam when journalists had shared in the dangers of operations.
21. Minute PM to SofS, 4 July 1950. FO 371/84170.
22. Gascoigne: Telegram no. 677, 16 July 1950. FO 371/84170.
23. Minute by A. S. Fordham, 28 July 1950. FO 371/84159.
24. Sawbridge Korea tel. no. 61, 9 August 1950. FO 371/84065.
25. 'Censorship Censured', *Broadcasting*, 24 July 1950, quoted in Benson Fraser, *Broadcast Coverage of the Korean War*.
26. 'Needed: A Rule Book', *Time*, 24 July 1950.
27. Ibid.
28. 'Censorship Question', *Broadcasting*, 24 July, quoted in Fraser, *Broadcast Coverage of the Korean War*, p. 81.
29. Marguerite Higgins, *War in Korea* (New York: Doubleday, 1951) quoted in Fraser, *Broadcast Coverage of the Korean War*, p. 81.
30. 'Needed: A Rule Book', *Time*, 24 July 1950.
31. 'More Chances', *Time*, 14 August 1950. Associated Press also irritated the British government. On 5 December 1950, they carried a story attributed to British informants that it had been agreed that UN forces would reinvade Korea if forced to leave in a 'Korean Dunkirk'. The story originated with the London correspondent of AP and in the view of the Foreign Office was 'pure fabrication'. The correspondent, Arthur Gavshon, was described as 'tricky and unscrupulous' (FO 371/84109).
32. John Edward Wiltz, 'The War and American Society' in Francis H. Heller (ed.), *The Korean War: A 25 Year Perspective*. This essay describes also the widespread comment and conjecture on the political implications of the war.
33. Memorandum for CIGS from COS, COS(W) 913, 7 December 1950. FO 371/84170.
34. Minute by P. Dalton, 5 December 1950. FO 371/84120.
35. Letter from H. C. Hainworth British Embassy Tokyo 289/22/50 dated 16 December 1950. FO 371/84170.
36. Mott, *American Journalism*, quoted in Fraser, *Broadcast Coverage of the Korean War*, p. 86.
37. Letter from H. C. Hainworth, UK Liaison Mission Tokyo dated 23 December 1950.
38. Headquarters Eighth US Army Korea, Information Section, Press Security Division APO 301. Memorandum entitled 'Information for Correspondents' dated 9 January 1951.
39. *The Times*, 16 February 1951.
40. E.g. 'Heartbreak Ridge', *The Times*, 11 October 1951. Correspondence on FO 731/92795 concerns reactions in Korea and China.
41. Wiltz, 'War and American Society', p. 128.
42. Ibid., p. 148.
43. *The Protection of Military Information: Report of the Study Group on Censorship*; Chairman General Sir Hugh Beach GBE KCB MC (subsequently referred to as the *Beach Report*) para 134.

44. *Beach Report*, para 62.
45. Air Marshall Sir Philip Joubert, 'What I Think', *Daily Express*, 2 November 1956.
46. Historical information taken from Hugh Thomas, *The Suez Affair*.
47. The media were perhaps less happy. According to the Beach Report, there were many problems in field censorship, with copy going astray. An Army report written shortly after Suez found a number of shortcomings in the organisation and quality of both the Army PR staff and some correspondents (*Beach Report*, paras 65 and 71).
48. In *Suez: The Double War*, Fullick and Powell state: 'There is small doubt that the extensive publicity given to the movement of ships, aircraft and men was designed deliberately to build up the tension which Eden and Mollet hoped might scare the Egyptians into submission' (p. 51).
49. 'Battle for Minds in Borneo', *The Times*, 4 October 1963. The 14th Army in Burma had made a similar complaint in the Second World War and earned the soubriquet 'The forgotten Army'.
50. H. James and D. Sheil-Small, *The Undeclared War*, p. 192.
51. See for example Major Edgar O'Ballance, 'Revolt in Borneo', *Army Quarterly* (October 1963); Anthony Harrigan, 'Borneo: Center of Crisis', *Military Review* (February, 1964); 'Guerrilla Warfare in Borneo the Main Threat', *The Times*, 20 September 1963.
52. *Beach Report*, para 75.
53. James D. Ladd, *Royal Marine Commando*.
54. In *War Since 1945*, p. 95, Field Marshal Lord Carver relates that General Sir Walter Walker asked for and received permission to carry the war over the border into Kalimantan, the Indonesian part of Borneo, and states: 'Maintaining secrecy about these operations posed many problems, knowledge of them was restricted to the minimum . . . Not only did this cause staff and public relations problems, but it was also a test of morale . . .'
55. HCDC *Report*, vol. II, p. 47. The BBC's Memorandum states: 'It seems also that the suppression of media coverage of the campaign in Borneo is regarded by the MoD as a success.'
56. For details of the tactics adopted see General Sir Walter Walker, 'How Borneo was Won', *The Round Table* (January 1969).
57. 'Conferences to follow Malaysia ceasefire: movement of British troops unaffected', *The Times*, 24 January 1964.
58. For example, *The Times*, 4 March 1964 and 21 July 1964.
59. See for example Wayland Young, 'Britain's Toy War in Sarawak', *Manchester Guardian*, 2 November 1965.
60. For example Harrigan, 'Borneo'.
61. Robert Elegant, 'Word War: Vietnam lost on front pages but not on front lines', *Soldier of Fortune* (December 1982). A detailed account of this argument is given in Hooper, *The Military and the Media*, Chapter 9, 'Vietnam'.
62. Elegant, 'Word War'.
63. HCDC *Report*, vol. II, Q1211 and 1212.
64. C. Richard Hofstetter and David W. Moore, 'Watching TV News and Supporting the Military', *Armed Forces and Society*, vol. 5, no. 2 (February

1979). A detailed critique of the kind of argument put by Robert Elegant appears in Michael Mandelbaum, 'Vietnam: the Television War' in *Daedalus: Journal of the US Academy of Arts and Sciences* (Fall 1982).

65. For example HCDC *Report*, vol. II, p. 126 (Memorandum by the *Daily Mail*) and p. 167 (Memorandum submitted by Mr Michael Nicholson, ITN correspondent with the task force).
66. Peter Braestrup, *Big Story*, p. 4.
67. Ibid., p. 17.
68. Edward Behr *Anyone Here been Raped and Speaks English?*, p. 259. See also Mary McCarthy, *Vietnam*, p. 53.
69. Braestrup, *Big Story*, p. 22.
70. 'Panels of Officers and Journalists to Review Grenada Press Limits', *New York Times*, 7 November 1983.
71. Braestrup, *Big Story*, p. 623.
72. Ibid., pp. 630ff, 641.
73. Ibid., p. 303.
74. For example, Braestrup quotes one incident in which, in a live CBS broadcast from Hue, the reporter identified a bridge which the US forces were planning to destroy.
75. Colonel Harry G. Summers, *On Strategy: A Critical Analysis of the Vietnam War* (Presidio, 1982), quoted in *Los Angeles Times*, 13 November 1983, pt IV, p. 1.
76. 'Panel of Officers and Journalists to Review Grenada Press Limits', *New York Times*, 7 November 1983.
77. Colonel William V. Kennedy, 'It Takes More than Talent to Cover a War', *Army* (July 1978).

3 Correspondents and Commentators

THE WAR CORRESPONDENT

The media report wars in two ways. The first is the straight reporting of events and impressions from the theatre of war. The second is the more detailed analysis and commentary which the media impose on the basic news. These are two separate functions, generally carried out by different people. The war correspondent reports from the front; he does not provide a detailed commentary on the war. That is the province of the defence correspondent or the specialist called in for the purpose, who may be an academic or civilian expert, but more probably will be someone with military experience – frequently a retired Service officer. While the commentators are the subject of this study, the role of the modern war correspondent bears analysis. An understanding of his priorities and problems goes some way towards explaining the controversy that arose over the reporting of the Falklands campaign.

It is clear that the modern war correspondent has the same priorities – and encounters much the same problems – as his Victorian and Edwardian predecessors.[1] His preoccupation is two-fold: to get to the story and to get the story back to his editor. In wartime, the actual scene of fighting is frequently difficult to get to either because it is remote, or because the military have sealed off routes of access, or because the journey there is too dangerous to be undertaken without military assistance. Edward Behr, in his book about his experiences as a war reporter, *Anyone Here been Raped and Speaks English?*,[2] describes his difficulties in getting to the front in the 1962 war between India and China as typical of the 'archetypal situations which keep repeating themselves generation after generation'. Philip Knightley records that the ludicrous incidents in Evelyn

44

Waugh's *Scoop*, where journalists are debarred from the front and then sent off on a wild goose chase to report on non-existent operations, were not imaginary but were based on the reality of the Abyssinia campaign.[3] More recently, the civil war in Chad and the US invasion of Grenada have shown how dependent the media can be on military assistance. In Chad, access to operations was considerably restricted by uncertainty as to their exact location, and by the lack of transport, while in Grenada, the media were simply not told about the invasion until it was fully underway and then were debarred for a time from observing operations.

Having got his story, the reporter then has to get it out to his newspaper. Behr's account is a catalogue of unreliable telex and telephone lines, interrupted transport services and unhelpful or even obstructive officials. Knightley records that for the correspondents recently arrived in Abyssinia, 'It did not take them long to find out that the filing facilities were not only primitive, but laughable as well . . . Incoming communications were, if anything, worse.'[4]

As we have seen, such problems are common in war reporting, and are only resolved (if at all) when the war continues for some time, allowing those who control communications to learn about and then arrange to meet the needs of the media. It seems that this learning process has to be gone through afresh for each war.

What of the actual content of the story which the war correspondent goes to such lengths to secure? It operates at two levels: first, as a straightforward narrative of events (either witnessed, heard about or perhaps imagined) and second, as a means to satisfy a more general public curiosity: the war correspondents tell us what it's like. In the case of the Falklands, the straightforward factual reporting caused much of the friction between the journalists with the task force and the MoD. The former wanted their stories to be scoops, preempting official announcements and making headlines. 'Colour' stories were less closely tied to deadlines, but none the less still represented every reporter's first objective – to get his story in print. Articles of this kind also ran the risk of being seen as trivial and their transmission delayed, with obvious justification in some circumstances. Captain Jeremy Black of HMS *Invincible* read to the HCDC the following copy submitted for transmission from his ship, at a time when communications were already heavily burdened: 'The page 3 girls are going to war. 50 outsize pin-up pictures each one 2 foot by 6 inches were airlifted to the Task Force and are now on their way to the Falkland Islands . . .' There was more in the same vein, then, a couple of hundred words later, the article described some of the people on board including the following:

> Skinhead Ian Walter Mitty would put the frighteners on anyone. With his close-shaved head, tattoo-covered body and heavy bovver boots he looks every inch what he is – a hard man. But Walter, 20, from Richmond, Yorkshire was near to tears yesterday when he learned that his dearest wish, to get at the Argies with his bare hands, had been denied.[5]

Some reports from the task force were however outstanding; probably the most celebrated is that by BBC reporter Brian Hanrahan, on the first Harrier raid on the Falkland Islands on 1 May 1982, when he said: 'I'm not allowed to say how many planes joined the raid but I counted them out and I counted them all back.'[6] This tells us something about the nature of successful war reporting. It's succinct; it manages to convey important information – the fact that there were no losses – without offending the censor or damaging security; and it is not so much historical as dramatic: indeed Wynford Vaughan Thomas, describing his experience as a war reporter in the Second World War, said, 'This is drama of the highest order.'[7] Behr writes

> Missing out on a war, for a reporter, is like missing out on an invitation to a particularly coveted party . . . My motive in seeing as much of the war [i.e. Vietnam] as possible was neither machismo nor a craving for camaraderie (though both elements entered into it) but a genuine curiosity . . .[8]

The continuing popularity of war stories attests to the fact that, whatever its horrors, war is exciting. Taking part in it inspires a range of emotions – fear, affection, sorrow, anger; and it accentuates human strengths – comradeship, bravery, kindness, self-sacrifice and humour. To the war reporter the most interesting aspect of war is, perhaps rightly in the scale of human values, the people caught up in it. Reporting from the Falklands bears this out. In one newspaper there were constant references to the mood of the men involved – they are jubilant, their faces show strain, or they remain calm and alert. They just have time to pick up a favourite photograph as the call to action stations sounds; they have no qualms; failure is not a word in their vocabulary. Losses are greeted with shock; the men out on the hills want to go in and get it over with; the Royal Marines celebrate victory with a snowball fight.

These are not human interest stories culled from the tabloids, but a small selection of those which appeared in *The Times* between April and June 1982. Almost every report from the task force published in *The Times* included, and even gave prominence to, this kind of material. It is the staple matter of war reporting. The war correspondent is often dependent on his military companions not only for food and shelter, but also for his information and his personal safety. He becomes caught up in their world and, not surprisingly, identifies with them to some extent at least. Christopher Wain, the television defence correspondent, wrote some years ago of the 'latent partisanship which can occur':

> No matter how detached and impartial you may believe yourself to be, I defy anyone to sit through a heavy mortar or artillery barrage or spend an hour cowering under sniper fire in a ditch and not feel a sense of identity with and therefore a certain support for your fellow sufferers.[9]

Wain goes on to point out that 'such front-line distortion can impair the reporter's ability to judge the quality of the information he receives'. Others deliberately tailor their material; Max Hastings of the *Standard* not only identified with the military but obviously saw it as his duty to be helpful:

> Most of us decided before landing that our role was simply to report as sympathetically as possible what the British forces are doing here today ... When one's nation is at war, reporting becomes an extension of the war effort.[10]

The war correspondent is usually visiting or attached to one particular unit, where he is not in a position to comment on the progress of the war as a whole. He is dependent on instant information as to what's going on, whether it's a unit briefing or the latest rumour. He can only write with any accuracy about what he sees, and he is too close to events to get an all-round view of them. Thus the war reporter gives a piecemeal picture of the war – an advance here, a loss there, a single failure in logistics. Explaining what is really happening requires different conditions – access to several sources of information, political as well as military, an understanding of the relationship between different events, an awareness of relative strengths and weaknesses. For this, the media must rely not on their man at the front, but on the material available to them for more considered analysis, away from the fog of war.

THE FALKLANDS 'STORY'

The Falklands crisis was for two months the single main news story in the British media. Other major events in both domestic and international politics were set in the context of the Falklands: How would members of the European Community react? How would members of the Organisation of American States react? How was Mrs Thatcher's standing affected? Would the Pope still visit Britain?

In the newspapers, the Falklands crisis not only dominated the headlines, but many newspapers regularly devoted whole sections to it, with some of the tabloids even developing a Falklands 'logo' to identify reports. Two major American papers, the *New York Times* and the *Washington Post*, gave the conflict lengthy coverage, with the *New York Times* in particular going into considerable detail. Falklands stories were given precedence in almost every broadcast news bulletin until the invasion of the Lebanon, and many programmes were extended to allow for more detailed coverage. It dominated current affairs programmes on both television and the radio. Neville Taylor, Head of MoD's Public Relations, described the coverage as 'saturated':[11] certainly it ran to literally millions of words. It is relevant to ask whether this was really what the public demanded.

The relationship between media coverage and public opinion does not admit of easy categorisation.[12] At one extreme the media are seen as responsible for 'agenda setting' – that is, focusing attention on particular events to the exclusion of others, thus creating a public perception of priorities. On the other hand, editors and journalists can be viewed as exercising their judgment about those priorities in the light of a common – or common-sense – perception of what is important and what is not; a perception which they would expect to be widely shared. In this latter case, the relationship appears symbiotic – the media reflect public opinion, but they also help to shape it.[13] Within the media, there seems to have been little doubt that what the public wanted was to know what was happening in the South Atlantic and why.

There appears to be some evidence of an increased public interest in the news during the conflict. The editor of the *Observer* reported that '*The Times* usually receives an average of 1,200 [letters] a week . . . This average roughly doubled during those weeks when action was in train. Similarly, the *Guardian* reports that its postbag was doubled.' He went on to say that the May sales of the *Guardian* were 50 000 up on its figures for the same month in the previous year, while those for *The Times* were also up, but less strikingly.[14] These figures, although small in the light of the population as a whole, are significant for newspapers with a relatively small circulation in an already saturated market. A comparable increase does not seem to have occurred in the sales of tabloid newspapers, but that may be explicable in the light of evidence that the proportion of the population which regards newspapers as a reliable source of news is declining. For all but socioeconomic group A, television is reportedly superseding the newspapers as the main source of information.[15] There is certainly evidence of increased viewing figures for television news. ITN's *News at Ten*, which normally attracts a viewing figure of around 14 million, actually headed the list of the ten most popular television programmes in the week following the recapture of South Georgia, with a peak audience of 17.5 million for Sunday, 25 April,[16] and David Nicholas, of ITN, told the HCDC that ITN's audiences were up averaging around 16 million a day.[17] Alan Prothero, Assistant Director General of the BBC, told the HCDC that 10 million to 12 million people were estimated to watch the BBC news bulletins at the time (as opposed to the normal 7 million to 8 million for the BBC's *Nine O'Clock News*).[18] London's theatres apparently suffered even greater difficulties in filling seats than normal because the public wanted to stay at home for the news. Certainly most people can attest to a high level of interest and expectancy during the period of the conflict. This should have been predictable: as one editor said of the First World War, 'War not only creates a supply of news but a demand for it.'[19]

It is thus not surprising that the media sought to fill pages and programmes with news and discussion about the Falklands. Much of the reporting and discussion focused on political aspects of the crisis – especially during the first six or seven weeks, when there were still hopes of a diplomatic settlement and when the Labour Party's reactions provided more evidence of dissent within its ranks. Much also focused on the human aspects – the effects of the invasion on the Falkland Islanders, the risks to them in a British counter-attack, the views of those who left the Islands, of the Anglo–Argentine community, and in due course, reports about the families of servicemen involved. Inevitably, however, much of the interest centred on the task force, whose dispatch was announced to the House of Commons by the Prime Minister on 3 April. It was natural that there should be curiosity about the role and the capabilities of the task force and it would hardly have been realistic to expect the media – and by implication the public – to restrain themselves from asking what the task force was intended to achieve and how it might accomplish its objective.

MOD'S OUTPUT

In the first place, the media appear to have looked to the Ministry of Defence to satisfy this curiosity. They were quickly disappointed. This was due primarily to MoD's concern about prejudicing the security of the operations. Some basic information about the composition of the task force was bound to be of considerable interest to the Argentines: and the British were particularly keen to keep them guessing about the precise size of the Harrier force – because it was so small, any minor Argentine intelligence error would be disproportionate in its implications. The MoD consistently refused to speculate on the likely role and activities of the task force.

This reticence was quite understandable and had a simple

explanation: in the early stages, no one in the MoD actually knew what the task force was going to be required to do. The decision to dispatch it was by all accounts taken rapidly.[20] It was a political decision, taken to further political objectives: to force the Argentines by diplomatic means to withdraw from the Falklands. Sending a military presence into the South Atlantic was one further way of bringing pressure to bear on Argentina. The government believed that it had to keep its military options open in order to avoid prejudicing negotiations or, subsequently, operations.

The point has been repeatedly made that if MoD had provided more information, the media would have used it and devoted proportionally less time and effort to running their own commentary on the conflict. This argument is implicit in Alan Hooper's assessment, quoted in Chapter 1 above; it was made to the HCDC by ITN, by *News of the World*, by David Fairhall of the *Guardian*, by Reuters, who referred to 'the inadequacy of official statements which raised more questions than they answered', and by Jon Connell of the *Sunday Times* among others; it was put to the author by producers and editors at the BBC. At first sight it may be a persuasive claim, but on reflection it can be argued to be unconvincing and even potentially dangerous.

The idea that more material from MoD would have prevented speculation is open to challenge on several counts. First because it seems beyond the bounds of credibility that MoD could have produced sufficient information to fill, for example, half of the ITN's main *News at Ten* each day and a subsequent half hour's *Falklands' Special*. It simply would not have been possible for MoD to produce the volume of material required – at least without seriously compromising the security of task force operations.

Second, even if MoD *had* produced this much material, it seems implausible (to say the least) to suggest that the media would have been content to use it all, without their own assessments and analysis. This approach may have been generally acceptable twenty years ago, in the context of the Borneo operations, although passing references in the HCDC evidence suggest it was resented even them, but it is not credible in the context of 1982. Sir Frank Cooper implicitly recognised this when he suggested to the HCDC that off-the-record briefings by MoD would have led to more rather than less speculation.[21] This brings us to a further counter-argument. The dangers of allowing governments to monopolise the means of news dissemination are obvious: the result can only be a practical suspension of democracy. During the Falklands campaign, and particularly when their coverage of the war came under fire, the media were, quite rightly, anxious to stress the importance of their independence and objectivity. Against that background the following comments made to the HCDC by ITN, make interesting reading:

> in our view, through lack of imagination, great opportunities were missed for the projection of single-minded energy and determination by the British people in their support of the Task Force ... Flair in high places could have led to a nightly offering of interesting, positive and heart-warming stories of achievement and collaboration borne out of a sense of national purpose.[22]

There is no suggestion that ITN would have reported anything but the truth; none the less, this kind of approach must surely rank as soliciting propaganda and inviting governments to practise news manipulation by playing up the 'positive' stories and excluding or downgrading those with a negative aspect. In referring to 'single-minded energy and determination' it certainly seems to overlook the fact that there was substantial opposition to operations involving casualties in the Falklands, and that most of the British population was not actively involved in the provision of material support for the military effort.   MoD in fact resisted ITN's blandishments to provide facilities for 'positive' stories and appears to have continued in its obdurate and uncooperative course. In practice, not only was the Ministry unwilling to comment and speculate on events, but officials and even senior military officers often simply did not know what was going on. At one point, Brigadier Julian Thompson, Commander of 3 Brigade, is rumoured to have simply refused to communicate with Fleet Headquarters at Northwood (the command centre for Operation Corporate) for a period of some twenty-four hours, so concerned was he at the damage which could result from premature announcements about operations. In their evidence to the HCDC, the *Sunday*

Mirror state that 'the major events were allegedly unknown at MoD';[23] Portsmouth and Sunderland Newspapers told the HCDC that their defence correspondent ' "understood" that Fleet Headquarters, Northwood were not informing the Defence Ministry in Whitehall about all that was happening'.[24] David Fairhall of the *Guardian*, in a generous mood, wrote

> I have been surprised to discover how little detailed and specific information filtered back even to the highest levels of government while operations were actually under way. Much of what suspicious journalists regarded as news management could probably be explained as a mixture of ignorance, wishful thinking and a natural desire to put the best light on things when seen from a particular point of view . . .[25]

This view was confirmed by MoD evidence to the HCDC: Ian McDonald, commenting on the problems of censoring material, described how 'Whitehall tends always to be a little behind . . .' with the news.[26]

MEDIA SOURCES

If MoD could not or would not help out, the media have their own ways of tapping expertise. Reporters are used to commenting on and questioning government policies and in current affairs programmes it is standard practice to do this by interviewing people from outside government: Members of Parliament, trade unionists, businessmen or other experts. In the case of the Falklands, the media intensified this standard practice.

The first source of expertise for both newspapers and the broadcasting media was the defence correspondent. Most major newspapers have a permanent defence correspondent; the BBC has two – one for television and another for radio; ITN has one. The defence correspondents tended to be given the responsibility for the detailed reporting of the Falklands War from the UK end. They could draw on various sources of information in addition to the meagre official statements. First, there was their own background knowledge. Then there were whatever contacts they might have developed within the Ministry of Defence or the armed forces who could be relied on to pass them the occasional items. They might also have contacts among backbench Conservative MPs who could be expected to have some 'inside information' obtained from Cabinet members. The correspondents also fed off each other:

> Because information was so thin one was picking it up sometimes from one's colleagues, sometimes from reading other newspapers and getting what were not really confirmations but probably talking to somebody in the House [of Commons] or somebody in MoD who might indicate, yes, there was a submarine on the way, or something to that effect . . .[27]

One further source of information not widely publicised, but vital to the reporting of the campaign, was material leaked to American journalists in the United States. On 27 May, Jeremy Harris interviewed Charles Cawdrey of the *Baltimore Sun* on *PM*. Cawdrey explained that while the task force did not communicate directly with Washington, it was his belief that 'information that goes to London also goes to Washington'. (He did not specify by what means, but one explanation would be that the British were using US communications satellites, and that presumably the Americans could 'tune in' to messages being passed. Cawdrey also referred to US satellite intelligence in the area, although the poor weather conditions must have hampered intelligence-gathering by this means.) *Weekend World* apparently had a source in the White House, while the leaks emanating from the CIA prompted official remonstration by the British.[28] Certainly some information published in the United States was drawn upon heavily by the British media, the outstanding case being the dispatch of part of the task force ahead of the main fleet, to retake South Georgia. This was first reported in the *Boston Globe* and subsequently picked up by the British newspapers.

'OPEN' LITERATURE

Additionally, an enormous amount of information about military matters is available in open sources. These range from scholarly studies to encyclopaedias to specialist journals. Newspapers, radio and television all maintain libraries of varying degrees of excellence: they could be expected to contain at least the main reference works and probably also files of relevant cuttings. Also available are the resources of such bodies as the International Institute of Strategic Studies (IISS), and the Royal United Services Institute (RUSI).

The first and most obviously well-used source of material about the forces of Britain and Argentina was *The Military Balance*.[29] This gives, in note form, brief details of the size, composition and equipment of the armed forces of every country in the world, and is generally considered to be authoritative. In practice, when used alone it serves little purpose other than to provide numerical force comparisons which are not, in themselves, particularly useful. Material from *The Military Balance* was however widely supplemented by more detailed information drawn from the 'Jane's' series of books, particularly *Jane's Fighting Ships*, *Jane's All the World's Aircraft* and *Jane's Weapon Systems*.[30] These works not only give force strengths, but describe in detail the systems they cover: this reflects their function not only as encyclopaedias but also as sales catalogues.

Jane's Fighting Ships[31] gives *inter alia* numbers of each type (including numbers in refit), class, date of commissioning, tonnage, speed, main armaments and major modifications or change of role, as well as details of naval aviation including combat radius.

Jane's Weapon Systems[32] describes roles, capabilities and performance data, except where the latter are classified. Even when official performance data are not available, they are estimated – for example, Sea Dart's range is estimated as being at least 30 kilometres. Not only does *Jane's Weapon Systems* cover 'conventional' weapons – missiles, artillery and so on – but it also gives details of electronic warfare equipment, sonar, electro-optical equipment and other sophisticated systems. To give an almost random example of the kind of detail available – for the G1 777 Sonar, it describes frequency, modulation, transmission modes, detection ranges, target doppler, range accuracy, bearing accuracy and resolution.

Clearly detail of this kind is neither very meaningful nor very interesting to most members of the public. It could, however, be of great assistance to the defence correspondent in attempting more sophisticated comparisons of force strengths and capabilities than the purely numerical assessments widely given. It could also have helped in any assessment of the progress of the task force in its journey south. Once action had started, it provided a basis on which to develop informed commentary about the performance of different weapons systems. Most importantly perhaps, in the light of the subsequent criticism of the media commentary on the campaign, reference works such as *Jane's* would have been freely available to Argentine intelligence.

A number of readily available periodicals and journals also give detailed assessments of armed forces and accounts of weapons' performance, for example: *Armed Forces*, *Aviation Week and Space Technology*, *Flight International*, *Miltech*, *Interavia*, *Navy International*, *Air Pictorial*, *Air International* and many others. Cuttings from these as well as from newspapers and from Hansard are available in the libraries of the IISS and the Royal Institute of International Affairs (RIIA), to which many defence correspondents and other defence analysts belong. As the crisis developed, both the RUSI and the RIIA produced their own publications giving details of force levels.[33]

For commentators wanting to study equipment matters in greater depth, a little more research effort might have been required, but it would have been possible to get a wealth of detail from the many books and rather more 'heavyweight' journals which were available.[34]

For example, weapon developments of all types are covered regularly in the annual publication *RUSI and Brassey's Yearbook*. In the 1981 edition,[35] four chapters were devoted to that topic, written in language that would have been easily intelligible to the informed layman. Of particular interest given their significance in the Falklands War is the discussion of anti-ship missiles which described their capabilities and gave details of air defence against them.

Because the Falkland Islands were so unfamiliar to commentators and public alike, information about the Islands themselves was in demand. The Central Office of Information had prepared in March 1982 a reference paper describing their population, terrain, history, economy and so on. This was revised to include a brief reference to the Argentine invasion and released to the public.[36] It was quickly followed by another government publication covering the history of the Islands and the background to the dispute.[37] Both these pamphlets contained small-scale maps: reportedly HMSO had no ordnance survey maps of the Falklands in stock. A number of books and articles on the Falklands and on the Anglo–Argentine dispute had been published: these would have provided a reasonably comprehensive background briefing.[38]

Detailed facts about manpower, ships, weapons, aircraft and geography were thus readily available. What is harder to find is material about the *theory* of military operations – how would a task group position its various components? How should an amphibious operation be conducted? What are the criteria for selecting a landing site, what forces would land in what order and by what means? What tactics should be used to bomb an airfield or avoid enemy air defences or counter enemy aircraft? What would be the crucial targets for naval bombardment or air attack or special operations? What tactics should be used to dislodge static defences? What is the role of artillery in support of infantry operations? The questions are endless: finding the answers from published material would require more time and effort than any reporter could spare, especially since relatively little published material is available. The market for such material is limited and the military would certainly not wish to see information published which would be of such assistance to enemy intelligence. An acquaintance with modern tactical theory can most easily be acquired by talking to people with military experience.

THE 'ARMCHAIR STRATEGISTS' – RETIRED SERVICE OFFICERS

Some defence correspondents have seen military service themselves, others had cultivated close contacts with the military. There was, however, a body of up-to-date expertise waiting, as it were, in the wings and it was to this source that many journalists and presenters turned – the retired Service officers. There is a long-established tradition of employing retired servicemen as commentators on military affairs. Over thirty years ago, Major E. W. Sheppard, OBE, MC wrote of the military correspondent:

His role is not that of gathering news but of digesting and commenting on what others gather for him . . . In the early days of the profession the tendency was for a paper to call in an officer of high or highish rank, usually retired, or a civilian with special interest in and knowledge of military matters to write comments on such items of news as concerned the British Army or national defence . . .[39]

During the Falklands campaign, these commentators were in great demand. The *Guardian* reported that RUSI kept a list of suitable 'experts' to meet particular requirements and, by the end of the first week in May, were 'already poised' to produce an authority on using landing craft to invade a defended island.[40] This story was an exaggeration, but both the RUSI and IISS received many requests for information and interviews.

A list of the main commentators – that is, those who appeared in print or on the radio or television to make some reasonably substantial comment on the military aspects of the campaign – appears in Annex B. About thirty retired Service officers and, apart from defence correspondents, some twenty civilian commentators can be identified. These were mainly academics or journalists with specialist publications. They tended on the whole (but not exclusively) to be interviewed about either Argentine operations or about equipment on which they had particular expertise (although this often involved implicit comment on fighting techniques and other operational matters). The commentary about the intentions and tactics of the British forces was primarily provided by the retired officers and defence correspondents.

Outside commentators were used far more by radio and television than by newspapers, which frequently did not identify those experts whom they had consulted: phrases such as 'defence analysts say . . .' and 'experts on naval warfare believe . . .'

The greater use of commentators on radio and television, particularly the latter, was intended to add to the interest and authenticity of what was being broadcast. Transcripts confirmed the view put by one television presenter that the military commentators appearing on current affairs programmes rarely added much to the factual information being imparted, but they made it more interesting by bringing a military flavour to the proceedings: 'On the whole we found them useful just to give one a flavour of the sort of attitudes and language and temperament of the people involved in this exercise . . . It was atmospheric.'[41] Clearly a visual medium such as television can make more use than the press of such 'atmospherics'.

In deciding who to invite to give their views, defence correspondents and programme editors relied in the first place on known and proven contacts. There was, however, a certain amount of competition in broadcasting to avoid using the same people as appeared on other programmes, again in an effort to keep a high level of audience interest.

What was it that the 'armchair strategists' were intended to add to the material in the media, over and above the heightening of interest? It has already been noted that the commentary arose in part at least because of genuine uncertainty about what the task force could or would do. The demand for it also reflected a gap in public knowledge. Although defence has attracted considerable public attention in recent years, this has mainly focused on nuclear matters. The possession of relatively small professional forces (as opposed to conscripts) and the rarity of their use in full-scale fighting (as opposed to low-intensity operations such as counter-terrorism) mean that fewer people than was once the case come into contact with the armed forces and fewer still know much about their conventional equipment and fighting capabilities. This affected journalists as well as their readers: Patrick Bishop and John Witherow comment '. . . the military were a foreign country to most of us'.[42] The unofficial commentators were called upon to remedy that ignorance and that is how the majority of them seem to have seen their role. They were also used to embellish or reinforce or authenticate the views being put forward by journalists and programme presenters. A common technique was for an interviewer to offer a statement in the form of a question, so that the interviewee, the commentator, could endorse it. Occasionally, panel discussions were used – ITN's *Falklands Special*, BBC Radio's *The World Tonight*, *Weekend World* and *TV Eye* for example. On the whole, these worked quite well, although, as one *TV Eye* programme showed, they could get out of hand.[43]

Occasionally, one of the commentators gave a performance which for one reason or other fell short of the desired standards of a particular programme and would not be invited to appear again. On the whole, however, the relationship between the media and the outside experts appears to have been harmonious: the majority of editors and programme presenters felt that these 'experts' gave good value. In the following chapters, we look at how these experts and the media's own commentators, the defence correspondents, went about the task of informing the public.

NOTES

1. War correspondents have usually been male, although a few women have achieved distinction in this field, the outstanding example being Marguerite Higgins, an American who reported on both the Second World War and the Korean War. Even the Boer War boasted one female correspondent – Lady Sarah Wilson, who offered to write for the *Daily Mail*, but was captured by the Boers at Kimberley.
2. Behr, *Anyone Here been Raped*, p. 101.
3. Knightley, *First Casualty*, p. 173.
4. Ibid., p. 174.
5. HCDC *Report*, vol. II, Q1179.
6. Brian Hanrahan and Robert Fox, *I Counted Them All Out and I Counted Them All Back*, p. 21.
7. 'Trumpets and Typewriters', BBC, 19 July 1983.
8. Behr, *Anyone Here been Raped*, p. 240. A more impressionistic celebration of the excitement and glamour of covering the Vietnam War appears in Michael Herr, 'The War Correspondent: A Reappraisal', *Esquire* (April 1976).
9. Christopher Wain, 'Television Reporting of Military Operations – a Personal View', *RUSI Journal* (December 1974). Harris quotes Robert Fox on this: 'The world of the Falklands campaign was so enclosed that it was hard not to identify with the troops on the ground; in the heavier engagements it was the only means of psychological survival' (p. 135).
10. Quoted in *The Falklands War* by the *Sunday Times* Insight Team, p. 213.
11. Interview with Professor Freedman and the author, 25 February 1983.
12. The debate about this relationship is a long-running one: the main arguments on both sides are to be found in the Glasgow Media Group *Bad News* and *Report of the Committee on the Future of Broadcasting*, Cmnd. 6753 (*The Annan Report*) p. 276.
13. This is the view taken in the case of the Falklands by one commentator at least – see Patricia Holland, 'Public Opinion, the Popular Press and the Organisation of Ideas' in *Falklands/Malvinas: Whose Crisis?* (Latin America Bureau).
14. Charles Wintour, 'What War has done for Fleet Street', *Observer*, 6 June 1982, p. 8.

5. Glasgow Media Group, *Bad News*, pp. 2–4; Harris, *Gotcha!*, p. 58.
6. Reported in the *Daily Mirror*, 1 May 1982. According to this report only four times since 1977 have news programmes had an audience of more than 17 million.
7. HCDC *Report*, vol. II, Q228.
8. Taken from 'The TV Top Ten' television viewing figures for the week ending 4 September 1983, reported in the *Daily Express*, 12 September 1983. The BBC's Saturday evening 'News and Sport' is occasionally watched by over 10 million people, cf. 'TV Top Ten' for the week ending 27 November in *The Times*, 6 December 1983.
9. Knightley, *First Casualty*, p. 85.
20. Franks Report, passim.
21. HCDC *Report*, vol. II, Q91 & 92.
22. HCDC *Report*, vol. II, pp. 76–7.
23. Ibid., vol. II, p. 108.
24. Ibid., vol. II, p. 139.
25. Ibid., vol. II, p. 107.
26. Ibid., vol. II, Q1801.
27. Jon Connell, defence correspondent of the *Sunday Times*, quoted in Harris, *Gotcha!*, p. 98.
28. Interviews with Professor Freedman and the author.
29. *The Military Balance* 1981–2, International Institute for Strategic Studies (London, 1982).
30. Although other similar works have been published, the 'Jane's' series continues to be preeminent among military reference books.
31. *Jane's Fighting Ships 1981–82*. See also *Jane's All the World's Aircraft 1981–82*.
32. *Jane's Weapon Systems 1981–82*.
33. *Chatham House Special: The Falkland Islands Dispute: International Dimensions* (Royal Institute of International Affairs, London, April 1982). *The Falkland Islands Aide Memoire* (Royal United Service Institute, 1982).
34. See for example: *Sea Power and Influence: Old Issues and New Challenges*, ed. Jonathan Alford, Adelphi Library 2 (IISS, London, 1980). Essays include: Hubert Feigl, 'The Impact of New Maritime Technologies'; George R. Lindsey, 'Tactical Anti-Submarine Warfare: The Past and the Future', *Tactical and Strategic Anti-Submarine Warfare* (Stockholm International Peace Research Institutes; MIT Press with Alnquist and Wiksell International, 1974). The *RUSI Journal*, the *Proceedings of the US Naval Institute* and *The Military Review*, passim.
35. RUSI and Brassey's Yearbook 1981, ed. RUSI (Brassey's, Oxford, 1980).
36. *The Falkland Islands and Dependencies*, Central Office of Information Reference no. 152/82/revised (London, 1982).
37. *The Falkland Islands: The Facts*, Foreign and Commonwealth Office (HMSO, London, 1982).
38. See for instance M. Cawkell, D. Maling and E. Cawkell, *The Falkland Islands* (1960) and I. J. Strange, *The Falkland Islands* (2nd edn, 1981); R. Johnson, 'The Future of the Falkland Islands', *World Today* (June 1977) and *Falkland Islands and Dependencies: Report for the Years 1972 and 1973* (HMSO, 1976) and Shackleton Report.

39. Major E. W. Sheppard, OBE, MC, 'The Military Correspondent', *The Army Quarterly* (January 1952).
40. 'The Stage – Army on Standby', *Guardian*, 7 May 1982.
41. Peter Snow: interview with the author.
42. Patrick Bishop and John Witherow, *The Winter War*, p. 22.
43. *TV Eye* on 29 April 1982, see pp. 88–9 below.

Part II
The Commentary

4 The Fleet Sets Sail: 2–25 April 1982

Speculation about naval movements in the South Atlantic began even before the departure of the task force had been agreed by the Cabinet, and became intense soon after that decision had been announced. The speculation focused initially on submarine movements and in particular on the whereabouts of HMS *Superb*. The report by the Franks Committee on events leading up to the Argentine invasion of the Falklands noted that a British press report on 31 March had referred to the sailing of a nuclear-powered submarine. This appears to have been an article in *The Times* stating that an SSN, possibly HMS *Superb*, had sailed from the Mediterranean for the South Atlantic.[1] This story quickly gained currency so that by 2 April *Newsnight*, drawing on an Argentine source, reported that HMS *Superb* 'is already off Argentina, south of Buenos Aires'. By the time the task force sailed, it was regarded as common knowledge that HMS *Superb* was either en route for the Falklands or already there.[2] It was not until the submarine's presence at her base in Scotland was noted on 21 April (when MoD broke their normal rule and confirmed that it was HMS *Superb* which had been sighted) that the rumour was scotched.

These early reports and claims about the task force illustrate how fact and speculation can become intertwined to produce an outcome which bears little relationship either to reality or common-sense. The idea that either HMS *Superb* or, as reported elsewhere, ships from Exercise Spring Train in the Mediterranean[3] could have reached the South Atlantic so quickly could only have been plausible had the ships sailed a couple of weeks before the Argentine invasion! The media fed on leaks and rumours; MoD followed its customary practice of refusing to comment on the whereabouts of the Navy's nuclear-powered submarines and this was seized on as confirmation.

When the truth about *Superb*'s location emerged, the media were outraged at what they saw as a deliberate piece of deception; in fact they had scored an 'own goal' – although even if MoD were not responsible for the error, they certainly welcomed it.

BALANCING THE FORCES

The business of establishing what ships comprised the task force occupied a considerable amount of media attention, particularly in the first week after the task force had sailed, when something like half the newspaper articles commenting on the operation dealt with the force levels of both sides. Initially, the media focused on the naval and air forces: rather less information was published about the land forces.

Comment on force levels took various forms. First there were straightforward attempts to make numerical comparisons between the forces of the two sides by listing ships, and perhaps aircraft as well, sometimes with details of armaments and often with recognition silhouettes culled, for example, from *Jane's*. Some of these comparisons were clearly ill-conceived; for example, three newspapers, in describing the naval forces available to Britain, listed the entire active strength of the Royal Navy without questioning whether all of these vessels were likely to be used.[4] The majority were however more reasonable, if not always accurate. The total size of the task force was generally reckoned to be between thirty and forty vessels, though some reports arrived at figures of this order by counting in all, or a larger number than was really the case, of the ships thought to have participated in Exercise Spring Train.[5]

Finally, on 9 April, the MoD published the names of the ships that were currently in the task force. This list (far shorter than the final roll of task-force vessels) totalled twenty-nine ships, including five landing ships and twelve supporting vessels. Of the media, only *Newsnight* had shown an appreciation of the scale of the logistical support needed to mount so remote an operation.[6]

There was intense speculation about the number of fixed-wing aircraft available to each side. Normally HMS *Invincible* and *Hermes* carry one squadron of Sea Harriers apiece.[7] Reporters watching the task force assemble at Portsmouth counted eight Sea Harriers landing on each ship,[8] and the number was widely reported as being sixteen, although further aircraft joined the carriers as they steamed down the Channel, bringing the total to twenty. (Later, in May, this was increased by reinforcements to thirty-eight.) On 7 April, *The Times* reported accurately that there were twelve Harriers on *Hermes* and eight on *Invincible* and this figure was soon widely, although not universally, accepted. When the dispatch of reinforcements to 'nearly double the size of the Harrier force' was announced by the Prime Minister, most commentators concluded that the total number would be about forty. MoD regarded it as important to maintain secrecy about the size of the Harrier force and consistently refused to publish the exact figure. The Argentine assessment of Harrier numbers appears to have been cautious: according to one report, they believed the initial force was 'between twenty and forty', with twenty more en route.[9]

Assessments of Argentine naval and air strength were clearly based for the most part on the standard reference works, although there were differences of interpretation, with some reports failing, for example, to take account of the Argentines' Dagger aircraft[10] and many omitting reference to the Super Etendards, of which fourteen had been ordered and five delivered.[11]

Television and radio, particularly the latter, made much less use than the press of these straightforward numerical comparisons of the two sides. This reflected in part the constraints of the media. Detailed tables of forces would need considerable simplification to have any visual impact on television and were not usable by radio. It may also have reflected the much greater use made by the broadcast media of expert commentators, for they would recognise that comparing forces simply on a numerical basis is a fairly pointless exercise. It says nothing about the numbers of vessels and planes operational: that depends on other commitments and factors such as reliability and the availability of spares. It says nothing about the relative capabilities of the two sides: that depends on factors such as equipment performance, standards of maintenance and of training and expertise. Moreover, equipment capabilities must be related to tactical and strategic objectives –

are these the right means to achieve whatever goal the force commander may have?

A second kind of comment on force levels came closer to dealing with these issues as commentators compared the British and Argentine force levels in terms of *capability*. In the broadcast media such analysis was generally the province of the military commentator rather than the general reporter or even the defence correspondent, although occasionally the latter would be drawn into it. In the press, defence correspondents provided most of the material. Discussions of capability appeared throughout the conflict (unlike the more basic numerical comparisons which tailed off after the first few weeks) and took two forms – either general assessments or more detailed comment on particular types of capability, e.g. for submarine warfare, or the quality of land forces. In the first weeks, as the task force began its journey south, assessments focused on two areas – naval and air capability.

NAVAL CAPABILITY

Most newspaper reports analysing naval capability were sensible and reasonably well informed. The general view seems to have been that the British fleet was bigger, its ships more modern and their crews more experienced and better trained. Assessments ranged from the cautiously optimistic to the ebullience of the *Sun*'s headline 'OUR SUBS COULD SINK THEIR FLEET.'[12]

A number of newspaper articles drew attention to the commonality of some Argentine and British equipment, particularly missiles. Here again, experience and the modernity of equipment were seen as crucial, and Britain was generally estimated to have the edge: indeed the *Sunday Times* reported this as the Argentine view, expressed in a leaked classified security report which apparently described the task force as having superior fire-power, allowing it to dominate at sea.[13]

In general, commentators on television and radio took a similar view of Britain's prospects in any naval engagement, although again few people seem to have underrated the Argentine Navy: Major General Edward Fursden spoke of their zeal and determination; Captain Peter Stewart RN, a former defence attaché in Buenos Aires, described the Argentine Navy as 'proud and competent', with officers and chief petty officers of high calibre, although he felt that there was 'no comparison' with the Royal Navy.[14] Rear Admiral Edward Gueritz noted the presence of Type 42 destroyers on both sides, but thought that the British crews were likely to be better and that the forces 'advertised as forming part of the task force' were well balanced in their capabilities.[15] These were typical of the assessments by expert commentators. They went into relatively little detail and were sober but reassuring on the British chances of success. With regard to Argentine naval training, there were references to the fact that a number of Argentines had been trained by the British, but no one mentioned the fact that in their regular annual exercises with the Brazilian, Uruguayan and US Navies, the Argentines used the English language and standard NATO operating procedures, which might have been presumed to improve their intelligence about the British.[16]

Two aspects of naval warfare were to prove of particular importance in the conflict: submarine and missile warfare. There was widespread media interest in the former since it rested with the nuclear-powered hunter-killer submarines (SSNs) to enforce the Maritime Exclusion Zone which took effect on 12 April. A number of newspapers produced detailed descriptions, with diagrams, of an SSN. In general, commentators were optimistic about the likely performance of the submarines. Rear Admiral Gueritz described them as 'first class, with the right equipment and training'.[17] Admiral Lord Hill-Norton saw no major problems for the submarines in enforcing the blockade,[18] while the *Sun* simply announced that the Navy's Tigerfish torpedoes could 'blow the entire Argentine fleet out of the water'.[19] This last comment has a certain irony, given the system's unreliability which led the commander of HMS *Conqueror* to use the old Mk 8 torpedo against the Argentine ship, the *General Belgrano*.

The imposition of the Maritime Exclusion Zone (MEZ) around the Falklands was announced on 7 April, to take effect on 12 April. As most observers correctly concluded, this timing meant that the task of enforcing the MEZ fell initially to the SSNs (although even they did not reach the area for some days after 12 April). The ability of the submarines to do this was questioned several times. On 8 April, Christopher Lee of the BBC and Geoffrey Archer of ITN spoke of difficulties – shallow coastal waters, problems of detecting Argentine ships, Argentine anti-submarine warfare (ASW) and the possibility of minefields, while on 10 April, the *Financial Times* gave a detailed account of the problems facing the SSNs. Correcting an earlier assessment, it also acknowledged that the Argentine diesel electric submarines were quieter than the SSNs. These problems eventually led the Royal Navy to send one of its own non-nuclear submarines to the area. At this stage, however, most of the military commentators seem to have been more optimistic: detection and identification of Argentine ships was relatively straightforward, and while no one could guarantee that no Argentine ships would get through, the exclusion zone was likely to be sufficiently effective to deny the Argentines supplies.[20]

Before the loss of HMS *Sheffield*, when it was hit by an Exocet missile on 4 May, there was much less interest in missile warfare than in submarines. None the less, it was mentioned on a number of occasions, the most detailed being in *Newsnight* on 3 April when, in what the *Newsnight* team regard as something of a scoop, Peter Snow described how the men and ships of the task force had to face the possibility of a 'new kind of warfare, fought not just with guns but with naval missiles . . .' After a piece of film, he continued,

> nobody can be sure how ships and men would react to this kind of exchange of deadly accurate missiles which could cause appalling casualties. Most deadly of all is this one, the Exocet. It's a ship-to-ship missile which skims on the waves and homes in on its target twenty miles or more away . . .

Snow went on to say that Britain had the advantage of Sea Wolf for anti-missile defence but a further major threat lay with the Argentine Skyhawks which could enable the Argentine Navy and Air Force to carry out 'massive missile attacks' on the Royal Navy.[21]

CAPABILITY IN THE AIR

During the first month of the crisis, the attention given by the media to the air threat to the task force was very patchy, particularly in the press. Initially, in assessing the air capability of the two sides, many newspapers dealt solely in terms of air-to-air combat; few followed *Newsnight*'s example and focused on the threat to ships. A number declared that Britain had air superiority.[22] Henry Stanhope, then defence correspondent of *The Times*, was less bullish; he described air support as 'an open question';[23] air superiority 'could be crucial' but achieving it could present task force commanders with 'their greatest problems',[24] while Max Hastings wrote that the task force was being despatched without air cover and could suffer great losses.[25]

As time passed there seems to have been a greater recognition by the press of the task force's lack of air superiority, although even at the end of April, the *Scotsman* carried a report that 'air superiority may favour the task force, given the range at which Argentine aircraft would have to operate'.[26]

The commentary on television and radio went much further in spelling out and debating the air threat to the task force, although again there seems to have been some initial uncertainty about the range of Argentine land-based aircraft, despite the fact that information on this was readily available.[27] Most commentators suggested either that task force defences would be adequate to meet the threat, or that tactics would be geared to avoiding it. Brian Walden on *Weekend World* described the possibility of mounting a long-term blockade, and went on:

> In mounting such a blockade our ships would be vulnerable to air attack. Argentinian Mirage and Skyhawk fighter-bombers flying from bases along the Argentinian coastline would have our ships within range. But Sea Harrier warplanes launched from our two aircraft-carriers and Sea Dart surface-to-air missiles on some of our smaller ships, should be able to prevent the majority of any attackers getting through.[28]

Rear Admiral Gueritz suggests the threat would be taken account of in planning, and said: 'It's unwise for surface naval vessels to engage land-based air power where there's a high concentration of aircraft and therefore naval deployments will be geared to avoid that.'[29]

On the whole the commentators seem to have been broadly in agreement that while Argentine aircraft posed a threat, it should be manageable. The message that came across was that no one could guarantee that no Argentine aircraft would get through, but the task force's defences were strong. Few spelt out explicitly the consequences of any gap in these defences, although Brian Walden did state bluntly that 'some [Argentine warplanes] might get through and sink our ships', and Peter Snow in *Newsnight* referred more than once to the possibility of the fleet's air defences being swamped.[30]

*   *   *

In retrospect, and taking the material as a whole, the coverage given to the forces of the two sides seems to have been reasonably thorough, in view of the pressures of time and the limited information made available by MoD. Given, however, that the public have to be selective in their reading, listening and viewing, there is no guarantee that they would have received consistent, comprehensible and accurate information. There was, moreover, a considerable amount of uncritical use of material from open sources, such as the numerical 'balance of forces' tables which appeared widely in the newspapers, and which served little useful purpose as a means for assessing the likely outcome of any combat between the two sides. Other force comparisons relied quite heavily on the concept of comparing like with like – our submarines against their submarines, Sea Harriers against Mirages. Again, this was of limited use, the crucial comparisons being between capability and counter capability – for example, British submarines against Argentina's ASW capability; Argentine aircraft and stand-off missiles against British air defences. This last is particularly relevant. The threat from Argentina's land-based aircraft was frequently underestimated or glossed over: many people talked about the likelihood of 'dog-fights' between Harriers and Mirages without confronting explicitly the threat of bombing attacks. In retrospect, it seems fair to conclude that the public would on the whole have been reassured that, while the task force faced certain risks, it should be able to cope with them: this of course was true – but the coping was a more painful process than many people had expected.

OPTIONS AND OPERATIONS

As a number of commentators pointed out, the government's objective was to bring Argentina to withdraw her occupying forces from the Falklands and enter negotiation, and the task force served a dual function, both as a means of persuasion and, if necessary, of reoccupation:[31] the dangers of the latter course were widely and openly recognised: it was described as 'the most awful military operation one could contemplate'.[32]

In the first few weeks it was far from clear to the public what the task force would do once it reached the South Atlantic, nor did the government have any firm plan: it continued to hope that diplomacy and the threat of force would prove successful. The imposition of the Maritime Exclusion Zone was announced on 7 April; thereafter an Air Exclusion Zone was widely and accurately forecast before it was announced on 25 April.[33] The embarkation of 3 Commando Brigade reinforced with two battalions of the Parachute Regiment made it clear that land operations of some kind were at least possible. Moreover, it suggested that British options would be constrained by certain time limits, given that soldiers could not be kept at sea in troopships indefinitely.[34] Discussion of the options open to Britain at any one time, and speculation about the kind of operations that would be undertaken, dominated the media commentary on military aspects of the crisis even at this early stage.

An article in the *Sunday Times* on 4 April, by the defence correspondent Jon Connell, set the tone for others considering the options open to the government and to the task force commanders. The article suggested that although only 1000 Marines might embark initially with the task force, this number would be increased. Retaking the Falklands was a daunting prospect since an airborne landing was ruled out. Attacks on the mainland were unlikely on the grounds that they would not be tolerated by the Soviet Union and would not in any case be an effective way of regaining the Islands, and the same applied to the sinking of the Argentine Navy. An assault on the Islands would therefore be necessary; a blockade could provide cover for reconnaissance and landings.

Whilst not precisely accurate in every detail, this report gave a sensible appraisal of the problems and a fairly good forecast of what was to follow. And if the reference to the Soviet Union seems slightly surprising in the context of assistance to a right-wing military government, it must be remembered that at the time, the Soviet Union was making definite noises of support for Argentina, to the extent that there was a fairly widespread but wrong belief that the Russians were helping Argentine intelligence.

Detailed assessments of this kind have little place in television news programmes, but such analyses and speculation as do appear may have a disproportionate effect on public attitudes because of the size of the audience reached. Television commentators did identify the choice between a prolonged blockade and a landing: ITN's defence correspondent, Geoffrey Archer, commented 'The decision of what to do when the fleet arrives is desperately difficult' and went on to suggest that to try to recapture the Islands could involve 'colossal' loss of life, including among the Islanders. The risk to the Islanders was raised on a number of occasions – for example, by Brian Walden and Rear Admiral Gueritz in *Weekend World*, the former describing an assault on the Islands as 'fraught with danger'.[35] This programme also recognised that a long-term blockade carried the risk of losses. *Sunday Times* correspondent Jon Connell said: 'if we ever did mount a blockade with surface ships, we would be bound to sustain heavy casualties'.[36] Several reports however advocated or at least expected a blockade. The *Guardian*'s defence correspondent described it as 'the only comfortable option', despite his recognition in an earlier article of the difficulties of enforcing it without adequate air reconnaissance.[37] According to the *Financial Times*, Admiral Hill-Norton apparently believed that a blockade need involve no British casualties, although there is a question how far his publicly-stated view was influenced by considerations of morale.[38] The *New York Times* of 15 April carried an article quoting unidentified 'military sources at NATO' as saying that the task force was not strong enough for an amphibious landing, while the *Washington Post*, again using unidentified military sources (a retired US Admiral 'long associated with NATO') argued that Britain had lost the capacity for independent action due to its concentration on its NATO role and its reliance on US carriers for naval air cover.[39] *Newsnight* forecast 'A long war of attrition accompanying the naval siege. It would take months and would be expensive and dangerous.'[40]

A number of commentators noted the real difficulty in sustaining the blockade given the severe weather conditions, the possible deterioration in the fitness of the embarked troops, and the Argentine air and submarine threats.[41] Group Captain David Bolton referred also to the problems of logistic back-up, but none the less thought a blockade feasible and saw signs that there were 'cracks in the facade' of the determination of the Argentine military leadership.[42]

Clearly some of the most acute fears about the dangers of a British landing on the Falklands stemmed from the idea that this would be an opposed landing. Vice-Admiral Sir John Roxburgh pointed out in *The World Tonight* that while an invasion would not be easy, it should be possible to establish a beach-head away from Argentine defences.[43] This point was picked up in *Weekend World* and *Newsnight* and by Admiral Hill-Norton in *The World at One*.[44] Other commentators thought the British forces more than capable of dealing with Argentine resistance. The *Daily Mail* quoted Admiral Hill-Norton as recommending a landing by Marines, who would bombard Argentine defensive positions with CS gas prior to an all-out attack[45] although in the *Sun* he acknowledged that landings could involve heavy casualties. Another article in the *Sun* on 17 April quoted naval expert Anthony Preston as saying that the Argentine armed forces could not resist the task force for more than two weeks; their fighters would be grounded by lack of supplies, their troops would lack support, and the garrison would be starved out in two days.[46] This particular scenario was clearly highly remote from a reality in which Argentine aircraft continued to fly supplies into Stanley airfield up until the day before the Argentine surrender, which took another eight weeks to materialise.

During the first three weeks of April, speculation and comment about operations thus tended to be in fairly general terms. It was in a sense a period of education for media and public alike. What would the task force be able to do? What were the dangers? Would there be casualties? The idea of an actual landing on the Falklands themselves still seemed remote: it was generally reckoned that the task force would take three weeks to get there and that it would then concentrate on mounting a blockade of the Islands. A landing was not unthinkable (although it was seen as carrying great dangers), but neither was it felt to be an immediate likelihood. What was, however, widely and accurately forecast was the retaking of South Georgia, some miles south of the Falklands.

NOTES

1. Falkland Islands Review: Report of a Committee of Privy Councillors (subsequently referred to as the *Franks Report*) para 29.
2. References to HMS *Superb* appeared, for example, in the BBC TV *Nine O'Clock News* (8 and 10 April); *Weekend World* (11 April); ITN (3 and 4 April) and in a number of newspapers, including the *New York Times* (9 April); the *Financial Times* (6 April); the *Guardian* (6 April); *The Times* (5 and 7 April).
3. *Standard*, 2 April.
4. *Standard*, 2 April: *Sun*, 5 April: *New York Times*, 6 April.
5. For example the *Financial Times* and *The Times*, 5 April: *TV Eye*, 15 April.
6. On 8 April, the day before the MoD announcement, Peter Snow, the *Newsnight* presenter, had reported that twenty warships and ten RFAs were en route and on 23 April he referred to twenty warships being backed up by thirty-five support vessels.
7. See *Jane's Fighting Ships*.
8. For example 'Task Force ordered Full Speed Ahead', *The Times*, 5 April.
9. 'Argentines Predict Victory in the Air', *Guardian*, 20 April.
10. For example in the *Daily Mail*, 5 April, the *Washington Post*, 6 April and *The Times*, 9 April.
11. Jeffrey Ethell and Alfred Price, *Air War South Atlantic*, p. 26. In fact only four Super Etendards saw active service, the fifth being cannibalised to provide spares. In addition to the reports listed in note 10 above, the Super Etendards were overlooked by reports in the *Standard*, 2 April and the *Sunday Times*, 11 April. The *New York Times*, 8 April, overestimated the number of Super Etendards which had actually been delivered; Bill Gunston, writing in the *Daily Mail* on 15 April, suggested the possibility that the Super Etendards could be put into use without training being completed. This is exactly what happened.
12. *Sun*, 5 April 1982.
13. 'Operation Blue', *Sunday Times*, 11 April.
14. *The World Tonight*, 5 April; *The World at One*, 8 April.
15. *The World at One*, 9 April.
16. Robert L. Scheina, 'The Argentine Navy Today', *Naval Forces* (April 1981).
17. *The World Tonight*, 5 April.
18. *The World Tonight*, 12 April.
19. 'Menace of the Deadly Tigerfish', *Sun*, 14 April.

20. For example, Captain Peter Stewart RN in *The World at One*, 8 April; Admiral Lord Hill-Norton in *The World Tonight*, 12 April; Rear Admiral Gueritz in *Weekend World*, 11 April.
21. Among other earlier references to missile warfare were comments in ITN's *News at One*, 15 April, *World at One*, 1 May, *The Times*, 5 April, 21 April.
22. For example the *Daily Mail*, 5 April, *The Times*, 6 April, the *Daily Mail*, 20 April.
23. 'The Harsh Options Facing the Navy', *The Times*, 5 April.
24. 'Admiral Pinning Faith on Air Superiority', *The Times*, 7 April.
25. 'A Bitter Choice for the Iron Lady', *Standard*, 5 April. *Washington Post* raised similar doubts on 6 April, but some caution is needed in reading US reports since the Falklands conflict coincided with a domestic debate about the US carrier force: as one US commentator noted:

> If one already believed, for example, that big carriers were what the Navy needed, then the Falklands case *proved* it needed big carriers. If one believed the Navy should have small carriers, then the Falklands Islands *proved* that it needed small carriers. If one believed that the Navy needed no carriers at all, then it *proved* that it needed no carriers at all . . .

Commander Kenneth McGruther USN, 'When Deterrence Fails: The Nasty Little War in the Falkland Islands', *Naval War College Review* (April 1983).
26. *Scotsman*, 28 April.
27. For example, Peter Snow in *Newsnight*, 3 April: 'The British should be able to control the airspace directly around the Falklands and into the airport again out of range of those shore-based aircraft.' Christopher Wain, on the BBC evening news on 16 April, interpreted the information that Stanley airfield had not been extended as meaning that Argentina was 'losing total air superiority'.
28. *Weekend World*, 18 April.
29. *The World at One*, 9 April.
30. *Weekend World*, 25 April. *Newsnight*, 3 April, 23 April.
31. E.g. Peter Snow, *Newsnight*, 14 April; Geoffrey Archer, *News at Ten*, 20 April.
32. Professor Lawrence Freedman, *TV Eye*, 15 April.
33. For example in BBC TV News, 16 and 21 April; *Weekend World*, 18 April; *The World Tonight*, 15 April; *Daily Telegraph*, 5 April.
34. For example by Colonel Jonathan Alford in ITN *News at One*, 21 April.
35. *Weekend World*, 11 April.
36. Ibid.
37. 'Battle Options in the South Atlantic Strategy', *Guardian*, 26 April. Other forecasts of a long blockade appeared in the *Financial Times*, 5 April, the *Daily Telegraph*, 7 April and the *New Scientist*, 22 April, in which an editorial note described it as being 'generally accepted' that a long blockade was the best tactic.
38. 'First Test of a Modern Navy', *Financial Times*, 17 April.
39. 'US Naval Experts say they believe Distance too far for GB', *Washington Post*, 4 April.

40. *Newsnight*, 3 April.
41. For example in the *Daily Telegraph*, 5 April; *New York Times*, 12, 15, 18 April; *Weekend World*, 11 April.
42. *The World at One*, 16 April.
43. *The World Tonight*, 15 April.
44. *Weekend World*, 28 April; *Newsnight*, 26 April; *The World at One*, 23 April.
45. 'Deadly Harriers Face an Ageing Enemy', *Daily Mail*, 5 April.
46. 'Enemy Bangers Haven't a Chance', *Sun*, 15 April.

5   The Early Successes and Losses: 25 April–7 May

The first major action of the campaign was the retaking of South Georgia. This had been identified as probable as early as 5 April by Bridget Bloom, defence correspondent for the *Financial Times*. There was soon widespread agreement on the subject.

The main arguments advanced were that the recapture of South Georgia would provide a forward operating base, out of range of Argentina's land-based aircraft, and that its recapture would strengthen Britain's negotiating position.[1] There was, therefore, no great sense of surprise when, on 20 April, the *Boston Globe* reported that 'A swift task force of destroyers, two aircraft carriers and several troopships have broken off from the 40 ship British flotilla' and that these vessels were within twenty-four to forty-eight hours of South Georgia.[2] This item was picked up that day by the *Standard* and, with some caution, by ITN.[3] It became the subject of intense speculation.

David Fairhall wrote in the *Guardian* that for warships travelling at 25 knots, South Georgia was within five days of Ascension Island, but he noted that HMS *Invincible* and HMS *Hermes* had been at Ascension Island only three days earlier.[4] The *Daily Mail* reported the view of 'Pentagon officials' that by 22 April British ships could be in position for an attack on South Georgia.[5] The next day, 21 April, the BBC's *Nine O'Clock News* reported the South Georgia story as a rumour, but pointed out that the Foreign Secretary, Francis Pym, had added to the speculation when he returned to the dispatch box in the House of Commons to revise remarks he had made earlier, to the effect that the task force would not go into action while negotiations continued. ITN's Geoffrey Archer doubted whether fighting would start 'before next week'. Peter Snow thought that 'most experts reckon Mrs Thatcher has probably the capability from tonight onwards to mount a helicopter attack from this group of warships into South Georgia'.[6]

There were however some dissenting voices. Colonel Jonathon Alford, interviewed in ITN's *New at One* on 21 April, saw the retaking of South Georgia as a 'useful political gesture', but was unenthusiastic about the military benefits of the operation, which he saw as diverting effort. He argued that South Georgia was too distant from the Falklands and too inhospitable to be useful as a forward operating base. Air Vice-Marshal Menaul seems to have taken a similar view in ITN's *Task Force Special* the same night: he described an operation to regain South Georgia as having 'not much military sense but a lot of political sense'. These two commentators seem to have come closest to the view of the Royal Navy, who are reported to have opposed it not only because of the diversion of effort, but also because failure would have been a 'devastating blow'.[7] This point does not appear to have been made in any of the speculation about the South Georgia operation.

Meanwhile on 22 April ITN reported military sources in the Ministry of Defence as saying that 'some ships might already be very close to South Georgia'. The ITN reporter went on to say that the general feeling in Buenos Aires was that the British would try to take South Georgia which was defended by 'no more than 800' Argentines. He added that South Georgia would not make a good staging post since an airfield suitable for *Vulcans* (emphasis added) could not rapidly be built there. The point of this reference to an airfield for Vulcans in the context of troop reinforcements is unclear to say the least! Finally in this report, reference was made to another ministerial statement which had added to the mounting speculation. On this occasion it was the Prime Minister, who had said in the House of Commons that the position of South Georgia in law was different from that of the Falkland Islands.[8] It may not have been the Prime Minister's intention to stimulate further speculation, but her words did nothing to dampen it.

The link between ministerial activities and media speculation was further highlighted on 23 April when, despite denials that it was 'a dramatic dash', Mrs Thatcher's visit to the naval headquarters at Northwood was inevitably tied to speculation about the prospect of action.[9] There was an official attempt to defuse this speculation; but it misfired. Peter Ruff reported on

PM that the MoD would not discuss the position of the fleet. The MoD spokesman had referred to the rumours about South Georgia. It was, he had said, 'absolutely untrue' that the fleet had split into three, four or five parts. As Ruff pointed out, this did not deal with the question of whether the fleet had split into *two* parts, which was, as he put it, the 'consistent rumour'.[10] That night ITN reported an Argentine claim that some British ships were within helicopter range of South Georgia. The MoD refused to comment on this report.[11]

The attack on the submarine *Santa Fe* on Sunday, 25 April, was announced by MoD late that morning. Thereafter, the retaking of South Georgia was widely reported, with supposedly detailed accounts of how it had been achieved – not always very accurate ones.[12] Given the official reticence, inaccuracies are hardly surprising, since reporters had to rely largely on leaks and imagination. It was not until the true story of the near disaster on the Fortuna Glacier (when members of the SAS had to be airlifted off South Georgia in 'white-out' conditions) leaked out nearly a month later that MoD gave the full details of what had happened.

The South Georgia incident provides an interesting case history. It involved a number of features which were to be repeated throughout the campaign. There was persistent conjecture in the media about a current operation. That conjecture was, however, based on information available to Argentina from non-British sources.

The way speculation intensified following the *Boston Globe* report reflected the importance given to authoritative US sources and it appears that some officials in Washington were rather more willing to talk to the media than were their British counterparts. Whether inadvertently, or deliberately for psychological reasons, statements by British ministers and officials succeeded in stimulating rather than damping down speculation. There is some evidence (for example the ITN newscast on 22 April) to suggest that sources within MoD were actively encouraging or confirming the speculation – but even without these, significance was read into every event, including the timing of a Prime Ministerial visit. The MoD's official reaction to the speculation went rather further than the neutrality of 'neither confirming nor denying', the standard form of no comment. On 23 April, after special forces had landed on South Georgia, Ian McDonald told the press: '. . . The main task force is not involved in any landing action. There are many rumours going around but to put them at rest I have heard that the task force has not landed anywhere.'[13] The denial of a task force landing verged on the disingenuous: although the task force as a whole had not landed, elements of it had certainly done so.

Given that the Argentines clearly knew that British ships were off South Georgia, it may be argued that the MoD should have been less coy about admitting that there was an advance flotilla in the area. In practice, however, their reticence can be seen to have been justified. As late as 24 April, the Argentines were apparently uncertain about where and when the blow was to fall.[14] Uncertainty on the part of the enemy and the element of surprise combine to make an important tactical advantage. As it was, the British attack on South Georgia had to be improvised in the light of changing and difficult circumstances: without that tactical advantage, the operation might have run into much greater difficulty.

Two specific complaints were made by the BBC about the information given out by MoD after the operation. The first concerns MoD's statement on the *Santa Fe*, the Argentine submarine disabled off South Georgia. According to the BBC:

> . . . the spokesman announced that a 'hostile' submarine had been attacked by helicopters 'in the vicinity of South Georgia'. That was interpreted to mean the submarine was submerged and at sea and had been attacked by anti-submarine patrols using underwater weapons. The assumption had to be that it was sunk. Finally, the MoD confirmed Argentine communiques claiming the submarine had been attacked on the surface in Grytviken Harbour by rockets and machine gunfire from helicopters.[15]

This statement begs a number of questions. The fact that the BBC placed a particular interpretation on a statement is their responsibility rather than that of the MoD. It is not clear why 'the assumption had to be that' the *Santa Fe* had sunk; moreover, at the time it was attacked the *Santa Fe* was apparently heading from South Georgia out towards the sea and was about to submerge rather than sitting helplessly in harbour.[16] In any case, in the confusion of action and given their own reliance for information on the normally terse contents of signals dictated by harassed officers using overloaded communication systems, the lack of precision in the MoD's statement is understandable. It appears, however, that the Foreign Office shared the BBC's concern: their press desk was provided with 'defensive' briefing 'interpreting' the MoD's statement.

Another complaint by the BBC has, however, more force: 'the downing of two Wessex helicopters on South Georgia became known only when a serviceman wrote home about it'.[17] Nor was the near loss of several lives, when inflatable boats drifted, announced. Obviously it would have made no sense to announce the failed reconnaissance mission before South Georgia was recaptured, or even until there was time to ensure that the island was fully secured, but thereafter there can have been little good reason to keep the operation under wraps.

MoD gave the HCDC an account of its reasons for withholding the truth. At the time

> it would have prejudiced operational security in relation to the recovery of South Georgia and in the longer term in relation to the special forces' activities in the Falklands prior to the main landings. Moreover within MoD knowledge of this incident and all Special Forces operations was only made available to a very small number of people.[18]

The HCDC accepted this but, while the argument about the short term is sensible, the reference to the long-term implications is not convincing without fuller explanation, especially since, as it emerged, many people with the task force were aware of what had happened. The impression remains that the MoD sought to cover up a failure: Jim Meacham of the *Economist* described it as 'one of the major disinformation operations of this campaign'.[19]

The British media on the whole handled the South Georgia operation in a reasonably responsible way. There had been speculation by experts that the first landings would be on South Georgia but it was only after the rumour that elements of the task force were heading for the island had been broadcast on the US networks that it was published in the UK. Moreover, after the story started in Washington, it was consistently reported as 'rumour' or 'speculation'. Radio and television were in this instance particularly scrupulous in qualifying their reports in this way, and it is clear that the British media told the Argentines nothing that was not available to them from other sources.

South Georgia represented the acceptable face of warfare. A British victory was achieved without casualties. That latter fact, taken with the fact that South Georgia's legal status differed from that of the Falklands, meant that the British operation could stand up well to international scrutiny. It did not put on the UK the onus of having made diplomacy impossible. It is no wonder that the Prime Minister saw it as an occasion for rejoicing. It must also have been an occasion of considerable relief – so much could have gone wrong, but even those things that did so were not common knowledge at this stage. The operation could be represented as a triumph despite the last-minute changes in plan and the near disasters. The same was to be true of the first 'Black Buck' air raid; the air raid on Stanley airfield by an RAF Vulcan aircraft flying from Ascension Island.

THE BLACK BUCK RAID

Even before the conversion of a number of Vulcans to carry conventional bombs was announced, some commentators had recognised that Stanley airfield posed a threat to the task force, particularly if it was lengthened to allow Skyhawks and Mirages to take off. On 18 April, the MoD announced that a number of Vulcan aircraft were to be converted from their nuclear role to carry a conventional bombing load – subsequently known to be twenty-one 1000 lb bombs. The MoD spokesman refused to confirm that the conversion was for use in operations in the Falklands, but most commentators made the connection. This immediately led to speculation – in this case about what the Vulcan's role was to be. Having made the announcement, it would hardly have been realistic of MoD to expect the media to refrain from asking what it was all in aid of.

It had already been widely suggested that Britain could gain local air superiority by putting Argentina's mainland airfields out of action,[20] and, reporting the announcement that evening,

ITN said: 'our defence correspondent says that with extra fuel tanks and mid-air refuelling the Vulcans could be operated from Ascension Island to destroy Argentine airfields'. This was the conclusion reached by much of the press the next day.

A similar view seemed to be taken by two retired RAF officers speaking on BBC Radio 4. Air Vice-Marshal Norman Hoad suggested that the Chiefs of Staff must be worried about the threat posed to the task force by Argentine aircraft. 'Political constraints apart', he said, 'the neutralisation of air power would be attractive.' He saw difficulties, however, both in the distances involved and because of Argentina's defending aircraft, the Mirage IIIs, which could fly higher and faster than the Vulcans. If the latter operated out of Ascension Island, 'tactical routeing' (that is, the flight profile adopted to defeat enemy air defences) would involve air-to-air refuelling outside the zone of action of the Argentine fighters.[21]

Air Vice-Marshal Stewart Menaul described it as 'conceivable' but 'doubtful' that the Vulcan would operate in the Falklands. Any attack would almost certainly be on the mainland since 'there would be really very little point in attacking the Falklands themselves'. He was in any case uncertain whether the British would wish to destroy the airfield, since their objective could now be met by shooting down aircraft – a view which overlooked the political importance of minimising casualties. He thought the Vulcans would be effective in the strike role. Their electronic counter-measures (ECM) would make the job of Argentine interceptors and radars very difficult. The Argentines might find it difficult to pick up a low-level attack and to vector their Mirages onto a Vulcan. The Mirage operated best as a high-level interceptor and 'might have trouble with a low-flying Vulcan'; moreover, the bomber was a night flyer, the Mirage was not. In reply to further questions Air Vice-Marshal Menaul stressed that the Harrier was 'the key to the conflict'. It could match the Skyhawk, take out the Falklands Island airfield and give ground support; the Vulcan was a longer-term option.[22]

These interviews raise some interesting points. They contain quite a lot of factual information, much of which can be assumed to be known to the Argentines (particularly that on the Mirage) and all available in standard reference works, such as Thetford's *Aircraft of the Royal Air Force Since 1918*.[23] They give some idea of the sort of technical detail expert commentators

could get into – and also of the level of debate about tactics: is a
fast high-level interceptor a threat to a slower bomber, or can
the latter get through by virtue of its low-flying capability.
Finally, in the light of the subsequent commentary on the
'Black Buck' raids, Air Vice-Marshal Menaul's doubts about
the value of such an attack are particularly noteworthy.

It was to be nearly a fortnight before the actual raids took
place, and meanwhile the media continued to speculate about
the Vulcan's role, with a growing consensus that some sort of
action was likely against Stanley airfield although not necessarily
using the Vulcans.[24]

The Vulcan raid on Stanley airport finally took place early in
the morning of 1 May. The initial MoD announcement of the
raid was prompt but cryptic, so that initially the media
suggested that the attack had been carried out by Harriers.[25]

Gradually, more information about the raid filtered through.
At lunchtime, Ian McDonald gave some details and mentioned
the Vulcans. ITN's *News at 5.45* repeated this together with an
entirely spurious Argentine claim that two Harriers had been
shot down, and Geoffrey Archer gave his 'assessment' of the
attack. In the *News at Ten*, he asked Air Vice-Marshal Menaul
how difficult the Vulcan attack would have been, and was told,
reassuringly – although not entirely accurately – that, given the
good training the pilots received and the versatility of the
Vulcan, the crews wouldn't have had any difficulty.

In *The World Tonight*, Angus MacDermot had a panel of
guests 'to help us assess what's happened'. Vice-Admiral Sir
Ian McGeogh called the attack 'predictable' and thought
rendering the airstrip unserviceable was better than shooting
down aircraft. He expressed some surprise at the RAF's capacity
for such precise attacks at long range and, in reply to a question
suggested that the task force was now within ninety miles of the
Falklands for Harrier operations, and was probably acting as a
navigational beacon for the Vulcans. Mr Ian White, a former
pilot in the Falkland Islands, dampened the excitement a little
when he pointed out that there was plenty of gravel nearby
which would enable any craters to be filled in adequately to
take a Hercules.

The British daily press on 3 May gave considerable coverage
to the story, and all the papers followed the line in official
announcements that the raid had been a success. Most gave

detailed descriptions, presumably largely imaginary, of how it had been carried out. No one questioned the necessity for, or the value of, the operation.

In retrospect, this seems remarkable. Prior to the Black Buck raid, Air Vice-Marshal Menaul had expressed apparently sensible doubts about the value of using Vulcans to attack Stanley airfield. But now no one among the commentators queried what the operation had achieved or whether it had been worthwhile, given the immense risk to men and aircraft, and the costs. The fact that Stanley airfield had been put out of commission was thought to be a sufficient justification, while the epic nature of the operation ruled out anything other than praise and admiration: to question its value would have seemed to belittle the skill and courage of the men involved. In practice, the major benefits of the Black Buck raid appear to have been much more in the realms of psychological warfare – as a boost to British morale, as a symbol of capability and, perhaps most importantly, the attacks 'forced the Argentine air commander to reposition his Mirage fighters to meet possible attacks on the mainland', thus denying fighter cover to the Skyhawks when, in later weeks, they attacked the task force.[26]

ANALYSING THE OPTIONS

While the media published the detailed accounts of the Black Buck raid, they also set it in a wider context. It was generally thought to be the opening of real hostilities. The accompanying Harrier attacks were seen as a secure indication that the task force had reached the Falklands: at this stage it was not generally known that in fact the task force was divided into two main elements – the carrier group and the amphibious group, with the latter still at Ascension Island. The strongest response to the news of the attacks was to ask what would happen next. This took up and intensified a strain of speculation which had been in evidence ever since the task force left the UK and which had consistently examined all the options open to the task force commanders.

Several main alternatives were identified or canvassed by different commentators as the most likely approach. These were a long blockade: a landing on West Falkland; a series of 'hit and run' raids; or a landing at an undefended or remote site on East Falkland – two reports specifically mentioned San Carlos as a likely site.[27] There was disagreement as to whether an early landing was likely or whether the task force would await reinforcements.

Concern about potential casualties came over clearly in much of the commentary, although the appreciation of the risks was not always accurate. Typical of several commentators, Brian Walden, describing an 'attrition strategy', thought that 'the risk of a large number of casualties through military action would probably be low', although he drew attention to the possibility of Argentine 'preemptive strikes' which 'might sink some of our ships and prevent the strategy from ever succeeding'. He went on to say that the bloodshed involved in an invasion could be considerable.[28] In reality, British ships at sea were far more vulnerable than troops on land, particularly once the latter had set up their air defence systems.[29]

This particular edition of *Weekend World* revealed some of the limitations of using a 'panel of experts' to define a preferred course of action: the experts disagreed among themselves, shifted their ground and were drawn by Brian Walden to a 'consensus' view barely supported by the preceding discussion, which remained fairly general and superficial. This was typical of the way *Weekend World* worked during the crisis, when the immediacy of the subject matter prevented the programme's being 'polished' before it was broadcast.

Another programme revealed some of the pitfalls of the 'panel' approach. In *TV Eye* on 29 April, Denis Tuohy chaired a discussion between Rear Admiral Martin Wemyss, Air Vice-Marshal Stewart Menaul and Lieutenant-Colonel Colin Mitchell.

The discussion began in a reasonably calm way. Air Vice-Marshal Menaul stressed the importance of controlling the air and sea around the task force and the Islands. He noted the Argentine air superiority 'at least on paper' but was confident that the Harriers 'would be able to take care of almost any type of air operation that the Argentines could mount'.

Rear Admiral Wemyss advocated an early landing which should be both 'brutal' and 'bloodless'. This paradox, he explained, meant putting 'the best of our people in very soon'. Lieutenant-Colonel Mitchell was more doubtful: the political limitation on what could be done militarily made the operation 'a nightmare for anybody. Even for an Admiral I should think.' Rear Admiral Wemyss believed however that '. . . when time really comes, even if we land away from Port Stanley . . . very many of those Argentine troops will run for the nearest white flag'. After further discussion about the options, the panel returned to discussing the Argentine armed forces. The assessments included the following:

They're national service boys, ten thousand, who aren't even a formation . . . They are very untrained, they've never seen a shot fired in anger, none of their officers have . . . I should think the morale of the Argentines in the Falklands is absolute zero now . . .

And I should think the appearance of ten Royal Marines will be enough to make them have this dysentery we've heard about in the newspapers . . .

They don't know where we're coming. They don't know where we're going to land, they don't know what we're going to do. I think they're in complete confusion.

. . . if the Argentinians get very stupid and try and fight us the hard way, there will be a lot of very dead Argentinians.

As a serious means of informing the public about the prospects of fighting and the likelihood of casualties, statements of this kind seem to be of minimal value. They seriously underestimated the determination and fighting capability of the Argentine forces. They came closer to propaganda than to informed discussion and had much in common with that element of the popular press which one analyst subsequently described as falling naturally into place 'at the level of boys' comics'.[30]

THE *GENERAL BELGRANO*

The popular press were stimulated to a further excess of jingoism by the sinking on 2 May of the Argentine battle cruiser, *General Belgrano*, with the loss of 368 lives. This occasioned the *Sun*'s notorious headline 'GOTCHA!', although once the number of casualties was known, the *Sun*, in common with other newspapers, muted its tone.

News of the successful attack on the *General Belgrano* was broadcast early on 3 May and it received detailed coverage in that day's news programmes and in the following morning's newspapers. Several newspapers described in some detail – presumably mostly supposition – how the attack would have happened. A number quoted a report from the Press Association that it had been disclosed that HMS *Conqueror* sank the *General Belgrano*. This appears to have stemmed from a leak by ITN's Mike Nicholson, on board HMS *Hermes*. According to one account, on 3 May:

> Mike Nicholson on board the MARISAT ship *Olmeda* happened to overhear on the bridge the name of the nuclear submarine responsible, HMS *Conqueror*. This was confirmed to him by what he calls 'a senior naval source'. Nicholson promptly broadcast the information in a dispatch to ITN's *News at One*.[31]

The HCDC did not ask Nicholson about this incident, but Captain Middleton of HMS *Hermes* told them:

> In point of fact, Michael Nicholson was not in the ship at the time because on 1st May he went across to RFA *Olmeda* to use the Marisat satellite and he was in *Olmeda* when the *Belgrano* incident happened. He got the name of the *Conqueror* from his editor in London.[32]

It is thus unclear where Nicholson received his information. However, publishing *Conqueror*'s name broke a cardinal MoD rule – that the whereabouts of SSNs is never revealed. It certainly seems likely to have reinforced the military view that, in Nicholson's own words, 'The press will always do the dirty because it is their instinct to do so . . .'[33]

The death toll following the sinking of the *General Belgrano* clearly shocked media, politicians and public alike. Even at the time, the sinking was controversial – but the controversy was different from that which was to develop after the end of the Falklands War. This later (and continuing) debate centred on the timing of the sinking in relation to the peace plan put forward by President Belaunde Terry of Peru: it was in effect claimed – and disputed – that the Prime Minister authorised the attack on the *General Belgrano* in order to scupper the peace talks. At the time, it was recognised that the sinking would have implications for Britain's diplomacy, but these were generally considered to be the risk that support for Britain would be diminished in Europe and elsewhere.[34]

Diplomatic issues apart, the contemporary controversy focused on three main questions: Was the sinking necessary since the cruiser had been outside the Total Exclusion Zone (TEZ)? Why had the loss of life been so high? Had the action been approved by ministers? Speaking on ITN, Rear Admiral Wemyss was adamant that 'the only reason we would have taken out that cruiser' was to prevent serious loss of life[35] – an argument that was deployed by ministers and, in a rare interview a few days later, by the Chief of Defence Staff, Sir Terence Lewin.[36] In an 'Insight' article on 9 May, the *Sunday Times* described it as 'a matter of dispute' whether the *General Belgrano* was an active threat to the task force, justifying the sinking, and questioned whether the commander of HMS *Conqueror* equated the sinking of a cruiser 'with over 1000 men on board' with 'his Goverment's policy of minimum force'. Elsewhere, the media discussed whether the attack had been permitted by the Rules of Engagement (ROE) which set out the conditions under which the task force could open fire. What was not known at the time was that the Rules of Engagement had been changed to permit attacks outside the exclusion zone.

The question of casualties was to the fore. Several reports claimed that the British had fired only two torpedoes in order to damage and not sink the cruiser, in an attempt to minimise loss of life.[37] Gareth Parry, with the task force, reported that the latter had shown 'some compassion' by allowing the cruiser's escorts to sail away,[38] while the *Sunday Times* article quoted above suggested that HMS *Conqueror* had attacked the cruiser rather than the escorts with the intention of saving life.

All these reports missed two fundamental points. The first relates to the concept of minimum force. This is a widely quoted phrase, but one which has no categorical legal – or military – definition. It means the least amount of force necessary to secure a particular objective; but to be sure of securing an objective, the military must use *adequate* force: that is, enough to be reasonably sure of putting an enemy out of action. The British armed forces do not 'shoot to wound' – to do so is risky and uncertain. The degree of uncertainty is demonstrated by the fact that HMS *Conqueror* fired not two but three torpedoes – but one missed. There was no intention to minimise – or maximise – casualties; *Conqueror*'s aim was to ensure that the *General Belgrano* was put out of action.

The second misconception related to the way in which submarine operations affected the number of casualties. HMS *Conqueror* could not search for survivors without surfacing and so endangering herself. Much was made of the failure of the Argentine escorts to search for casualties – but their movements too were governed by prudence, and by the need to avoid risking even more lives. They were not to know that HMS *Conqueror* was not waiting to attack them; accordingly they dropped depth charges and sailed away from the scene of attack – in naval terms a perfectly sensible course. This was not, however, widely appreciated by the media, although it was noted by David Fairhall in the *Guardian*.[39]

The issue of political control remains contentious even now. Like other aspects of the continuing Belgrano controversy, this – in part at least – is because of the way the government responded to the initial questioning. The central issue at the time was who had authorised the firing? The first MoD statements reported simply that the action was 'fully in accordance with the instructions given to the task force commander'.[40] The media interpreted this as meaning that the decision to fire had been taken within the task force – *The Times* reported that the submarine commander probably 'conferred with the task force commander'.[41] The *Sunday Times* claimed that the 'crucial blow was delivered without consultation, political or otherwise', because the submarine was unable to communicate with the UK since to do so would have given its position away.[42]

This view was quite widely shared: confusion was not dispelled by ministerial and official statements. Asked whether she had personally sanctioned the attack on the cruiser, Mrs Thatcher assured the House of Commons that 'the task force is under full political control . . .', which implied that she had been consulted, but failed to give explicit confirmation. The

Ministry of Defence pointed out that 'ships' commanding officers in the RN are allowed to exercise their own discretion at least to some extent in deciding when to fire . . .',[43] which implied that the decision had been the commanding officer's. Both statements were of course true – the Prime Minister and her colleagues had agreed that HMS *Conqueror* could fire on the *General Belgrano* and changes made in the Rules of Engagement some days previously to allow attacks on Argentine vessels outside the TEZ accommodated this; the actual decision *when* to fire had been taken by *Conqueror*'s commanding officer. This dual process of decision-making was possible because HMS *Conqueror* actually followed the *Belgrano* for some thirty hours, having detected it on 1 May. In May 1982 and thereafter, all official statements said that the *Belgrano* had been detected on 2 May – the day it was sunk. It was not until two years later that the truth emerged.[44]

The government have claimed that this and other discrepancies arose in part because of the 'fog of war', and in part because of the need to protect sensitive operational and intelligence information. The government's critics have claimed that there have been consistent attempts to cover up the truth. It is difficult to credit that a sustained government effort to manipulate and conceal information would have resulted in such a clumsy and inconsistent cover-up. It seems probable that having made incorrect statements due to genuine confusion, the government were at first reluctant to put the record straight for fear of prejudicing current operations. Then, after the war, concern about political embarrassment and the mistaken desire to close the subject led them to decide against publishing the full story.

In these circumstances, it is understandable that the media accounts were often confused and inaccurate: they did however succeed in identifying the main issues arising out of this action which so undermined the international support for Britain.

HMS *SHEFFIELD*

Another tragedy that same week redeemed Britain's international position, for the victim was the Royal Navy. On the evening of 4 May the BBC's *Nine O'Clock News* was interrupted for a statement by Ian MacDonald at the MoD, announcing that HMS *Sheffield* had been hit. John Nott was forced to return to the dispatch box in the House of Commons to announce the loss of the *Sheffield* after it had been hit by an Exocet missile.

The next few days saw the media and the public alike receiving an education in modern warfare – what was an Exocet, how could it be stopped, what was Sea Wolf, why had *Sheffield* burned so quickly?

There was disagreement in the press about the value of a new shipborne surface-to-air-missile, Sea Wolf. A number of reports described it as the only defence against Exocet – indeed one report, in the *Standard*, described the missile as specifically 'designed to combat the Exocet'.[45] The *Daily Telegraph*'s air correspondent, Air Commodore Cooper, wrote however that the task force had no defences guaranteed to stop the Exocet – the Sea Wolf missile was not of the type to do so.[46] This point was taken up by Bridget Bloom, who reported that both Sea Dart and Sea Wolf were alleged to lack adequate tracking radar to deal with sea-skimming missiles.[47]

Other articles referred to alternative measures of defence. Several were identified: chaff, ECM and the possibility of shooting the missile down with a gun.[48]

One commentator who commanded much media attention was Anthony Preston. Appearing on *The World at One* on 6 May, he questioned whether there had been a 'lapse in operational procedure'. The Captain's statement that he had seen the missile implied that the ship was not at action stations and an unconfirmed report of radar silence would mean the big 965 air-warning radar was not switched on, although switching radar off was a device used to conceal ships. Preston believed that in theory *Sheffield*'s Sea Dart missiles should have been capable of engaging the Super Etendard and he listed various passive counter-measures that could have been used. Finally he described the 'severe political constraints' that had surrounded the Type 42, leading to a design which prevented its being fitted with Sea Wolf when that became available.

As well as asking how the *Sheffield* had come to be hit, the media focused considerable attention on the implications of the loss. Argentina was estimated to have anything from five to twelve Super Etendards and not more than twenty Exocets.[49] In fact the lower figure for the aircraft was correct and one of the five was cannibalised to provide spares for the others, while a total of only five missiles had been delivered. Several commentators suggested that the threat posed by these systems would lead to a change in Britain's plans. The *Daily Express* and *New York Times* surmised accurately that Admiral Woodward would have ordered his ships out of range of the Argentine Air Force.[50] The *Scotsman* stated that the task force ships were believed to have closed together as a defence against air attack,[51] while the *Washington Post* had them scattering rather than fight it out with the Argentine Navy in the face of a major Argentine naval attack.[52] Thus, as usual, expert opinion not only differed but was even contradictory.

The loss of the *Sheffield* was in several ways a turning point in the commentary on the Falklands conflict, particularly following so closely on the sinking of the *General Belgrano*. The media now saw that the fighting was for real: 'bloodless brutality' was not practical. The prospects of a negotiated settlement seemed to be fading, despite the efforts of Peru and of the UN Secretary General: the loss of life was mounting. The confidence that came from the apparent ease with which South Georgia had been captured and the mounting of the record-breaking Black Buck raid, was shaken; particularly when, the day after the loss of HMS *Sheffield*, two Sea Harriers – 10 per cent of the Harrier force – were lost in a mid-air collision.

NOTES

1. These arguments were advanced variously by, for example, Rear Admiral Gueritz, *The World at One*, 9 April; Brigadier Hunt, *PM*, 9 April; Professor Freedman, *TV Eye*, 15 April, Brian Walden and Brigadier Hunt, *Weekend World*, 18 April.
2. Quoted in 'Change of Course', *Standard*, 20 April.
3. In the *News at Ten* Geoffrey Archer reported that it was 'possible' that a small group of ships was sailing for South Georgia, and that there was speculation that the Marines would recapture it with little difficulty.
4. 'British Squadron is Heading for South Georgia at Full Speed', *Guardian*, 21 April.
5. 'Fleet Ready for Action', *Daily Mail*, 21 April.
6. *Newsnight*, 21 April.
7. Hastings and Jenkins, *Battle for the Falklands*, p. 125.
8. Reported in *News at Ten*, 22 April.
9. For example, in both the BBC's *Nine O'Clock News* and ITN's *News at Ten*.
10. *PM*, 23 April.

11. BBC *Nine O'Clock News*, 24 April.
12. In his evidence to the HCDC, Max Hastings said: 'Reports published in the newspapers in London of the way in which South Georgia had been retaken were complete and absolute rubbish from beginning to end . . .', HCDC *Report*, vol. II, Q675.
13. Memorandum by the MOD, HCDC *Report*, vol. II, p. 417.
14. According to *Newsnight* on 24 April, the Argentines thought that the attack on South Georgia might not now be 'imminent', while US sources also were not expecting any immediate action.
15. Memorandum by the BBC, HCDC *Report*, vol. II, p. 45.
16. Hastings and Jenkins, *Battle for the Falklands*, p. 129.
17. Memorandum by the BBC, HCDC *Report*, vol. II, p. 46.
18. Memorandum by MoD, HCDC *Report*, vol. II, p. 415.
19. HCDC *Report*, vol. II, Q731.
20. For example the *Sunday Times*, 11 April, *Sun*, 14 and 15 April, *Daily Express*, 19 April, *PM*, 9 April, ITN *News at Ten*, 11 April.
21. *The World at One*, 19 April.
22. *The World Tonight*, 19 April.
23. Owen Thetford, *Aircraft of the Royal Air Force since 1918* (London: Pitman & Co., 1968).
24. For example in the *New York Times*, 21 April, *Daily Telegraph*, 29 April, *Scotsman*, 28 April and *Guardian*, 29 April.
25. For example ITN *News at One*, 1 May, *The World at One*, 1 May.
26. Ethell and Price, *Air War South Atlantic*, p. 218; for a detailed account of the Black Buck raid and the difficulties it posed see ibid., pp. 43–73.
27. *Newsnight*, 26 April, *New York Times*, 29 April.
28. *Weekend World*, 2 May.
29. Comparison with the *General Belgrano* is not entirely fair since that was an older ship than any in the task force and its conscript crew may have had less training and skill in damage control than their RN counterparts, but the speed with which the cruiser sank and the heavy losses give some idea of how much worse the British would have fared had one of their ships been hit by torpedoes below the water level rather than by a missile or bomb above it.
30. Patricia Holland, 'Public Opinion, the Popular Press and the Organisation of Ideas' in *Falklands/Malvinas: Whose Crisis?* (London: Latin American Bureau, 1982).
31. Harris, *Gotcha!*, p. 108.
32. HCDC *Report*, vol. II, Q1120.
33. Ibid., Q471.
34. The *Financial Times*, 5 May 1982. At the time reports about the Argentine response to the Peruvian peace proposals did not generally relate it to the sinking of the *General Belgrano*; Rudolfo Baltierrez, the presidential spokesman, said the peace plan was 'essentially similar to the last peace proposal presented by Mr Alexander Haig in Washington and turned down by Buenos Aires . . .' (*Financial Times*, 4 May). Although the Argentine position was initially said to have hardened as a result of the sinking, by 11 May the *Guardian* was reporting a *softer* Argentine line on sovereignty.

35. ITN *News at One*, 4 May.
36. *The World Tonight*, 7 May.
37. *The Times*, *Financial Times*, 4 May.
38. *Guardian*, 4 May.
39. *Guardian*, 5 May.
40. *The Times*, 3 May.
41. *The Times*, 4 May.
42. *Sunday Times*, 9 May.
43. *The Times*, 5 May.
44. In a letter from the Prime Minister to Mr Denzil Davies MP, 5 May 1984.
45. 'Has this Missile Changed the Whole Strategy?', *Standard*, 6 May.
46. 'Paris Halts Order for Jets . . .', *Daily Telegraph*, 6 May.
47. 'Navy Ships lack Defence against Exocet Missile', *Financial Times*, 6 May.
48. For example, in the *Daily Mail*, 6 May, *Scotsman*, 6 May and *ITN*, 5 May.
49. *The Times*, 5 May, reported that five out of fourteen Super Etendards had been delivered. The *Daily Telegraph*, 6 May, reported that up to twelve could be in service, and it was 'unlikely' that more than twenty Exocets had been delivered.
50. 'Target Invincible', *Daily Express*, 6 May. 'British Fleet's Options after Ship's Loss', *New York Times*, 7 May.
51. 'Task Force Worried over Air Cover', *Scotsman*, 7 May.
52. 'Successful Attack on Destroyer . . .', *Washington Post*, 5 May.

6 Building up to the Invasion: 8–21 May

FORCE COMPARISONS

The first engagements led to renewed efforts to assess the military strength of the two sides. This seems a sensible approach – to measure expectation against outcome and revise one's analysis accordingly.

These later force comparisons were more sophisticated than their predecessors. Some straightforward numerical comparisons did still appear, particularly relating to air and ground forces, but these no longer dominated attempts to weigh up the two sides. Material comparing forces covered all three fighting environments – sea, land and air – but more emphasis than before was placed on the relationship between them, particularly between air and naval power.

NAVAL FORCES

The surface ships of the Argentine Navy (ARA) were no longer generally thought likely to threaten the task force, particularly after the sinking of the *General Belgrano* had demonstrated the capabilities of the British hunter-killer submarines. The extension of the Total Exclusion Zone to within twelve miles of Argentina's coast reinforced the threat to the ARA. So, while on 7 May, the BBC's *Nine O'Clock News* suggested that '... What may be worrying the Defence chiefs most is that Argentina could be planning an attack on the British troop convoy which is steadily approaching the Falklands ...', only a few days later, the Argentine fleet could be dismissed as 'basically a coastal defence rather than a blue-water fleet'.[1] Argentina's submarines continued to pose a more serious threat. One submarine was known to be in port, one had been captured off South Georgia and two were believed still to be at large – although one of these was actually also in port, undergoing repairs. The submarine threat was the subject of a number of analyses which were not only more detailed, but also more sophisticated, than some earlier material. The difficulties facing British ASW operations were identified,[2] as was the threat to the task force's supply chain.[3]

AIR FORCES

After the sinking of HMS *Sheffield*, the air threat, and particularly the Exocet missile, became something of a media obsession. Headlines ranged from 'TASK FORCE WORRIED OVER AIR COVER'[4] to 'HOLE IN THE MISSILE UMBRELLA'[5] and (perhaps predictably) the *Sun*'s 'MENACE OF THE ARGY SKY FORCE'.[6]

Two typical articles dealt in some detail with air operations. The first, in the *Sunday Telegraph*, described some of the new weapons being tested in the war – the advanced radar and bombing computers of the Vulcans, and radar-guided missiles. It reported accurately that Argentine anti-aircraft missiles lacked a night-firing radar package, and inaccurately that the Sea Harriers did not have the latest AIM9L model of the Sidewinder missile.[7] A later article in *Flight International* gave a blow-by-blow account of air operations so far. It reported what was then the currently-held belief that the *General Belgrano* had been sunk by two Mark 24 wire-guided homing torpedoes: it was not until much later that it became known that the older Mark 8 had been used in preference.[8]

Following its extension to within twelve miles of the Argentine mainland, there was considerable debate over the purpose and effectiveness of the Total Exclusion Zone, particularly with regard to aircraft. Christopher Lee, BBC Radio defence correspondent, described it as a 'step before bombing the mainland'. He agreed with the interviewer, Brian Redhead, that extension of the TEZ was 'us taking another initiative' to exert more military and more political pressure.[9] The BBC was not always impartial: Redhead replied enthusiastically to Lee's comments 'Good!'

The effectiveness of the Exclusion Zone was clearly called into question by an Argentine TV film, purportedly shot in the Falklands and flown out by Argentine aircraft. Speaking on Radio 4, Major Bob Elliot of the IISS pointed out that with seventeen aircraft, the British could not put a tight blockade over the whole area – hence the bombing of Stanley airfield.[10] Airfields could be repaired, but he thought the resupply pattern to the Falklands must have been cut down. It was also possible that Hercules C-130s were making air drops on the Islands. The Harrier reinforcements en route might not necessarily make the blockade more effective, since most were designed for close support of the ground forces. Major Elliot also picked out a gap in Argentine tactics – one which, when remedied, brought heavy losses on both sides: he pointed out that 'so far we haven't seen a large Argentine air component over the Islands'. This, he suggested, might be due to differences in the junta, or might be because the air commander was holding back until it was really necessary, because of the difficulty in maintaining aircraft in combat at that range. Within Argentina, controversy continues over the reasons for the delay in committing the air force to action: political as well as operational factors seem to have been involved.[11]

Speculation continued as to whether the Argentines were still getting air supplies through, with *Newsnight* on 11 May reporting a claim by Argentine television that 'Stanley airport is still being used by these very hardy Hercules freighter aircraft' (this proved to be one truthful Argentine news report).

The *Economist* reported that there was evidence that the damage to Goose Green and Stanley airfields was much less than had been previously believed.[12] By this time, there had been two Vulcan attacks on Stanley airfield, several Harrier raids and, for several days, daily naval bombardment: it was clear that the success of the initial Black Buck raid had been limited, although some confusion was understandable given the simple but effective deception measures taken by Argentina to make the damage to the airfield look worse than it was.

THE MISSILE AGE – EXOCET AND SEA WOLF

The 'missile war' was the subject of the most detailed analysis, with the debate over Sea Wolf still raging. This now went beyond initial basic claims that the 'only' defence against Exocet was Sea Wolf, indeed the capability of the latter was still being questioned,[13] to the extent that its manufacturers, Marconi, found it necessary to issue a press statement confirming Sea Wolf's capability against Exocet.

The adequacy of the Type 42 destroyer's armaments continued to be criticised. Anthony Preston blamed the 'defence procurement bureaucracy' for being too slow in providing the development of the new lightweight Sea Wolf which might have defended *Sheffield*: Michael Mates MP, a member of the HCDC (which had just examined defence procurement), denied that MoD had been dilatory: once the Operational Requirement had emerged, he said, the decision to allocate a contract had been taken reasonably quickly 'within overall naval priorities'.[14] *Newsnight* and ITN continued the debate on 12 May, asking specifically whether HMS *Sheffield* would have been saved if she had been equipped with Sea Wolf. Their conclusion was that this would not necessarily have been the case.

THE FIRST UXB

Few analyses of the air war prior to the San Carlos landings identified the threat (which was to prove very serious) of 'iron bombs'.[15] On 12 May, HMS *Glasgow* was hit by a bomb which failed to explode. During the next month, seven further vessels were hit by UXBs: only one, HMS *Ardent*, was lost when a bomb disposal expert attempted to defuse the bomb. The Argentine bombs failed to explode because in order to evade the task force's Sea Dart missiles, the Skyhawk pilots came in low. This allowed insufficient flight time for the bombs to fuse. Had the Argentines remedied this, British losses could have been disastrously higher.

Later, the MoD came to appreciate this and clamped down on news of UXBs, but when *Glasgow* was hit, the need for secrecy was not recognised and MoD announced the bomb's failure to explode. On 14 May, Peter Snow reported on *Newsnight*: '. . . we do now know that the Argentine Skyhawk attack on the British warship two days ago was a very lucky escape for the Royal Navy. The bomb, dropped at very low level, passed right through the side of the ship and out the other without exploding.'

LAND FORCES

As the likelihood increased that there would be a British invasion of the Falklands, so the media devoted more attention to the land forces of the two sides. The total manpower of the task force numbered some 28 000 people, of whom 10 000 men were eventually put ashore.[16] These comprised about 5000 in the first wave – 3 Commando Brigade and supporting units, reinforced with 2nd and 3rd Battalions the Parachute Regiment (2 Para and 3 Para) – and another 5000 in 5 Infantry Brigade which was to land at the beginning of June. Argentine forces in the Falklands appear to have numbered about 14 000, although this may include airmen, sailors, administrators and other non-combat troops.

The estimates of force sizes in the media varied widely. Those of the Argentine forces ranged from 5000 to around 10 000; estimates of British force levels ranged from about 2000 to about 7000.

Different figures were reported by the same paper from day to day or by different papers on the same day. Those reports which gave details of the units involved also varied in accuracy: several referred only to two Marine Commandos instead of the three – 40, 42 and 45 Commandos – actually involved.[17] One omitted 2 Para.[18]

Perhaps because human qualities are less obvious than those of equipment, there were fewer comparisons of the relative capabilities of the ground forces. Although there were references to the higher quality of the British troops and to the Argentines' limited overland mobility,[19] less was made than hitherto of the poor condition and morale of the Argentine troops.

SPECIAL OPERATIONS

One aspect of operations which attracted some attention, perhaps because of the glamour which attaches to their activities, was the British use of Special Forces. Members of the SAS and SBS had landed on the Falklands as early as the beginning of May.[20] The official silence and the aura of mystery surrounding these units endow them with an irresistible magnetism as far as the media are concerned, but little hard fact emerged about their operations.

One of the most detailed reports was by *Newsnight* on 14 May. A Royal Marines training film was shown and Peter Snow interviewed Jim Short, whom he described as having 'made a special study of the SBS'. The interview was actually conducted sitting in a Gemini inflatable boat of the sort used by the SBS. Short described the equipment carried by the SBS for escape and evasion purposes, but refused to say how or where it could be concealed. He also described their underwater breathing apparatus and their weapons. Peter Snow asked various questions about SBS operations in the Falklands. Short made it clear that he could 'only speculate' as to how the SBS had got ashore – one possibility was that they had parachuted into the sea near the equator, been taken by submarine to the Falklands, then gone ashore by Gemini, canoe or surf board. Their task once ashore would be primarily beach reconnaissance – to check the gradient of the beaches for landing craft; to observe, identify and then 'neutralise' any barriers to landing; to locate Argentine observation posts and create diversions. He had with him a radio of the type carried by the SBS which, he said, was used in conjunction with special computerised equipment to code messages.

The line between giving away information which could serve an enemy and meeting the public right to information can be fine; a less cautious response to Snow's enthusiastic questioning might have got onto dangerous ground. As it was, however, the interview gave nothing away while bringing a measure of practical reality to the mythology surrounding the Special Forces. Moreover, although Short provided all the kit which was shown, his appearance, according to Peter Snow, had the 'blessing' of the SBS.[21]

OPERATIONS

By the end of the third week in May, most force comparisons were being set in the context of operations. Reports on the task force's movements accompanied speculation about the timing and tactics of any British landings. For weeks there had been predictions that an invasion was imminent; most commentators seem not to have realised that the amphibious group was several days' sailing behind the main task force. The amphibious group rendezvoused with the carrier force on 18 May. This was not formally announced to the media, but it is clear from the comments made on BBC News and in *Newsnight* that day that the news had got out. It had been thought that the troops were simply waiting on board ship at sea and that they risked losing their 'fighting edge'. Now it was assumed, correctly, that the rendezvous meant that the troops would not be kept at sea, but would land shortly. There was a widespread recognition that the weather was a crucial factor in determining that the landing must be soon.

The likely location of the landing had been the subject of considerable speculation. So far as can be judged from open sources, the task force commanders initially considered landings on West Falkland, at Lafonia, then in Berkely Sound, before deciding on San Carlos.[22] The commentators' early enthusiasm for a landing on West Falkland diminished with the passage of time, although some still advocated it – indeed, when the news of the landings first filtered through, some commentators appear to have believed West Falkland was involved.

Although most speculation focused on the likelihood of an unopposed landing, there remained a current of opinion which thought that an opposed landing possibly at, or close to, Stanley was likely. Not only was this represented as the view of the military commanders on *Canberra*,[23] Drew Middleton of the *New York Times* also quoted military analysts in London as considering it the most likely scenario.[24] It may also have been the expectation of General Menendez; this would explain the intensive mining of the waters around Stanley and the concentration of troops there.

Other Argentine sources seem to have taken a different view – in so far as real intelligence and disinformation can be disentangled. An Argentine analysis which was passed to several journalists as an 'official leak' expected a 'five-prong attack' on various locations, but including a landing on the East Falkland side of Falkland sound – that is, somewhere along the same coast as the actual landing site at San Carlos.[25]

Most commentators were deliberately vague about the possible landing site – understandably, since there seemed to be a number from which to choose, particularly in the absence of knowledge of tides, gradient of the beach and other local conditions. Some were, however, more specific. Frank Draper, writing in the *Standard* of 20 May, quoted unnamed experts as believing the assault was more likely to be away from Stanley at Foul Bay, Port Louis, San Salvador or *San Carlos*. San Carlos had already been mentioned specifically in earlier reports (see p. 88). None of these references seems likely to have given anything away to Argentina (even when the landings took place the Argentines were not at first convinced that San Carlos was a serious target), but it is understandable that the military planners may have felt at times that the media were trying to give all their secrets away.

Speculation about the timing of an invasion appears on two occasions at least to have been fuelled by statements or leaks from official sources. On 13 May, Trevor MacDonald reported for ITN on the view at the UN that Britain would go ahead with its plan to invade the Falklands, probably in a couple of days' time. Two pieces of evidence were quoted: Sir Nicholas Henderson, the British Ambassador to Washington, had spoken on US television of 'events taking their inexorable course'; and Sir Anthony Parsons, the UK's representative at the UN, had said that the military option would not be held back indefinitely. Five days later, on 18 May, Peter Snow reported on *Newsnight* '. . . the mood here among the military chiefs in London is that an invasion may be only hours away – and will almost certainly come this week'. The reporters interviewed by the authors all stated categorically that references of this kind to the view of the military or 'in Whitehall' meant that an official or military source had provided the information.

One other *Newsnight* programme deserves special mention in the context of the run-up to the San Carlos landings; that of 19 May, in which Peter Snow examined 'the way an invasion might take place'. First he described the landing 'on a beach that's virtually undefended . . . unlike the D-Day reinvasion, the landing is sure to be in the dark'; *Fearless* and *Intrepid*, the main assault ships, could take 700 marines and 'a whole load of heavy equipment which we saw on *Fearless*'s deck at Ascension Island two weeks ago'. Together with the five Landing Ships Logistic, these ships would edge close inshore. The SBS would have carried out a reconnaissance, looking for approaches clear of kelp. The first wave of assault troops would 'sweep onto the beach'. Rapiers would be landed to provide air defence. RAF Harriers would operate 'right inside' the beach-head, providing close support and air defence. The landing must be complete by first light, when the entire supporting and amphibious force would be withdrawn.

The description was marvellously dramatic. It described a classic amphibious landing operation and did not go beyond the bounds of what could be discovered in open sources about such operations (although the reference to the sighting of *Fearless* off Ascension suggests that the Chiefs of Staff were wise to be concerned about the intelligence that might be collected there). It does however raise questions about the role and objective of such commentary. This was not historical information – the landings, after all, had not yet taken place. It was rather a preview of a forthcoming event. It not only informed the audience about the details of how an amphibious landing would take place but, by imbuing the occasion with a sense of excitement and anticipation, it came close to entertainment – offering the same vicarious participation as a film or play.

In the final resort the speculators were out-manoeuvred by the Ministry of Defence in the person of Sir Frank Cooper, the Permanent Under-Secretary at the MoD. On 20 May at a routine briefing (the unattributable briefings having been reinstated from 11 May), Sir Frank replied to a question about operations:

> But what I think is likely to happen is that there will be an increase in pressure – the screw will be turned – and it will be in a variety of ways. I think we have all tended to think this is a rather dramatic way of the landing ships dashing up to the beaches and chaps storming out and lying on their tummies and wriggling up through barbed wire. I don't think that is the kind of picture that one has. But I think the screw will be tightened at a variety of points . . .

The transcript concludes with Sir Frank Cooper pointing out that the task force commander now had more forces and a wider variety of forces at his disposal, and was therefore likely to 'step up action in a whole different variety of ways'.[26]

This briefing influenced almost all reports in the British media that evening and the next day, 21 May. *Newsnight* reported that 'hit and run' attacks were to be expected rather than a major battle; the same phrase, 'hit and run', appeared in accounts in the next day's *Daily Mirror*, *Guardian* and *Sun*. The *Daily Mirror* and the *Daily Express* both carried the same headline 'SMASH AND GRAB'; while the *Daily Telegraph* and the *Sun* both referred to 'attrition'.

The Ministry of Defence had good reason for wanting to mislead the Argentines about the San Carlos landings when both ships and land forces were at their most vulnerable. The hills around San Carlos water limited the effectiveness of the ships' air defence radars and it was to be several hours before the land-based Rapier anti-aircraft missiles were effective. Forceful opposition would have made the landings a much more hazardous and bloody operation. The task force commanders were becoming increasingly alarmed at the volume of speculation in the media: undoubtedly anything which deceived the Argentines as to their intentions would be welcomed by them. Moreover, the media had themselves prepared the ground for what they subsequently saw as a major piece of misinformation. There had been much speculation that an early raiding operation would be repeated[27] – although it is unclear to what extent this was prompted by official sources, particularly in the week prior to the San Carlos landings.

Sir Frank Cooper told the HCDC that on the morning of 21 May at 11.45, which was first light in the Falklands, he met the editors and asked them

> quite openly and specifically to be rather 'confused' during the day as we would like to hold on as long as possible the whole question of establishing the beach-head because light was breaking in the Falklands and we had got the whole of the stores and a lot of people still to get ashore, and we did not want to give any information to the Argentines as to where we were, what our intentions were, and what forces were going there.[28]

The media complied, up to a point, but they still attempted, with the help of the expert commentators, to interpret MoD's announcements. The first of these, Ian MacDonald's noon statement to the media, was distinctly misleading: 'The task force has landed a number of raiding parties in the Falklands during the night. These raids are still in progress. Early indications are that they are achieving their objectives.'[29] This seemed a logical follow-on from the Cooper briefing, but the commentators began to sense that something more was involved. By lunchtime that day Cooper was hinting that this was the real thing. ITN's Michael Green reported from MoD that 'the feeling here is that the raids are moving from a hit and run to a hit and hold phase'. Later, in the *News at One*, Rear Admiral Wemyss commented that

> MoD are being very careful and I deeply approve of this, of not giving the impression of a full-scale invasion . . . This is not a wartime invasion to kill people, it is a reoccupation of territory annexed by illegal means and we're going ashore to establish a presence to defend ourselves and to persuade the Argentines to go home.

Air Vice-Marshal Menaul interpreted the MoD announcement of Harrier raids on West Falkland as implying that landings had taken place there. By 5.45 p.m. the picture was still unclear: ITN's Geoffrey Archer said of the operation that 'it cannot be called an invasion'. Rear Admiral Gueritz, interviewed on the BBC's *Nine O'Clock News*, thought that a bridgehead had been established for further exploitation. It was thus becoming clear that there was a main landing site and by the time *Newsnight* went on the air, the uncertainty was diminishing. Peter Snow described the day's operations as 'a number of raids all over the Islands' but said that some troops were ashore at San Carlos.

It was only when the Defence Secretary made a press statement later that evening that the full scale of the landing became definitely known. The deception appears to have worked. It built effectively, if unintentionally, on the reported Argentine speculation that the task force would invade at five points, and the Argentines seem initially to have been confused by the various diversionary operations. ITN's *News at 5.45* reported that 'According to Argentine reports, one of the main British raids took place at San Carlos' but this was interpreted as a diversionary attack. Serious as the later air attacks on the task force were, this initial confusion meant that at least the major part of the landing had been accomplished before the main air attacks began.

The media complained bitterly after the event about the way they had been manipulated. The harsh fact is that through their willingness to publish speculation they lent themselves to the deception. It is conceivable that if MoD had taken editors more into its confidence, as subsequently suggested by the HCDC, the deception of the Argentines could have been maintained with media connivance, rather than with their unwitting assistance – but the grounds for believing this are not firm. Despite the fact that editors were asked to keep things 'confused' on 21 May, the media interpretation of events sought to go beyond the MoD statement and the subsequent case of the reporting of unexploded bombs despite a request to editors to suppress the material showed how ineffective such measures could prove. Some of the defence correspondents interviewed by the author were similarly sceptical about the practicality of collusion between MoD and the media (see Chapter 10).

NOTES

1. 'Argentina's Next Move', *New York Times*, 16 May.
2. For example, in the *Financial Times*, 20 May.
3. *Newsnight*, 11 May.
4. *Scotsman*, 7 May.
5. *Observer*, 9 May.
6. *Sun*, 22 May.
7. *Sunday Telegraph*, 9 May.
8. 'Casualties Mount in Falklands Hostilities', *Flight International*, 15 May.
9. *Today*, 8 May.
10. *The World at One*, 10 May.
11. See for example 'Malvinas Post-mortem Hits the Fan', *Latin America Regional Reports Southern Cone RS-83-07* (September 1983).
12. 'Task Force Closing In', *Economist*, 15 May.
13. For example by Admiral Robert Falls, chairman of NATO's Military Committee, as reported in the *Guardian*, 7 May, and *Newsnight*, 10 May.
14. *The World at One*, 12 May.
15. One exception was an article in the *Guardian*, 20 May: 'The News from the Bridge'.
16. Cmnd. 8758, para 108.
17. *New York Times*, 16 and 19 May, *The Times*, 18 May; *Daily Telegraph*, 19 May. BBC TV also deliberately omitted reference to 45 Cdo RM because their departure had not been officially confirmed (interview with Chris Wain).
18. *New York Times*, 19 May.

19. For example in the *Guardian*, 15 May.
20. Hastings and Jenkins, *Battle for the Falklands*, p. 176.
21. Interview with the author.
22. Hastings and Jenkins, *Battle for the Falklands*, passim.
23. 'Chiefs of Staff Spell out Stark Options', *Sunday Times*, 16 May.
24. *New York Times*, 19 and 21 May.
25. 'Junta expects a Five-pronged Attack', *The Times*, 20 May.
26. HCDC *Report*, vol. ii, p. 432.
27. For example in *The Times*, 17 and 19 May; *Guardian*, 18 May; *Scotsman*, 19 May; *Washington Post*, 20 May.
28. HCDC *Report*, vol. ii, Q1910. One senior official told Professor Freedman and the author 'it would have been criminal not to create as much confusion as we possibly could'. His only regret was that MoD had not had a better formulated and concerted plan for the deception, rather than having to conceive it off the cuff.
29. Reported on ITN's *News at One*.

7 Consolidation and Advance: 22–29 May

The main British landing at San Carlos – codenamed Operation Sutton – began at about 4 a.m. local time – about 8 a.m. in the UK. The troops were ashore when, soon after full light, the air attacks began. The first raid was by four Pucara aircraft which unsuccessfully attacked 2 Para; two aircraft were shot down. Later a single Aeromacchi, possibly a reconnaissance flight, hit HMS *Argonaut* with cannon fire. Then began the massed air attack which was to last six hours and cost the British one ship, HMS *Ardent*, lost and four others damaged, two by unexploded bombs.

By the morning of 22 May, the news both of the San Carlos landings and the air attacks had made the headlines. In the circumstances it is unsurprising that the media commentary over the next week was dominated by two themes: the extent of the air threat and task force commanders' plans.

AIR THREAT AND AIR DEFENCE

The *Financial Times* followed the San Carlos landings with a detailed analysis of the task force's air defence. A serious problem, it suggested, was the lack of depth: the task force was believed to have had twenty Sea Harriers of which three had been lost, plus a further eighteen to twenty still at sea on the *Atlantic Conveyor*. Naval strategists demanded three levels of air defence – point defence, area defence and airborne early warning (AEW). The absence of the latter was the most serious gap. The priority on landing would be to improve area defence by setting up Rapier missiles and air defence radar.[1] Other press reports added little to this, although a number continued to emphasise the Exocet threat.

Air operations were discussed in some detail in a *Newsnight* 'Special' on 22 May. Air Marshal Sir Alfred Ball was asked about the 'disappearance' of the Argentine Air Force. He described the previous day's operations as a 'significant victory in the air' for the British, in which the Argentines had been given a 'pretty bloody nose' and they would be 'licking their wounds'. More raids could be expected, but the Argentines could not sustain that rate of loss for long. Asked what he would do if he were Argentina's Air Force Chief, he replied 'I'd be thinking very carefully about getting the maximum out of the aircraft left' – advice which did no more than state the obvious.

The next day, 23 May, Air Chief Marshal Sir Christopher Foxley-Norris was interviewed in *Weekend World* (repeated in ITN's *News at Ten*). In the former, the Air Chief Marshal described the Argentine Air Force as 'extremely dangerous'. He continued: 'It's already been mentioned, a figure that I was unaware of, that we're talking in terms of about 40 Harriers in all. That means 30 serviceable Harriers . . . you don't get 40 out of 40 in the air and we're losing them gradually one by one.'[2] He then explained that the absence of air attacks the previous day was a natural consequence of the intense operations on 21 May. 'The more you fly on one day the less you can fly on the second day' but, he said, 'I should be astonished if they didn't come in quick and fast and soon . . .'

Air attacks had in fact been resumed that day; HMS *Antelope* was severely damaged by a UXB which exploded in the night. Several Argentine aircraft were shot down. The next day, three Royal Fleet Auxiliaries (RFAs) were hit by bombs which failed to explode. The lower level of Argentine air attacks and the task force successes led to a greater degree of confidence about the British ability to win the air battle: the question of the moment was 'Has Britain achieved air superiority?'

ITN's defence correspondent, Geoffrey Archer, thought that the Argentine ability to carry out major raids 'must be in doubt'. Air Vice-Marshal Menaul, also speaking on ITN on 24 May, considered air superiority an old-fashioned concept. The task force aircraft had been successful in controlling the air over the Falklands and Argentina could not sustain its present rate of losses. Numbers were not the only criterion: the British technical and professional skills were greater. While the assertion that the task force controlled the air over the Falklands was premature, these comments on air superiority avoided the simplistic number-crunching approach of much of the press comment.

The next day, 25 May, Argentine intentions were also discussed in *The Times*, the *Guardian*[3] and *The World Tonight*. In the last of these, Harold Blakemore of the Institute of Latin American Studies referred to the politicisation of the Argentine armed forces and the division between the three commands – air, naval and army. William Perry, Fellow in Latin American Studies at Georgetown, also spoke of the 'sharp differences in political philosophy' between the Argentine armed forces. He agreed with Major General Loudon that the British would succeed, but pointed out that the Argentine Air Force still had 'a few days of punch' left in it.

This warning was particularly timely given the day's events. 25 May is Argentina's National Day and the Argentine Air Force had mustered its depleted resources to mount a series of attacks. After destroying three enemy aircraft, HMS *Coventry* was hit by three 1000 lb bombs and sank. In the same attack, HMS *Broadsword* was hit by a bomb which failed to explode. Later, the container ship SS *Atlantic Conveyor* was hit by an Exocet missile and abandoned when fire blazed through the ship. The *Atlantic Conveyor*'s cargo of Harriers had already been off-loaded, but lost with the ship were three of the four Chinook helicopters sent to the task force and a considerable quantity of tents, protective clothing and vital engineering supplies. The loss of the *Atlantic Conveyor* was a serious blow and made the task of the ground forces and the remaining helicopter resources very much harder; a fact which some commentators failed to appreciate at the time.

That night, the Defence Secretary revealed that an unidentified ship (later named as HMS *Coventry*) had been sunk – an announcement which with hindsight the Ministry of Defence accepted had been a mistake.[4] The next morning, 26 May, details of the losses were made public. In an ITN *Falklands Special* that night Air Vice-Marshal Menaul departed from his earlier comments about the success of the task force's aircraft, to remark that he was 'disturbed' by the ease with which ships had been sunk by conventional bombs and that with relatively inexperienced pilots, aircraft should have been able to come in low, under the ship's radar. Certainly little of the previous weeks' commentary had prepared the public for losses to the old-fashioned 'iron bomb'. The success of the Exocet was, once it was understood, less surprising; this at least was, as Admiral John Nunn pointed out in *The World Tonight*,[5] a sophisticated modern weapon system. Four issues arising out of the air war received particularly widespread media attention and deserve further examination: the question of whether Argentine airfields should be attacked; the role of the Sea King helicopter found burnt out in Chile; the reporting of unexploded bombs; and the debate over ship design.

ATTACKS ON ARGENTINE AIRFIELDS

The suggestion that Argentine airfields should be attacked to prevent land-based aircraft striking the task force had first been raised in early April. During the week after the San Carlos landing it was repeatedly aired – and repeatedly dismissed.

Air Chief Marshal Sir Christopher Foxley-Norris, speaking on *Weekend World*, was quite categorical:

> It's appallingly frustrating for any air force such as our own to realise that they can bomb our airfields, in other words, the carriers and we can't bomb theirs. But the fact remains that in my opinion we are incapable of carrying out a sustained attack on a large number of Argentinian airfields from 3000 miles away with a minimal force of Vulcans which requires an enormous amount of refuelling. It's been proved since 1940, it's no good knocking out a runway unless you can attack it again and again and again – we haven't got the forces. I think we . . . militarily it's not a very good option but practically – it's not practicable.[6]

The government was not always consistent on this issue. On 26 May, John Nott told the House of Commons that bombing the mainland was 'not militarily feasible',[7] but the next day on *TV Eye* the Foreign Secretary refused to rule it out as a possibility, saying 'we have closed no military option'. None the less, Mr Nott's view had been heard. Christopher Wain in the BBC's *Evening News* on 26 May described Tory backbench demands to bomb Argentine airfields on the mainland as being 'regarded as unnecessary by most British military chiefs – and certainly undesirable'. On *The World at One* Air Chief Marshal Foxley-Norris repeated his view: advocates of bombing Argentine airfields, he said, 'haven't the faintest idea of what they're talking about'. Eventually, this authoritative view seems to have percolated through the system and laid the proposal to rest.[8]

THE CHILEAN INCIDENT

The wrecked Sea King helicopter found in Chile was immediately linked by the media to operations against Argentine airfields. The loss of the helicopter was announced on 20 May and covered in that evening's broadcasts. ITN's Geoffrey Archer pointed out in *News at Ten* that only 100 miles away from the site of the crash was the Argentine airbase of Rio Gallegos, from which Argentine aircraft were believed to operate. Speculation about the helicopter's activities was intense. All agreed that the Sea King's range meant that it must have taken off from a ship that had sailed nearer than the main body of the task force to the mainland. The *Daily Telegraph* suggested it might have been on ASW patrol[9] and *The Times* that it was listening to Argentine naval radio transmissions.[10] On 26 May, however, following the reappearance of the missing helicopter crew, several newspapers suggested that the helicopter had been involved in landing SAS troops for clandestine operations involving either the destruction of Super Etendard aircraft at Rio Gallegos or the installation and use of monitoring equipment to improve the warning of airborne attack available to the fleet.[11] When the helicopter's crew members gave their widely reported press conference in Chile, all they said was that 'While on sea patrol we experienced an engine failure. Due to adverse weather conditions it was not possible to return to our ship . . . we therefore sought refuge in the nearest neutral country.'

This may have been true so far as it went, but it omitted the crucial question of what the Sea King was doing at the time. The MoD have not added anything to this initial explanation, but the view accepted by most commentators subsequently appears to be that the helicopter had landed Special Forces who hid up near Argentine airfields and signalled to the task force or to the SSNs lying off-shore intelligence about Argentine air operations.[12] Presumably the men involved then retraced their steps and got out of Argentina through Chile, or were retrieved by submarines.[13]

UXBs

Comment on the failure of Argentine bombs to explode was potentially more dangerous to the task force than the attempts to penetrate the mystery surrounding the crashed Sea King. During the air attacks on 21 May, two further ships – HMS *Argonaut* and HMS *Antrim* – were hit by UXBs. On 22 May dispatches from the task force arrived referring to the failure of bombs to explode; US correspondents were briefed unattributably on the subject by MoD. On 23 May, the MoD's morning press release included reference to the successful defusing of two UXBs.[14] That afternoon, the Chiefs of Staff decided that there should be no further press releases on unexploded bombs and some correspondents were informed of this in an unattributable briefing; the MoD account of this briefing suggests that correspondents were asked not to refer to UXBs. None the less on 24 May, the *Daily Mail* ran an article on 'The Bomb Squad', including an interview with an expert who suggested that the Argentines might have been forgetting to fuse their bombs. The same day, Michael Evans, defence correspondent of the *Daily Express*, for example, suggested that 'the Argentinians have failed to get the fusing right'.[15] That day too, the Chief of Public Relations signalled the task force prohibiting the use of the phrase UXB in copy or voice transmissions and MoD announcements of damage to ships were thereafter unspecific about the name of the ship or the cause of the damage. On 25 May, HMS *Broadsword* was also hit by a bomb which failed to go off, but this was not announced. On 27 May: 'At defence correspondents' briefing MoD reiterated concern that there should be no mention of UXB on *Broadsword* or detailed discussion about the damage to her.'[16] The defence correspondents seem to have complied and there was a temporary lull in the reporting and comment on UXBs until early June, when the attack by a Hercules on the merchant vessel *British Wye* was reported in the press.

The handling by MoD of the press coverage given to UXBs seems to have been a little clumsy. In their evidence to the HCDC, Rear Admiral Woodward and Captain Middleton (of HMS *Hermes*) spoke of their concern about the release of information on UXBs,[17] yet for several days there seems to have been no attempt to censor references to them by embarked correspondents. By the time MoD did clamp down, the incidence of UXBs had been widely reported and commented on. The Argentines would not have had to conduct a very vigorous perusal of the British and American press to find references to them. Indeed, the *Sunday Times* of 20 May reported an interview between an Argentine pilot and an Argentine journalist in which the pilot referred to the failure of delayed action fuses to detonate when the bombs hit a light ship.[18] In their evidence to the HCDC, MoD themselves argue that the record of Argentine bomb attacks 'does not dictate any substantial or dramatic improvement in making their bombs explode on impact'. The attempt to suppress mention of the UXBs thus seems to have been a clear case of closing the stable door too late; fortunately the horse came to no harm. It was suggested to the author by one official in the MoD that this was an instance when the press should have exercised self-censorship. The criticism seems unmerited – if MoD were actually informing the media about the bombs, and if reports were coming through uncensored from the task force when the flow of other information was being so restricted, it would be natural for the media to assume that they had licence to publish this story.

SHIP DESIGN

A final side-show to the media comment on the air threat was the long-running debate over ship design. There had been some earlier articles following the sinking of HMS *Sheffield* when it was claimed that fire had spread so rapidly through the ship because of its aluminium superstructure. This claim was in fact wrong. HMS *Sheffield* had a steel superstructure, and the argument temporarily died down, to be resurrected as if by common consent on 25 May when it was carried in several newspaper articles and on the television news.

The focus was again on aluminium. Anthony Preston had an

article in the *Daily Mail* headlined 'BLUNDER THAT LEFT OUR SHIPS IN PERIL' in which he described aluminium as an 'unacceptable fire hazard'. Other articles explained more fully and sympathetically the reasons for the use of aluminium; the *Daily Telegraph*'s naval correspondent, Desmond Wettern, pointed out for instance that HMS *Sheffield* had less aluminium than the Type 21s, but because of her top weight, was underarmed.[19] *The Times*, too, gave a clear explanation of the dilemma facing ship designers.[20]

Anthony Preston was interviewed in ITN's *News at One* and again for *BBC TV News*. In the first he was asked whether the task force ships had 'a major design or construction fault', in the second he was asked more specifically about aluminium. In both cases his answer was much the same; aluminium melts long before it burns, leading to the collapse of companionways and preventing fire parties from getting to the seat of the fire. He then went on to criticise the presence of other flammable material – PVC cable, 'flame-resistant' wood and other materials used purely for comfort's sake.

The next day the media continued the discussion. In an ITN 'Special' that night, Rear Admiral Wemyss was asked (in the much-quoted phrase) whether there was something wrong with our ships? He replied that, while the damage was 'hideous', the casualties could have been much greater; the risks in ship design had long been known. There were good reasons for using aluminium, and alloy, but steel withstands attack better. The low level of casualties suggested however that damage control was 'immensely advanced'.

The coverage of the aluminium/steel controversy was on the whole reasonably informative and accurate. Later the media focused on the further controversy in ship design which lay behind this – whether the classic 'greyhound' shape of the warship was essential – and on the alternative Vosper–Thorneycroft 'Osprey' design, which received considerable publicity up to the time of its trials with MoD in late 1983. The debate over ship design and armament continued with the subsequent evidence to the HCDC in February 1984 and seems unlikely to be resolved for some time. Meanwhile, there were more urgent matters for comment and speculation.

THE ADVANCE TO GOOSE GREEN

The speculation, comment and premature announcements surrounding the operation made the recapture of Goose Green perhaps the most notorious incident in media terms. Staff at the BBC are still sensitive about the charges levelled against them, whilst many among the military believe that the BBC acted with what can at best be described as recklessness. Before going on to discuss the government's and the media's handling of this operation it may be helpful first to describe briefly, as far as can be ascertained from open sources, what actually happened.

It appears that on either Sunday 23 or Monday 24 May, the order was given for elements of 2 Para to attack Goose Green and Darwin. On the evening of 24 May D Company set off for Camilla Creek House, but the operation was cancelled. The reason for the cancellation is in dispute; two sources claim it was because the SAS had commandeered the helicopters needed to move the guns' ammunition;[21] another source asserts, however, that it was because the Argentines had reinforced their garrison at Goose Green.[22]

On Wednesday 26 May, 2 Para recommenced their advance. That night they lay up at Camilla Creek House, some five miles north of Darwin, where the following morning (at 1400 GMT) they picked up a broadcast on the BBC World Service which announced that they were five miles from Darwin and about to take Goose Green.

> The Colonel's reactions were predictable. Everyone was incredulous – whose side were the BBC on anyway? 'H' [the Colonel commanding 2 Para] fulminated to all and sundry that he would sue the Corporation when the war was over, but he immediately ordered the battalion to disperse and find cover wherever possible, away from what must now be an obvious target for Argentine weapons . . .
>
> There was much conjecture as to how the Ministry of Defence and all those responsible could allow the media to jeopardise the whole operation, indeed possibly the outcome of the campaign, in this way.[23]

Fox makes it clear in his account of this incident that Colonel 'H' Jones, while angry about the report, was less inclined to blame the BBC than the MoD which he assumed was its source. The outrage of soldiers in the field on learning that their plans and position had apparently been divulged is wholly understandable. Their anger was shared by the task force commanders: at one point, Admiral Woodward, making a routine report on his operational plans, apparently referred Fleet Headquarters at Northwood to the BBC World Service for information.

The attack on Darwin and Goose Green was actually scheduled to begin several hours before dawn on Friday 28 May. By that night, after a day of fierce fighting in which Colonel 'H' Jones lost his life, Darwin had been retaken. The following day, 29 May, the Argentine garrison at Goose Green surrendered.

When the background to the BBC's report is examined, the announcement of the forthcoming attack seems much less extraordinary. Prior to the San Carlos landings there had been remarkably little speculation about what the British force was likely to do once it was ashore. From 21 May that changed dramatically. The only item of which 2 Para were aware was the BBC World Service report, but that was only one among the many items of comment and speculation. Between 21 and 28 May more than thirty such pieces came to light.

From the first, the Goose Green/Darwin complex was canvassed as a likely objective. On 22 May Sir Terence Lewin, Chief of Defence Staff, announced 'We're going to move and move fast!'[24] The next day, 23 May, Cecil Parkinson, then Chairman of the Conservative Party and member of the 'War Cabinet', and Bernard Ingham, the Prime Minister's Chief Press Secretary, briefed journalists in similar terms.[25] It would hardly have been reasonable to expect the media to resist the temptation to ask precisely where the British forces were going to move. Nor did this take much working out; as Neville Taylor subsequently told the HCDC: 'looking at the map, it was noted that we had two ways in which forces were likely to move, however promptly'.[26]

Few commentators seem to have been in doubt as to the objective. ITN's Geoffrey Archer, *Newsnight*'s Peter Snow, Christopher Lee of BBC Radio, Michael Evans of the *Daily Express*, Philip Tibenham of *Panorama* among others, were all confident that Goose Green and Darwin would be attacked, well before the order was given. Interestingly, these are all reporters and defence correspondents: our study uncovered no incident of a retired officer volunteering the suggestion that it might be planned: and some specifically refused to speculate.[27] The same day, 24 May, the *Daily Express* reported (quite inaccurately, since the land forces were by and large still at the bridgehead) that

> British forces are pushing relentlessly towards key Argentinian positions . . .
>
> [Admiral Woodward] has decided to take Goose Green because the Argentinians have put up such little resistance so far. A priority target will be Port Darwin, which will provide extra mooring facilities for British ships . . .[28]

while the *Daily Telegraph* published a pooled dispatch from their task force correspondent under the headline 'GOOSE GREEN SEIZED', describing unconfirmed reports of the seizure of Goose Green. Presumably this report had been cleared in the 'vetting' process.

Speculation continued over the next couple of days. On 27 May, the day of the much-criticised BBC broadcast, the *Daily Telegraph* carried an article referring to unconfirmed American reports that 'early today . . . Goose Green and Darwin had been captured'.

In ITN's *News at One* on 27 May, Peter Sissons reported a statement by Ian MacDonald: 'MoD confirm that so far as they know the Argentine positions at Darwin and Goose Green have not been taken . . . The government spokesman did point out that the government said it did intend the British forces on East Falkland to push forward quickly but so far there were no reports of major British advances.' That afternoon, the Prime Minister informed the Commons: 'Our forces on the ground are moving forward.' That evening ITN's Geoffrey Archer reported that radio reports from the task force commanders were scarce, indicating that action was taking place. Archer, Christopher Wain and Peter Snow all reported that operations were probably in train against Goose Green and Darwin. The report by Chris Lee which so angered 2 Para was thus far from being an isolated incident. It was, rather, part of a flood of conjecture.

The recapture of Darwin and Goose Green was the first

major land operation in the Falklands. It was a hard-fought battle, costly in lives. It is impossible to be categorical about the extent to which the speculation in the British and American media influenced the Argentines' decision-making. The options open to the British were clearly limited; the Argentines made use of reconnaissance aircraft and had observation posts outside the garrisons, although apparently their intelligence-gathering on the ground was not good.[29] Argentine staff officers, some of them familiar with British tactics and training, must at least have allowed for the possibility that the British would do the obvious and mop up the enemy outposts on their flank. According to General Frost, during the interrogation of prisoners after the recapture of Goose Green:

> Two Argentine Special Forces Officers taken earlier admitted that, following the BBC announcement the day before of the impending attack on Darwin and Goose Green, up to three companies of fresh troops had been brought into the area. (Their story was corroborated some two weeks later when the battalion eventually arrived in Stanley. The local librarian had kept a diary of arrivals and departures by helicopter to and from the race course: on 27 May up to 500 men had left for Goose Green by Chinook.)[30]

The fact remains that the coincidence of timing with the BBC World Service report could have been fortuitous; the decision to reinforce could well have been based on the Argentines' own intelligence and assessments of British plans.

In any case, it seems invidious to single the BBC out for criticism. Christopher Lee, whose report was broadcast on the World Service, recalls that his own assessment of the size, composition and logistics of the task force, and of the opposition facing them, led him to the view that the Paras would be used against Goose Green. Speculation was rife in the media when he was sought out by someone who knew what his 'amateur tactical assessment' was. This source, who he confirms was 'certainly' senior enough to make a sensible judgement on the matter, told him that the attack was currently in progress, and that there was no reason why Ian MacDonald should not have announced it: the source indeed advocated publication of the facts.[31] Lee thus acted in good faith and was certainly far from unique in publishing the move against Goose Green.

As to the speculation surrounding this operation in general: it was certainly intense and highly specific. Even when MoD refused to comment, the news black-out itself became the subject of conjecture. It is clear from the analysis above that some sections of the press elaborated detailed and quite inaccurate accounts, based on official hints, but going much further than the latter justified. There is no evidence of self-restraint on the part of editors or correspondents, although many of those who gave evidence to the HCDC stressed in general their concern to avoid putting operations and lives at risk.

Having said that, the media were quite evidently encouraged in their attitude by the readiness of senior military and political figures to stimulate speculation. This may have been intended as psychological warfare, to keep the Argentines under pressure, but it is difficult to avoid the suspicion that other factors were involved. Apparently ministers were intensely anxious over the slow build-up of the bridgehead, there was constant public and parliamentary pressure for news of operations.[32] Robert Fox in his account implicitly links the decision to retake Darwin and Goose Green to the losses on 25 May of HMS *Coventry* and the *Atlantic Conveyor*:[33] following major losses, announcing a victory is certainly politically attractive. Whatever the reasons, the government's approach to publicity over the Goose Green attack was inconsistent and muddled.

The media were led to follow up the government's spokesman's suggestions of early moves by their own expectations. Few appear to have understood why the break-out from the bridgehead was taking so long. It was not widely realised at the time that it would be several days before enough supplies had been landed to permit the advance. Naturally, MoD did not publish this fact – as has been widely noted since, if the Argentine aircraft had attacked the supply vessels rather than the frigates, the whole operation would have been jeopardised. So the impression was widely gained that once the troops were ashore, the advance could begin immediately.

At this stage too, many commentators did not fully appreciate the sheer physical difficulty of movement in the Falklands. In the 23 May edition of *Weekend World*, Brian Walden and Colonel Neil Maude, a former Royal Marine, talked about moving troops forward to Stanley by helicopter – something described as probable in a number of other reports. Few commentators seem to have realised that there would not be sufficient helicopters to permit this.[34] Even the military planners with the task force do not appear fully to have realised the difficulty of the terrain.[35] The media could not know that the troops would move forward at no more than a mile an hour – the expectation was that once the advance began it would be fairly brisk.

The media expectations and the lack of hard news combined with leaks and briefings to fuel a week of intense conjecture and speculation. Once the operation was actually under way, the MoD tried to keep quiet about it, but by then it was too late: the speculation would not be quietened.

NOTES

1. 'Air Defence in Depth is Key for Task Force', *Financial Times*, 22 May.
2. In fact serviceability was better than suggested here. Availability was 95 per cent at the beginning of each day and 99 per cent of all planned missions were flown (Cmnd. 8758, para 222).
3. 'Junta Shaken by Huge Air Losses', *The Times*, 25 May: 'British Forces turn Greatest Threat into Success', *Guardian*, 25 May.
4. HCDC *Report*, vol. II, Q1417–1418.
5. *The World Tonight*, 26 May.
6. *Weekend World*, 23 May.
7. Quoted in K. S. Morgan (ed.), *The Falklands Campaign*, p. 321.
8. At the beginning of June, when the *Guardian* reported a story carried on the Washington National Public Radio Network that the US had vetoed the British bombing of mainland airfields. No evidence has come to light to substantiate this claim (see 'Mainland Bombing Vetoed', *Guardian*, 2 June).
9. 'Sea King Crashes on Chile Beach', *Daily Telegraph*, 21 May.
10. 'Santiago Concerned about Effects on Neutrality', *The Times*, 22 May.
11. For example, the *Daily Express*, the *Daily Telegraph* and *The Times* of 26 May all carried reports on these lines. Claims that some Argentine aircraft had been destroyed on the ground were renewed in June 1982 following further reports from Chile; see 'Secret Base is Raided', *Daily Mirror*, 3 June, also *ITN*, 2 June.
12. For example, in Hastings and Jenkins, *Battle for the Falklands*, p. 162. After the war a special report on communications in *The Times*, 'Security comes in Short Bursts' (7 September 1982), suggested that although it was not known at the time, many Argentine aircraft did not get through to the task force. SAS personnel in Argentina alerted Harriers to aircraft taking off from the main Argentine airfields. To avoid detection, they used a new radio system transmitting high-speed data.

3. Argentina claimed at one point that seven British commandos had been captured near Rio Gallegos; these claims appear to have been without foundation.

4. This had already been reported in *The World at One*, 22 May. A detailed, if rather defensive, analysis of the reporting of the UXBs appears in a Memorandum by the Ministry of Defence, HCDC *Report*, vol. II, pp. 420–3.

5. 'Next Stop Port Stanley', *Daily Express*, 24 May.

6. MoD Memorandum, HCDC *Report*, vol. II, p. 423.

7. HCDC *Report*, vol. II, Q1153, 1154.

8. *Sunday Times*, 30 May.

9. 'Curbing Ship Fire Risk is Urgent Task for Designers', *Daily Telegraph*, 25 May.

10. 'Aluminium: Fire Risk versus more Stability', *The Times*, 25 May.

11. Major General John Frost, *2 Para Falklands*, p. 42; Robert Fox, *Eyewitness Falklands*, p. 147. The former was written at the request of the CO of 2 Para and draws on an account by the battalion's Signals Officer, while Fox was attached to 2 Para in the Falklands.

12. Patrick Bishop and John Witherow, *The Winter War*, p. 88.

13. Frost, *2 Para*, pp. 49–50.

14. Quoted in Hastings and Jenkins, *Battle for the Falklands*, p. 254.

15. Harris, *Gotcha!*, pp. 116–17.

16. HCDC *Report*, vol. II, Q1188.

17. E.g. Major General Nigel Gribbon refused to be drawn in questioning by Peter Sissons (ITN, *News at One*, 27 May) on how or where the British might advance.

18. 'Next Stop Port Stanley', *Daily Express*, 24 May.

19. Interview with Major General Jeremy Moore.

20. Frost, *2 Para*, pp. 82–3.

21. Interview with author.

22. Hastings and Jenkins, *Battle for the Falklands*, p. 254.

23. Fox, *Eyewitness Falklands*, pp. 150–1.

24. One exception was Andrew Wilson of the *Observer* who wrote on 23 May that the recapture of Stanley could involve 'a slogging infantry advance'.

25. Fox, *Eyewitness Falklands*, p. 109.

8   Reinforcement and Reoccupation: 29 May–14 June

The last two weeks of the Falklands campaign continued the
pattern of frantic activity apparently interrupted by long pauses
as the British forces moved across the Falklands, gaining ground
and then consolidating their positions. But now a British victory
seemed inevitable; the question was not whether it would be
achieved, but how.

There were, however, still reverses to be met. In some
instances, the Argentine troops put up fierce resistance. There
was still concern among commentators about the Argentine air
threat. This was justified when, on 8 June, air attacks struck
the RFAs *Sir Galahad* and *Sir Tristram* and HMS *Plymouth*,
leaving a total of sixty-two men dead. The heaviest casualties
were suffered by the 1st Battalion Welsh Guards, part of 5
Infantry Brigade, which had been sent south to reinforce 3
Commando Brigade, and ultimately to serve as the new British
garrison in the Falklands.

5 INFANTRY BRIGADE: SOUTH GEORGIA – SAN CARLOS

The departure of 5 Infantry Brigade aboard the liner *Queen
Elizabeth II* (known as the *QE2*) from Southampton on 12 May
was officially announced, and the emotional send-off was widely
reported. The liner actually met up with the *Canberra* and the
Norland off South Georgia on Thursday 27 May, when the men
of 5 Infantry Brigade transferred to the two latter ships which
were to transport them to the Falklands – the *QE2* was not to
be hazarded within range of Argentine air strikes. On 30 May

126

Major General Jeremy Moore, who had sailed south on *QE2* to assume command of the two brigades, landed in the Falklands, and over the next couple of days, 5 Infantry Brigade began their landing, which was not completed until Friday 4 May. This was, therefore, a most dangerous period – and not only for 5 Infantry Brigade. It had by this time become clear that 3 Commando Brigade were not strong enough to retake the Islands without reinforcements: successful air attacks on 5 Infantry Brigade at that vulnerable time before the landing was complete would have endangered the whole British operation. Both Fleet Headquarters and the MoD were desperate that the landing should take place in secrecy, and no official announcement was made until 6 June when it had been completed.

Official silence could not, however, guarantee secrecy. The movements of 5 Infantry Brigade offered the media not so much an open day for speculation as the chance to publish a blow-by-blow account of what was supposedly happening. From 22 May to 6 June, nearly forty articles and reports on the topic appeared in the media. The speculation was particularly intense in the week leading up to the landings on 1 June and covered their likely timing and location.

Those responsible were usually defence correspondents or programme presenters: when the retired Service officers joined in, it seems always to have been in reply to a question about 5 Brigade put by an interviewer.

On three occasions, the sources for the speculation have been identified as parliamentary or official. On 25 May, a report by *The Times* political correspondent, Anthony Bevins, referred to 'Tory sources'. On 28 May, Christopher Lee noted that 'It is being said in Whitehall . . .' that the reinforcements were ready to transfer from the *QE2*. Most important of all, however, was Mr Nott's statement to the House of Commons on 26 May, in which he said '. . . the build-up [of forces ashore] will continue and 5 Brigade is on its way'. This was immediately interpreted as a message to the task force that reinforcements would arrive shortly (although no commentator seems to have wondered why the Defence Secretary should use the House of Commons, rather than the Defence Communications Centre, as the means of transmitting that message).

All the reports underestimated the size of the reinforcements:

most assumed that they numbered 3000 but the total force put ashore was closer to 5000, because of the considerable number of supporting forces accompanying 5 Infantry Brigade.[1]

Many reports that landings were imminent were generally slightly premature; reports of the troops' transfer to assault ships were however for the most part timely and accurate. There was widespread emphasis on the opening of a second bridgehead, somewhere other than San Carlos, which proved in the event to be wrong. Although *Newsnight* several times referred to the possibility of landing the reinforcements at the latter site, the general view in the media was that the landing would be elsewhere. This possibility was apparently considered by the task force, but rejected because of the problems of providing air defence to a second bridgehead.[2]

Christopher Lee's comment of 18 May, referring to Whitehall sources, has already been noted. According to Lee, this timely report of the cross-decking which was then in progress off South Georgia particularly angered the government. He had worked out for himself the likely timing of the rendezvous, but before broadcasting it, he remembers checking the story with the MoD. The Press Office there refused to confirm or deny it, nor would they state that there was any specific objection to the story being published. Under these circumstances, Lee went ahead with his broadcast – but in retrospect he regards this as the one security leak which he allowed to slip through.[3]

By contrast Peter Snow of *Newsnight* gives his coverage of the 5 Infantry Brigade landing as an example of an occasion when he exercised a degree of self-censorship. He recalls that he knew that the Brigade had actually landed at San Carlos for nearly a week before he broadcast that information.[4] There was certainly a period of several days – 2, 3 and 4 June – when *Newsnight* made no mention of the landing, but the arrival of the reinforcements *had* been mentioned by Snow on 28, 29 and 31 May, and on 1 June. The report on 5 June that the British had up to 8000 troops ashore anticipated the following day's official announcement of 5 Infantry Brigade's arrival. Given the intense speculation which preceded it, Snow's restraint was probably of limited effectiveness: it did however cover part of the crucial period when 5 Infantry Brigade were disembarking.

It remains open to question whether the conjecture about the movements of the *QE2* and the landing by 5 Infantry Brigade was excessive. There was of course public anxiety about the whereabouts and safety of the ship and her passengers. Moreover, it could be argued that there was a public interest in knowing that the men already ashore in the Falklands were going to be adequately reinforced to enable them to carry out their task. However, satisfying the public on these questions did not demand the intensive coverage and repeated references the subject received.

Despite this, it seems unlikely that the speculation would have assisted Argentina: once the date of the *QE2*'s departure from Southampton was known, it would have required no great intelligence effort to establish the likely time of her arrival in the Falklands, even if air or submarine reconnaissance failed to locate the liner and her escorts: at least one defence correspondent, Christopher Lee, did precisely this. Equally, no great feat of imagination was needed to work out that the reinforcements would have to land either at San Carlos or else at some other site which would almost certainly have to be at a point on the coast closer than San Carlos to Stanley – since the former is almost as far from the latter as it is possible to get. The speculation might actually have misled Argentina in one respect – the size of the reinforcements – given the broad unanimity that there were 3000 to 3500 troops involved.

In this instance, as elsewhere, it seems clear that official statements and leaks from official sources did nothing to dampen speculation and may have encouraged it. The reference in *The Times* of 25 May to 'Tory sources' is interesting as one of the few explicit mentions of the role of the parliamentary lobby system in passing information to the media during the Falklands campaign.[5] What in practice seems to have happened is that Conservative ministers would informally brief their backbench colleagues on events in the South Atlantic – possibly simply in the course of a few minutes' chat – and some backbenchers would then pass snippets of information to favoured lobby journalists.

5 INFANTRY BRIGADE – BLUFF COVE

The timing of 5 Infantry Brigade's arrival in the Falklands was not the only aspect of their operations to be the subject of speculation. The story of the advance of 2 Para (which had now rejoined 5 Brigade) to Bluff Cove has been widely covered elsewhere. In brief, a phone-call made by members of 2 Para from a house in Swan Inlet, east of Goose Green, established that the Argentines had left Fitzroy and Bluff Cove and, on 2 June, 2 Para began a helicopter leap frog forward to these settlements. This was widely reported on 9 June as a victory resulting from a '50p phone call'.[6] The reports resulted from a leak back in the UK; Brigadier Tony Wilson described the story as 'wildly exaggerated'.[7] However, the leak did not breach the time ban imposed to allow the move forward to be safely completed.

5 Brigade had been intended to move up Sussex Mountain to Goose Green, but was now redirected to Fitzroy. The shortage of transport meant that rather than move en masse, the Brigade transferred piecemeal. On the night of 5/6 June, the Scots Guards arrived there after a dreadful journey culminating in a trip by landing craft which took seven hours. The RFA *Sir Tristram*, carrying stores and ammunition as well as some troops, arrived at Fitzroy at first light on 7 June; the Chief Officer apparently wanted to unload cargo first, and the soldiers had to ask to be put ashore. Before dawn next morning, RFA *Sir Galahad* came into harbour carrying two companies of Welsh Guards and other elements of 5 Brigade. Both ships remained at anchor, but no troops were landed. Some five hours later, four Skyhawks attacked and direct hits were scored on the two ships. More than fifty men were killed.[8]

On 9 June, the news of the attacks was announced, but no details were given of the number of casualties. Reporting the announcement on the BBC's *Nine O'Clock News* that night, Christopher Wain emphasised that the losses could have been worse; the fact that the ship was close inshore meant that it had been possible to rescue 'hundreds of men'. The setback was unlikely to have much effect on what he described as 'the coming assault on Stanley'.

The next day's papers were less sanguine – *The Times* was typical when it spoke of 'heavy casualties'.[9] By 11 June, the speculation began to crystallise around a set of figures. Terence Lancaster, political editor of the *Daily Mirror*, reported that as many as 200 men might have been injured in the attack on the *Sir Galahad*;[10] ITN quoted two sources, one suggesting sixty had died, another suggesting forty-three dead and 140 injured.

General Sir Jeremy Moore wanted the Argentines to continue to expect a British attack from the south – i.e. from the Bluff Cove area – in order to preserve the element of surprise for his forces north and west of Stanley. He therefore hoped that the Argentines would *under*estimate the impact of the British losses, or at least remain confused as to British intentions.[11] In practice this plan seems to have been over-subtle – even within MoD, it was thought that the idea was to make the Argentines *over*estimate the casualties and hence be off their guard when the attack came. The press thought that the military in the Falklands had deliberately encouraged the Argentines to believe that the losses ran to hundreds of men. Apparently 'Reports of 220 dead and more than 400 wounded emanated from a radio ham in the Falklands, doubtless briefed by the military . . . The Secretary of State's attitude was "You can print what you like in the newspapers" . . .'[12] Unfortunately, the concealment and speculation which were to the military advantage threatened to carry political penalties. Excessive losses could have undermined support for the government – that presumably was why Bernard Ingham briefed correspondents on 11 June that the casualties were somewhat lower than the figure of seventy which had appeared in that day's *Sun*.[13]

It appears that the attempt to confuse the Argentines was successful – ITN reported them as claiming that 500–900 men had been lost. This was clearly a case where speculation was encouraged by the Ministry of Defence because of the uncertainty it created: it was only the potential political damage which led officials to damp down conjecture by indicating the true scale of the casualties.

According to Andrew Wilson in the *Observer* of 13 June (in an article not notable for its accuracy in other respects), the air raid on Bluff Cove may have been prompted by a report from Mike Nicholson, with the task force.[14] On 6 June, ITN's *News at Ten* included the following from Nicholson:

There are under way at this moment operations which I can only describe as extraordinarily daring which until they are completed cannot be revealed but which almost certainly if they are successful will bring the end to this war that much closer . . .

This report, it is alleged by Wilson, was picked up by the Russians and passed to the Argentines who interpreted it correctly as meaning that Bluff Cove had been taken by the British.[15] Since Nicholson's report was widely published in the British press, it is hard to see why the Argentines had to rely on Soviet intelligence to inform them of it. There is no evidence to back up Wilson's allegation, but if the Argentines really needed the British media to draw their attention to the strategic position of Bluff Cove and Fitzroy, they had no need to interpret cryptic messages from the task force: it was specifically mentioned as a site of importance for British operations on several occasions.[16] Rather than take up a defensive position, for example at Fitzroy Creek, the Argentines simply blew up the bridge and left.[17] The media speculation does not appear to have alerted the Argentines to the potential significance of Bluff Cove. Perhaps they were not assiduously following the British media, or they may have preferred to rely on their own intelligence – perhaps because they could see no reason to assume that the British commentary was accurate.

After the conflict, various detailed accounts emerged of the circumstances surrounding the incident at Bluff Cove. Christopher Wain asked,

> Why weren't the Argentine Skyhawks shot down by Royal Navy Sea Harriers? Almost certainly they just weren't spotted in time. It's known that two Sea Harriers did destroy four Mirages but the Skyhawks probably came in by another route. In any case it's almost impossible to maintain permanent air cover at present; and it's clear that the Skyhawks arrived when they were least expected. An hour later and they'd have met a barrage of Rapier missiles.

It appears that through a series of unhappy coincidences, warning of the impending attack did not get through to Bluff Cove in time, and the Harrier strip at San Carlos was temporarily out of action. Wain's assertion that the Skyhawks arrived when they were 'least expected' is rather more dubious – it seems that 2 Para at least were amply aware of the risk of air attack, but the danger was not fully appreciated by all concerned.

OPERATIONS: SPECULATION AND INTERPRETATION

In this final stage of Operation Corporate there was, however, no sense that the threat still posed by Argentina might prevent the task force achieving its objective. What concerned commentators more was the tactics to be used, and particularly the issue of whether the British would retake Stanley by direct assault, or whether they would lay siege to it. In practice, the actual tactics adopted fell between these two alternatives: the British maintained a steady advance, increasing the pressure on the Argentine garrison, until the latter surrendered before a full-scale assault of the actual town of Stanley was needed.

The British Advance – 27–31 May

The advance on Stanley had begun the same day as that on Goose Green and Darwin. 45 Commando moved to Douglas, arriving there on 30 May. 3 Para moved direct to Teal Inlet, which they also reached on 30 May. The SAS had been patrolling Mount Kent, which dominated the hills around Stanley, since the beginning of May and 'had been established in strength since 27th May'.[18] On 31 May and 1 June, 42 Commando were flown to the mountain by helicopter. Although these moves out of the bridgehead were officially announced, no details were given and the media were left to speculate as to precisely what was happening. Peter Snow in *Newsnight* on 28 May described the aim of the operation as 'the decisive encirclement of Port Stanley itself'. The next day he was more specific:

> Stanley is fifty miles away, but in between there are settlements like Douglas – which we'd guess the British have now taken – and Teal Inlet seven miles further on . . . the going there is as bad as anywhere on the Falklands: this is the northern part of the wettest and boggiest of the islands: and most of these British troops will have been advancing on foot.

At the time Snow was speaking, 45 Commando were actually still several miles short of the settlement at Douglas: they reached it at 10 p.m. (local time) that night, having covered only thirteen miles during the day's march. Even at this stage none of the commentators, including those who recognised that the troops would have to move on foot, seems to have appreciated fully the difficulty of the terrain, or indeed the size of the load that the men would have to carry – for the Marines, often as much as 150 lbs. The magnitude of the task only became apparent when the first accounts of 'yomping' were received from reporters with the land forces in early June. Peter Snow had, however, accurately identified the task force objectives.

In *Weekend World* on 30 May there was a fairly detailed debate on the tactics open to the task force. Brian Walden explained that for the British the choice was between laying siege to Stanley, so allowing time for further diplomacy, and storming the town. The latter course, it was suggested, would have the advantage of giving Britain 'total and unequivocal control of the Falklands' but might involve considerable destruction of Stanley with high casualties on both sides. The defence experts on the programme – Jon Connell, Rear Admiral Gueritz, Colonel Neil Maude and Air Chief Marshal Steedman – were divided in their views. Two experts on Argentine affairs, Andrew Thompson and Harold Blakemore, both believed the Argentines would fight for the Islands; they thought a siege unlikely to bring the conflict to an end, while Philip Windsor pointed to a key factor when he said '. . . I think the British Government is more likely to favour a quick kill rather than a long-drawn out period of horse trading.' It is interesting to note that in this instance, where tactics were thought likely to be subservient to diplomatic and political considerations, it was the political commentators who were best able to forecast the course of events.

The next day's *Washington Post* was unconvinced by the political arguments: it reported that several thousand British troops 'are expected by military analysts' to lay siege to Stanley.[19] By that evening, however, it was being reported on *Newsnight* that fighting was now taking place for the ridge of hills some twelve miles from Stanley. This was the night when 42 Commando began to land on Mount Kent, and it was presumably to this move that the report referred.

During the last few days of May, the nature of the commentary was beginning to change. As the British forces advanced, there was less uncertainty about their objectives: the focus of interest was now on analysing what was actually happening. The emphasis was moving from speculation to interpretation. Typical was an article in the *Scotsman* on 1 June which reported that British troops were advancing on Mount Kent. 45 Commando had moved in a 'thrust from the north with 3 Para', while 2 Para and 40 or 42 Commando were likely to be pushing along the southern coastal plain and some of 5 Infantry Brigade had now been put ashore. The article went on to say that a news black-out had been imposed by MoD, but there was a suggestion 'from defence sources' that the battle was taking place for the strategic high ground. This could prove to be 'the bloodiest of the Falklands conflict', since the hills offered the defenders the chance to pin down the advancing troops.[20]

At lunch time on 1 June, ITN reported that Mount Kent had been taken, but there continued to be some uncertainty about what was happening. In the *Nine O'Clock News*, Christopher Wain reported MoD denials that the action around Mount Kent was anything more than 'patrol activity'. An hour and a half later, Peter Snow announced in *Newsnight* British confirmation that their troops had taken Mount Kent in the face of some limited resistance by Argentine troops.

Snow then moved on to his customary round-up of the situation and speculation about the next moves using photographs and models. The following extract gives the flavour of a typical *Newsnight* analysis

Now we assume that Two Sisters Mountain is fortified by the Argentines: it's only six miles out of Stanley and is divided from Mount Kent by a river valley. But from Two Sisters and the hills to the right of these the Argentines will still command the approaches to Stanley . . .

When you look at this from the British viewpoint with the ground forces now pushing forward on two fronts very roughly along the line of the two roads, you can see that with British troops on Mount Kent and perhaps the rest of that ridge too, Stanley is now almost cut off from the rest of the island. For the next day or two we're told British supplies will be helicoptered up to join this new front line: food, ammunition and guns . . . At the same time we can expect to see the 3000 reinforcements who've travelled out from Britain aboard the *QE2* landed either back at the main bridgehead or at some point up here where they'll now have their bridgehead covered from that range of hills . . .

As an emulation of a formal military briefing (of the type familiar to us all from war films) this was fairly successful. It resembles what is known in the Army as a 'Sitrep' – a situation report – and with material of this kind appearing nightly, it is little wonder that the military felt their entire operation was being exposed to public gaze. How damaging that exposure was is another question: nothing appears to have been said that would not be obvious to anyone familiar with military operations.

The British Advance – 1 June–13 June

As predicted by Snow, the first few days of June did indeed see a period of consolidation by 3 Commando Brigade holding the northern half of East Falkland, while 5 Infantry Brigade landed and moved forward to Fitzroy and Bluff Cove as described above. By 4 June, the forces around the north-eastern side of Stanley were closing in. There were however strong Argentine defences between the outer ring of hills held by the British and the capital: they occupied an inner circle of hills – Two Sisters, Mount Tumbledown, Mount Harriet, Mount Longdon and Mount William.

On 11 June, the attack on the inner circle of hills around Stanley was finally launched; 42 Commando were to attack Mount Harriet, 45 Commando Two Sisters, and 3 Para moved to take Mount Longdon.

All were defended and Mount Longdon was the hardest-fought land battle of the campaign, costing 3 Para twenty-three men dead and forty-seven wounded. By the morning of 12 June, however, all three units had taken their objectives, although for the moment they were unable to advance further.

5 Brigade then went into action: on 13 June the Scots Guards attacked Tumbledown Mountain where again the Argentines put up a fierce resistance. 2 Para atacked Wireless Ridge. The Argentine defences began to crumble, and the Welsh Guards and Gurkhas were able to retake Sapper Hill and Mount

William respectively with very little opposition. On 14 June, General Menendez, commander of the Argentine forces in the Falklands, surrendered.

At the beginning of this June period, the debate over tactics was still continuing. According to Drew Middleton of the *New York Times*, 'military analysts' expected the British commanders to prefer a direct assault, but the fact that the Argentines had had more time than at Darwin to prepare their defences might argue for a siege. British operations so far had been 'marked by rapidity and a sure sense on the part of ground commanders of the most vulnerable spot in Argentine positions'.[21] Middleton also referred to logistics problems which meant that the entire helicopter force was needed to move materiel instead of supporting combat.

3 June saw another news black-out which was itself the subject of interpretation in *The World Tonight*. The presenter, John Morgan, asked whether the enemy were as uncertain about what was going on 'as we are here?' Christopher Lee put the MoD case succinctly; there was still the problem of confirming the Argentines' staff work for them. In other words, official British .announcements could serve to confirm Argentine intelligence which might still be provisional or uncertain. The news black-out continued on 4 June. The next day's *Newsnight* suggested that a 'big move forward' by the British was imminent and by 6 June the *Observer* could almost accurately forecast that 'the task force seems likely to recapture Stanley in the next week . . .' The next couple of days brought little further news until the losses at Bluff Cove were announced.

There was speculation as to whether these would delay the British advance, but, supported by a reassurance from John Nott on the question, most commentators thought they would not. This reassurance was seen by some as undermining the purpose behind MoD's refusal to announce casualties – to keep the Argentines guessing about the implications of the British losses – but in fact it served Major General Jeremy Moore's objective.

By 11 June, it was becoming clear that the lack of action was puzzling some commentators. Geoffrey Archer of ITN reported that bad weather was slowing the rate of helicopter supply and that 'military sources' had denied that they were being held back by political contraints. (This latter comment was significant in that it implied that there had been some suggestion that the politicians were holding operations back.)

The following day, 12 June, John Nott announced the British capture of the high ground to the west of Stanley – i.e. the inner circle of hills. Geoffrey Archer reported that in consequence a British victory seemed certain. Christopher Wain of the BBC gave a more detailed analysis. This, he said, was the first full day of a battle which could last anything up to four or five days. The British forces now commanded Two Sisters, 'the most vital single piece of high ground'. He forecast the continued shelling of Stanley and concluded: 'For the moment at least it seems the Argentines are going to dispute every foot of ground over those final five miles.' This was certainly an accurate description of the battles so far and of what the Scots Guards were to face at Mount Tumbledown. The suddenness of the final Argentine collapse was not, however, foreseen by the media or perhaps even by the task force commanders.

The next day, 13 June, the Argentines admitted that their defences around Stanley had been breached. Commenting on *The World Tonight*, General Sir Peter Whiteley described the advance as 'a brilliant operation'. The night attack, on Two Sisters and Mount Longdon, which was a most difficult operation, had made 'a tremendous advance' with the minimum of casualties. It reflected the superior skill and field craft of the British troops. He foresaw the imminent surrender of the Argentine garrisons on both East and West Falklands.

This was one of the last substantial items of comment on the campaign. There were to be many reports of the final battles and articles congratulating the task force on its achievement, but as the Argentines surrendered on 14 June, the analytical commentary was leaving military matters and turning to the practicalities of victory – what was going to happen next, and what was the episode going to cost the taxpayer. With the passage of time, investigative journalism was to turn its attention to the conflict – how had the losses at Bluff Cove come about; what were the lessons for ship design and for other items of equipment; what should be the size and shape of the Navy and, dominating all these questions why had the *Belgrano* been sunk and what had the consequences been – a debate which still continues.

The commentary on military aspects of the campaign

diminished noticeably during June, as did the use of retired officers to comment. There may have been several reasons for this. First, as we have already observed, once Darwin and Goose Green were taken, there was little scope for detailed speculation. Secondly, the news black-out from the Falklands in the early part of June also discouraged speculation. Thirdly, and perhaps more importantly, other events were contesting the Falkland story for headline coverage: the Princess of Wales had her first baby; the Pope visited Britain and went on to visit Argentina; and most important was the Israeli invasion of Lebanon and the developing civil war there. In the words of one veteran war correspondent, 'New wars drive out old wars.'[22]

NOTES

1. Cmnd. 8758 para 108 states that 10 000 men were put ashore. The official announcement of the initial 21 May San Carlos landing referred to 5000 men; the reinforcements therefore numbered a further 5000.
2. Hastings and Jenkins, *Battle for the Falklands*, p. 270.
3. Interview with the author.
4. Interview with the author.
5. Robert Fox also refers to the lobby in connection with the case of Goose Green: 'Apparently on the afternoon of 26th May, Tory backbenchers had been assured that the break-out from the San Carlos Beach-head had begun . . .' This he links to premature reports of the retaking of Goose Green in the *Daily Express* and the *Daily Telegraph* on 27 May. *Eyewitness Falklands*, p. 156.
6. See for example '3 Navy Ships Hit', *Daily Mail*, 9 June: 'Brigadier Tony Wilson of Five Brigade found a telephone box . . . which appeared to be working. He put 50p in the slot and called up the manager of Fitzroy settlement.' The wording of other reports was almost identical, suggesting a single source.
7. HCDC *Report*, vol. II, Q1192–1194.
8. Detailed accounts of the incident appear in Frost, *2 Para*, and Hastings and Jenkins, *Battle for the Falklands*.
9. 'Heavy Losses Feared in Landing Ships Bombing', *The Times*, 10 June.
10. 'The Toll is Grim', *Daily Mirror*, 11 June.
11. Interview with the author.
12. Memorandum submitted by the Press Association, HCDC *Report*, vol. II, p. 310.
13. Harris, *Gotcha!*, p. 118.
14. 'Russian Tip Possible in Sir Galahad Disaster', *Observer*, 13 June.
15. The suggestion of Russian involvement presumably arose from the widely-held but inaccurate belief that the Russians were passing intelligence information to Argentina. While Soviet intelligence appears to have been

active in monitoring British operations, the evidence suggests that the Argentines received *no* Soviet assistance. See for example Dr R. L. Scheina, 'The Malvinas Campaign' in *Proceedings of the US Naval Institute* (1983).

16. For example in *Newsnight*, 23 May, 24 May, 29 May; ITN, 27 May; *New York Times*, 1 June.
17. Hastings and Jenkins, *Battle for the Falklands*, p. 272.
18. Hastings and Jenkins, ibid., pp. 264–6.
19. 'British Reported Moving towards Falklands Capital', *Washington Post*, 31 May.
20. 'Thrust for Gateway to Port Stanley', *Scotsman*, 1 June.
21. 'Tough British Decision: Assault or Lay Siege', *New York Times*, 2 June.
22. Behr, *Anyone Here Been Raped*, p. 106.

Part III
Assessment and Conclusions

9 How Did the Media Perform?

The media commentary on the Falklands covered every broad aspect of the British forces involved: morale; training; equipment and its capabilities; the whereabouts of the task force; the timing of reinforcements; the likely nature of operations. In some of these areas it was notably vague; in others quite detailed. Reports often contradicted each other and much of what was written and said was inaccurate; but much was extremely accurate.

The layman who tried to follow as much as possible of the material published and broadcast should have had a rough idea of the size of the naval and land forces involved, and a clear idea of the number of Harriers. He probably would not, unless he had been assiduous and expert at reading between the lines, have fully appreciated the scale of the logistic effort involved. Warning of the threat faced by the task force was there from the beginning, but might initially have been overlooked in the more general tendency to emphasise the superior calibre and equipment of the British forces. This hypothetical layman would have had a fair notion of the options open to the task force commanders at any one time and of the risk attendant upon them, although perhaps it is fair to say that the military risks of hesitation or caution were not always so fully appreciated as those arising from positive and bold action – for example, in the issue of whether to maintain a naval blockade or to land forces on the Islands, the dangers of the latter were on the whole more heavily stressed.

The appalling physical conditions in the South Atlantic and ashore were given coverage, although the commentary in general underestimated the difficulties of mobility across the wet and boggy country. There was perhaps a failure to recognise, or at least an unwillingness to dwell on, the physical discomforts of the campaign – it was not until its conclusion that tales of trench foot began to emerge. The greatest single weakness in the commentary, though, was in the assessments of the Argentine military position. It was easy to describe the military junta ruling Argentina as a 'fascist dictatorship' and to depict their troops as ill-trained, ill-equipped and unmotivated conscripts.

There was of course truth in this, but it was nothing like a rounded picture. It offered no real insight into the motives and determination of Argentina. Nor did it recognise the increasing professionalisation of Argentina's armed forces which had led to their involvement in the running of the country. Little weight was given to the political divisions between the different forces and these appear to have been reflected by divisions in the junta during the war.[1]

The complex interplay of military, political and nationalist factors in determining Argentine attitudes was not on the whole explored except by a few Latin American specialists. A firmer grasp of the situation would certainly have avoided some of the grossly misleading and jingoistic material emanating from some sections of the media. In this respect, a comment put by *Flight International* to the HCDC is of interest:

> We believe the national interest was poorly served by ill-considered jingoism which led to deception of the public about the casualties likely if hostilities started. Had knowledgeable technical press representatives been aboard the fleet, the resultant interchange of information amongst journalists might have helped to curb the wilder excesses of jingoism displayed by certain elements of the national press at the start of the campaign . . .[2]

It is questionable whether the presence of a technical journalist with the task force would have led to better-informed reporting – after all, the technical press were present back in the UK where most of 'the wilder excesses' in fact originated. None the less, there is a serious point to be made that a better understanding of the role, organisation and capabilities of the Argentine armed forces would have lessened the impression sometimes given of comic-opera generals and admirals backed by untrained troops, and might have better prepared the British public for the casualties which occurred.

The commentary and analysis in the media fell short of comprehensiveness in another aspect – in relating the military situation to the diplomatic and political circumstances. Considerable coverage was devoted to the diplomatic handling of the crisis, to the various attempts to reach a peaceful settlement, and to the domestic political situation. Much less effort was given to establishing the precise relationship between the diplomatic moves in train and the instructions given to the task force: the subject which lies at the heart of the *Belgrano* controversy. That there was such a relationship – and that its existence was at least recognised by the government, even if it was not always fully understood – is borne out by evidence of the tight political control under which the task force operated:

> The higher management of the crisis was conducted by a small group of Ministers which was chaired by the Prime Minister and met almost daily. This group of Ministers ensured that the diplomatic, economic and military strands of our policy were properly co-ordinated.[3]

Some commentators did set the role of the task force within a broad political context: for example, Group Captain David Bolton repeatedly spoke of military force being used 'to underwrite diplomacy'. There was however little detailed analysis of the way in which task force operations bore on the diplomatic efforts in train and vice versa.

There were several reasons for this. First, with the exception of a few cases such as *Weekend World*, both the press and the broadcasting media used different commentators to cover military operations and political developments. While the two teams would meet and discuss the day's news, there was frequently no one person responsible for drawing the two elements together.[4] Second, there was the difference in the speed with which news was released. On the whole, news about diplomatic activity was announced fairly promptly. Since journalists had only to watch the politicians and diplomats involved flying between London, Washington, New York and Buenos Aires to establish that meetings were taking place, this was inevitable: it is standard practice for such meetings to be followed by a formal communiqué or at least a brief statement of results. Moreover, the British government had an interest in publicising its active involvement in negotiations. News from the task force on the other hand tended to be delayed, and was often meagre; tying the events and decisions of a particular day together could only be done several days later, by which time there was other news to report. Thirdly, as the subsequent controversy over the relationship between the sinking of the *Belgrano* and the Peruvian peace plan showed, it was not always easy at the time or even in retrospect to establish a precise sequence of events. None the less, the public could have been forgiven for wondering at times whether and precisely how the military campaign and the diplomatic aspects of the crisis related to each other.

These two exceptions apart, it seems fair to say that for those who were interested – and who had the time and opportunity to make full use of the media – sufficient information was available for them to follow events, to understand what was happening and so to reach a judgement on the main decisions being taken by the government. In that sense, the media were able to fulfil their prime role within a democracy. To discuss the commentary in these terms is, however, to ignore the very great differences which exist between the different media, both in terms of the practical limitations on their handling of information and the attitudes displayed towards their role.

DIFFERENCES BETWEEN THE MEDIA

The first and most obvious distinction to be made is between the written and the spoken word – between the press and the broadcast media.

Some radio and television programmes are broadly comparable to newspapers in that they cover a wide range of items in a relatively short time, encompassing both news reporting and commentary. Nevertheless, the demands of the medium impose a considerable restraint. As the Annan Committee noted, 'All the words of a broadcast news bulletin could be printed in a single column of *The Times*.'[5]

The BBC distinguishes sharply between news and commentary. The news-reader reports facts (although these may include an element of interpretation, as when they identify a rumour of current speculation). Commentary on the news is then provided by someone else. In the *Nine O'Clock News*, this role generally fell to Christopher Wain, the BBC TV defence correspondent. Very little use was made of outside commentators. In the various Radio 4 programmes examined in the course of this study, the Radio 4 defence correspondent Christopher Lee played a major part, although outside commentators were widely used.

The distinction between analysis and news was sometimes less clear-cut in ITN's programmes, particularly in the *News at One* where the programme's presenter also took on the role of interviewer. In the *News at Ten*, however, broadly the same arrangement was followed as at the BBC: the news-reader gave out the news, with the tasks of analysis and interpretation falling to the defence correspondent, Geoffrey Archer. Of the three news programmes scheduled by ITN, the *News at One* made the greatest use of outside commentators, although the *News at Ten* also frequently featured retired Service officers and two, Rear Admiral Martin Wemyss and Air Vice-Marshal Paddy Menaul, were retained on contract.[6]

For both the BBC and ITN News, several items of information could be reported under the same introductory 'headline': this was particularly true of the *News at Ten*, which tends to carry a greater number of items in correspondingly less depth than the BBC's *Nine O'Clock News*. This apparently reflects ITN's policy: the Glasgow Media Group record that

> The staff [of ITN] on the whole are very partisan about their news bulletins compared with those of the BBC. They ... pride themselves on their more conversational style, better pictures, pace and immediacy.[7]

News reports are of necessity very brief. Current affairs programmes afford more time for detailed analysis of events. These programmes fall into two broad categories: those such as *The World at One*, where several issues are reported on and analysed, and those like *Newsnight*, *Panorama* and *World in Action*, which focus in much greater depth on one or two main topics. Both kinds of programme make extensive use of 'experts' either to comment on the events being reported or to provide background information and analyse the events under discussion.

The Annan Committee recognised the power wielded by the broadcasting organisations

> News programmes are the most important source of information for many millions of people: a similarly important influence in the formation of opinion in this country may indeed be current affairs programmes. As news and current affairs programmes are at the interface between broadcasting and politics, they are at the centre of controversy.[8]

This was reflected in the debate about the media, and particularly the BBC, during the Falklands conflict. There seems little doubt that television and radio have ousted the newspaper as the main source of news for a substantial proportion of the population. The BBC estimates that in spring 1974 nearly 60 per cent of the population of Britain listened to or viewed a full news bulletin.[9]

Radio 4 has, by comparison with television news, a relatively small audience. For *The World at One*, for example, it is normally two to three millions, with a possible high of around three to four millions during the Falklands campaign.[10] BBC TV news bulletins reckoned to achieve an audience of ten to twelve millions for one of their bulletins,[11] while the editor of ITN estimated in his evidence to the HCDC that in general during the Falklands campaign the total audience for all three ITN news bulletins was between fifteen and sixteen millions.[12]

These large television audiences may reflect public distrust of the popular press as a reliable source of serious information. Certainly there would be little point in looking for hard facts about world events in a newspaper which could declare of itself that 'Popular Sunday newspapers rarely seek facilities to cover foreign wars.'[13] A survey of the tabloids during the Falklands campaign uncovered almost as much material about the activities, habits and tastes of the royal family as about operations in the Falklands. Moreover, much of the Falkland coverage was given to 'human interest' stories and particularly to photographs of, interviews with and reports on the families of those killed.[14]

Although the 'quality' newspapers – the *Daily Telegraph*, *Financial Times*, *Guardian*, *Scotsman* and *The Times* and their Sunday equivalents – gave detailed coverage to the campaign, there were distinct differences between their approach and that of current affairs programmes. Although they published analysis of and speculation about operations, they tended to be relatively brief by comparison with the intensive coverage on radio and television, and they appeared more as an adjunct to factual reporting than as a subject in their own right. In that respect, the newspapers more closely resembled news broadcasts. On the whole, the quality newspapers seem to have relied much less than television and radio on the assistance of outside experts. Where they were used, it was common for them to remain anonymous – described, for example as 'naval analysts' or 'sources'.

MEDIA OBJECTIVES

In an article in *New Society* Stuart Hall asked: 'Do/can the media help us to understand these significant events in the real world? Do the media clarify them or mystify us about them?'[15] This, broadly speaking, is what the responsible editor or reporter would claim to have attempted in the context of the Falklands. Christopher Wain described his role as being 'to report and interpret the news as it came out'. Christopher Lee described reporting as 'broadcasting what you believe to be the factors in the order of their importance'. Similarly other reporters saw their first task as one of *informing the public*.[16]

The role of commentator was an additional one, intended to improve on the basic information by setting it in some kind of context: as ITN commented to the HCDC: 'Inevitably this . . . involved speculation, analysis of the options and the various arguments.'[17] Henry Stanhope of *The Times* saw the speculation about the options open to the task force commanders as 'All part of explaining to our readership what was going on and what might happen next.' Peter Snow, when asked about the purpose of the intensive speculation in *Newsnight*, said: 'We also reckoned it was our job to provide people with a prospect of the way things could go, of the balance of advantage and disadvantage in certain courses of action and so on.' In other words, speculation about the likely course of events was a serious aspect of the task of informing the public. In Snow's view, 'In a modern civilised society, the average viewer desperately wants to think about and discuss what's going on.' That meant knowing not only what had happened, but what the implications were. For him, speculation was 'part of what sophisticated viewers expect of a pretty sophisticated programme'.

The media are not, of course, purely motivated by a selfless concern for the truth. Every editor, producer and journalist has a more prosaic objective – to fill space. As Anthony Smith comments in *The Politics of Information*, 'television abhors a vacuum'.[18] Derek Lewis, a BBC editor, pointed out that programmes were going out around the clock; in the absence of hard news the media 'were going to find material from somewhere'.

The media's aim is to acquire and keep an audience. Robert Harris, in his analysis of the media and the Falklands, closely links the coverage in the popular press to the circulation war being waged in Fleet Street, and quotes some telling words by Derek Jameson of *The News of the World*.

> Readers were changing papers at a rate of 100,000 a week, thanks to bingo. Then along comes the war. War is an emotional business – blood, courage, guts, valour – it's something big enough to persuade people to change their paper. War and bingo.[19]

The Glasgow Media Group identified a comparable if less cut-throat trend in the television newsroom:

> On the one hand, the news was thought to be necessarily objective, authoritative, 'untouched by human hand.' On the other, it was seen as necessary that the news should hold a fickle and demanding audience by techniques that have more to do with 'show biz' than with the provision of information.[20]

Even serious programmes of minority appeal like *Weekend World* serve ulterior objectives – *Weekend World* was designed to persuade the Independent Television Authority (now the Independent Broadcasting Authority) to grant London Weekend Television the franchise to run commercial television in the London area at weekends.[21]

Not only does each newspaper or programme wish to outsell

its competitors, reporters also have their normal human ambitions. They want to publish, and they want to be heard. It is noticeable that many of the criticisms of the arrangements obtaining for reporting the war reflect annoyance that 'scoops' were being missed, or that a rival had got in first with his story. Most of the correspondents interviewed by the author were understandably keen for their achievements to be noted: 'we were the first' and 'we were the only ones who got it right' were expressions frequently employed.

The media saw themselves as meeting an existing public demand. This is probably fair – after all, once the decision to send the task force had been announced, the natural questions for anyone to ask were 'what is it going to do, and how? Has it the right equipment, what are the risks?' In the modern age, it seems inevitable that these questions will be posed about any decision to take military action: speculation cannot be switched off. As we have seen, even in the Second World War, it was not possible for the government to stifle discussions about operations even when they were potentially damaging.

How far the public interest was served by the commentary during the Falklands War is difficult to ascertain. Certainly adequate information was available to enable members of the public to be reasonably well-informed about what was happening – provided they were selective in their reading, viewing and listening.

A diet of certain tabloid newspapers alone, for example, would have aroused emotions of one kind or another, but would not have ensured an adequate level of understanding of the campaign and the issues surrounding it. The reader of the *Daily Mail* or the *Daily Express* who also regularly watched one of the main television news broadcasts would have received a fair amount of inaccurate or confusing information, but should none the less have had a reasonable appreciation of what was going on, as would anyone who relied on one of the quality newspapers or Radio 4 for their information. At the other extreme, anyone who managed the impossible task of watching, listening to and reading everything that was published would probably have found himself confused by the variety of contradictory material, unless he was sufficiently familiar with the British armed forces and their equipment and with military operations to form his own judgements about events. Even then, he could have been misled – several experienced defence correspondents recall incidents when they accepted and published inaccurate information. A classic example was the case of the Black Buck raids on Port Stanley airfield; one correspondent told the author that it simply never occurred to him that the Royal Air Force would have undertaken such a dangerous and costly mission in order to drop 'old-fashioned iron bombs which didn't even work against airfields in World War II', and to place only one such bomb on the runway itself.

In a war, the public interest is of course not always served by the disclosure of information. The HCDC devoted some time to considering this point and their comments describe clearly the issues that are involved.

These two principles – the public's right to information and the Government's duty to withhold information for reasons of operational security – need not be invariably opposed, but in practice they are very often in conflict. The question of operational security is a broad one which is open to very strict or very loose interpretation. If used too loosely, with phrases like 'that is an operational matter' being taken as a catch-all justification for not releasing inconvenient pieces of news, then the concept may be devalued and public and media confidence in the Government's spokesmen will suffer. If, on the other hand, too cavalier an attitude is adopted by the media and sensitive information is published because the security implications have escaped a layman's attention or are beyond his comprehension, then the Government's willingness to release non-sensitive information may be impaired. Where exactly the balance should be struck emerged as one of the major difficulties involved in formulating information policy.[22]

The Committee examined some of the difficulties in defining operational security: 'On a minimal interpretation ... the denial of vital intelligence to the enemy', and commented 'Much other information, while in principle best kept secret, is often assumed to be already known to the enemy.'[23] It was the tension between the objective of denying 'vital intelligence' and the assumption that the information was already known to the Argentines that lay at the heart of the controversy over the media commentary, and particularly speculation about future plans. The HCDC found that:

> Much has been made of the damage to the success of the campaign which would have resulted from speculation in the media by retired service officers as to military options open to task force Commanders. This argument cannot be resolved absolutely since, despite the activities of the media in this respect, we have received no evidence that any specific military operation was prejudiced.[24]

This was borne out by the findings of this study. In the material made available, no instance was discovered where a retired officer gave away information which could clearly be identified as prejudicing operations or which could not on any reasonable basis be assumed to be obvious to Argentine intelligence. One example cited was an occasion when a retired officer explained on *Newsnight* how a Mirage aircraft could shoot down a Harrier: we were not, however, able to trace this particular broadcast. The Ministry of Defence were also unable to trace any record of the precise grounds for the concern felt by the Chiefs of Staff on the use of 'armchair strategists'.[25]

Much of the analysis and speculation in the media came, however, not from retired Service officers but from the defence correspondents, the presenters and reporters assigned to cover the military aspects of the campaign. Chapter 10 looks further at the relationship and differences in the way the media professionals and the military pundits commented on the conflict, but at this point it is worth noting that the only definite instance of speculation damaging to British operations cited by the Ministry of Defence was that surrounding the move on Goose Green – and that was prompted by ministers and officials and reported by the defence correspondents. More generally, MoD commented:

> The majority of damage which speculation caused was probably to morale at home (e.g. damage to ships and casualty figures at Fitzroy). However, it represented a potential danger to our forces which we could not ignore and which we attempted to minimise.[26]

Although MoD saw speculation as 'a potential danger', it may in the case of the Falklands be fairer to describe it as a *perceived* danger. Alan Hooper claims that 'so much information was given to the public that one did not have to be a trained intelligence officer to work out the possible military options'.[27] In fact, the nature of the campaign was such that the military options were in practice extremely limited, and not difficult to identify. In any case, there can be little doubt that the Argentines did have trained intelligence officers – though Hooper's line of reasoning seems to imply that the British public had less right to information than they did. Argentine officers had been trained by the British, both with specific equipment as part of the follow-on to defence sales, and more generally by attendance at staff colleges. Thus they had access to recent British military opinion and theory. They were apparently familiar with NATO operating procedures and they had access to the open sources described in Chapter 3. Indeed, MoD invited ridicule when they behaved, in the words of Alan Protheroe of the BBC, as if they assumed 'that the Argentines did not have a copy of *Jane's Fighting Ships*'.[28]

In any case, it must be open to question how far Argentina would have relied on the British media as a source of intelligence. In the first place, it may be doubted whether a government which itself shamelessly controlled its national media could possibly accept that the British media were not being similarly manipulated. In other words, material which appeared in the British media may well have been assumed to be government disinformation. Second, the commentary and speculation which appeared in the media was so varied and so contradictory that even if the Argentines had had the resources to monitor it all (which may be doubtful) they would have been hard pressed to decide what was valuable to their intelligence effort.[29]

On the other hand, certain institutions within the British media, in particular the BBC, pride themselves on their worldwide reputation for telling the truth. It is not implausible that, as far as the British media were concerned, the Argentines would have concentrated their intelligence effort on monitoring those broadcasts and publications which they believed were particularly reliable. This suggests that the BBC has a special responsibility: if they object to being fed inaccurate information because this undermines the credibility of which they are rightly proud, they must also accept that in times of conflict whatever they publish may attract the special attention of hostile intelligence sources and that they have accordingly a duty to be circumspect.

Thus while, in the case of the Falklands, it seems fair to say that little or no damage resulted from the widespread and detailed analysis and speculation in the media, the same may not be true of other conflicts. Moreover, it has been claimed there is a special sense in which commentary by retired Service officers may assist an enemy – by giving an insight he would not otherwise have obtained into the British military way of thinking. These two considerations are discussed further in the following chapters.

NOTES

1. It is an interesting reflection that it was the Argentine Navy's experience of action against *their own* air and land forces in the 1955 overthrow of General Perón that established two major features of naval power which were to prove highly significant in the Falklands War: the importance of naval aviation and the essential role of the Marine Corps. See R. L. Scheina, 'The Argentine Navy Today', *Naval Forces* (April 1981).
2. Memorandum by Flight International, HCDC *Report*, vol. II, p. 97.
3. Cmnd. 8758, para 204, p. 15.
4. The Glasgow Media Group commented on this in their study of the way the news is broadcast: 'One very important effect of newsroom organisation and the processing of news is to compartmentalise events as they arrive in the newsroom.' *Bad News*, p. 59.
5. *The Annan Report*, p. 281.
6. 'Stage Army on Standby', *Guardian*, 7 May 1982.
7. Glasgow Media Group, *Bad News*, pp. 60–1.
8. *The Annan Report*, p. 266.
9. Ibid. A recent study by Professor Jeremy Tunstall (*The Media in Britain* (London: Constable, 1983)) suggested that in fact newspapers and not television are the dominant source of news in Britain, although the latter may be considered more reliable.
10. Interview with Derek Lewis, Editor BBC Radio 4, Afternoon Schedule.
11. HCDC *Report*, vol. II, Q140.
12. Ibid., Q228.
13. Memorandum by the *Sunday People*, HCDC *Report*, vol. II, p. 94.
14. Not only were the families of casualties the subject of intense press interest, the relations of any task force member identified by the press ran the risk of harassment. MoD signalled the task force to say 'naming

individuals in messages passed on press net unhelpful. Press in UK reac by visiting and telephoning homes day and night seeking comment from wives of those named.' HCDC *Report*, vol. II, p. 478.

15. Stuart Hall, 'A World at One with Itself', *New Society*, 18 June 1970 pp. 1056–8.
16. Interviews with the author.
17. Memorandum by ITN, HCDC *Report*, vol. II, p. 78.
18. Anthony Smith, *The Politics of Information*, p. 7.
19. Harris, *Gotcha!*, p. 43.
20. Glasgow Media Group, *Bad News*, p. 64.
21. For a detailed account of the programme's origins see Michael Tracey, *I the Culture of the Eye*.
22. HCDC *Report*, vol. I, para 23.
23. Ibid., para 24.
24. Ibid., para 128.
25. Letter from MoD (Defence Secretariat 11) to the author, 30 April 1984.
26. Ibid.
27. Hooper, *Military and the Media*, p. 158.
28. HCDC *Report*, vol. II, Q153.
29. Some sidelight was cast on Argentine attitudes to the British media in April 1983, when *The Times* published in its 'Moreover' column (written by humorist Miles Kington) an entirely facetious and fictitious article supposedly contributed by General Galtieri, caliming that Argentina wa holding the kidnapped horse Shergar and would exchange it for the Malvinas. This story was picked up by an Italian news agency and was apparently given front page coverage in Argentina, where it was treated seriously. (See 'General Alert', *The Times* (Diary) 21 April 1983.)

10 The Commentators – Disclosure and Discretion

Some seventy-five commentators took a substantial part in the media's analysis of and speculation about operations in the South Atlantic. These fell into two main groups – defence correspondents and retired Service officers. It is clear that, although individuals in each group had similar broad objectives, there were differences in the way they were used and in what they were willing and able to say.

THE DEFENCE CORRESPONDENT

Some of the reporters accredited for the purpose of covering the Falklands conflict had little knowledge of or expertise in the subject of defence.[1] Others were highly experienced. Chris Wain, of BBC television had, for example, spent three years in the army as a regular soldier during which time he was trained in photographic interpretation. He read military history at Oxford, and had been a BBC defence correspondent since 1975. Peter Snow of *Newsnight* had specialised in reporting on defence and foreign affairs since 1966. Christopher Lee had been a defence correspondent since 1977 and Henry Stanhope since 1970, while both the defence and air correspondents of the *Daily Telegraph* were quite recently retired senior officers who had seen extensive military service.

Correspondents like these had two kinds of expertise which they could and did bring to bear in their reporting – their experience of covering other wars and their knowledge of the British armed forces. They were therefore unlikely simply to report the Ministry of Defence's bland statements: they wanted to put them into some kind of context – as Christopher Lee described it, 'to pull together and analyse reports and to present a balanced picture at the end'. This they were well equipped to do. Their familiarity with military operations and equipment meant that they could not only interpret individual reports, but that they were able to put separate pieces of information together to present a broad picture of a particular event or operation. Chris Wain claimed that if a defence correspondent was to do his job properly, it was important that he should understand capabilities – he should, for example, know what was involved in mounting a Sea Harrier sortie, the fuel and weaponry it could carry, what would be reasonable attrition rates, and so on.[2]

This kind of understanding meant that defence correspondents were able to make their own deductions about the whereabouts of the task force, the likelihood of certain operations and even about some of the details of operations which were not released by MoD. Wain, for example, enjoyed analysing the pictures from Argentine television; his earlier training in photographic interpretation gave him a great deal of information about Argentine logistics and hence troop dispositions. Christopher Lee was able to work out for himself the likely timing of the *QE2*'s arrival off South Georgia and, on another occasion, the whereabouts of SS *Canberra*. Peter Snow in *Newsnight* and Geoffrey Archer of ITN similarly speculated on the basis of their own assessments of what was going on – it would, Snow thought, have been irresponsible if he had been given and broadcast details of actual British plans, but this was not what happened, and he found 'the idea of hamstringing television because of uninformed speculation totally unacceptable'.[3]

Some correspondents were less happy about taking this approach: Henry Stanhope described himself as 'not a great speculator – I tend only to write things when I'm 80–90 per cent sure of them. Speculative reporting carries a high risk.'[4] None the less, Stanhope too thought that conjecture about the likely nature of operations was 'all part of explaining to the readership what was going on and what might happen next. It was helping the layman to keep in the picture.' Jon Connell of the *Sunday Times* saw himself less in the role of educator, and more as simply typical of what was in everyone's minds: 'Everybody was curious to know what was going on – it was being discussed everywhere, and what was going to happen next was a matter of absorbing interest. Speculation was one way of keeping the public informed – but also I was very curious about what was going to happen next.'[5]

THE MEDIA AND OPERATIONAL SECURITY

Clearly conjecture of this kind could and did lead defence correspondents to make accurate assessments of British intentions. They appear, however, to have taken the view that, as long as this was *uninformed* speculation – that is, based not on official leaks, but on their own analysis of what was happening – it gave nothing away. In general, the media professionals responsible for the commentary on the Falklands campaign accepted that the safety of British forces was a paramount consideration and that the success of operations should not be put at risk. In a letter to *The Times*, Chris Wain wrote

> For a Defence Correspondent, the rules of engagement are clear. You do not reveal British military secrets. You do not put British lives at risk. You do not put interviewees whom you know to be in possession of secret information into the position where it may be inadvertently blurted out . . .[6]

Subsequently he added: 'You cannot knowingly jeopardise lives and anyone who does should not be a reporter. It would truly be wicked.' Geoffrey Archer would have been 'appalled if I reported something which resulted in the deaths of British servicemen'; Jon Connell described it as 'Worse than irresponsible'; Christopher Lee was equally categorical: 'First and foremost, you don't want to get people killed.' No one, he said, had the intention of giving away too much information. He added also that for a defence correspondent, considerations of security were not something new, they were a normal feature of life.

These views might give the impression that the security issue was seen in relatively clear-cut terms, but this was not so. Two aspects were controversial: who should decide what can safely be published and on what basis should information be withheld from the public? On the first of these, the HCDC's view was quite clear:

> The military obviously needs to apply common sense in assessing what are operational secrets in order to ensure that their judgment is respected when absolute silence is vital. In general where there are conflicting views as to what constitutes an operational secret, the military view must prevail.[7]

Thus, provided the military are not unreasonable, they should be the final arbiters of what can safely be published. In practice, it is clear from the evidence to the HCDC that the media's views often *did* conflict with those of the MoD and the military. There were several reasons for this – the too-frequent use of the phrase 'That is an operational matter' as a catch-all excuse for not commenting on particular issues, the inconsistencies in censorship and the media's reluctance to sit on stories when the information was believed to be freely available elsewhere – for example, in the foreign press.[8]

Some of the media seem also to have believed that it was their responsibility to determine whether publication of a particular story was in 'the national interest'. This lies at the heart of the controversy between MoD and the media. The MoD described the dictates of security as 'overriding':[9] *The Times* stated to the HCDC: 'The "national interest" as such was served by the fullest disclosure consonant with avoiding jeopardising lives,'[10] There is a difference of emphasis between these two definitions – the MoD stress security, *The Times*, publication. Disagreements between the media and MoD are however unsurprising, given that even the task force commanders and the Ministry were not always in agreement about what could and could not be released: for example, it was the MoD which announced that Argentine bombs were failing to explode, while Admiral Woodward told the HCDC that he 'would have preferred there to be no mention of unexploded bombs'.[11]

Different defence correspondents took different views as to who was best placed to decide what should be published and what withheld. The *Glasgow Herald* saw it as the newspaper's duty 'to determine what [it] was and was not in the public interest', to publish, on the basis of information which the government should make available.[12] Henry Stanhope did not believe that it was the reporter's responsibility. No journalist, he said, could afford to allow himself to become an arbiter of morality or security. If he came by a story, he would write it although, in a case of extreme doubt, he would consult the editorial staff as to whether the story should be published. He would have been willing in principle to accede to an MoD request not to publish information, provided it was for a limited period of time, but he did not think news could be suppressed indefinitely: 'Confidentiality leaks at the edges'.

Peter Snow put the issue of confidentiality into the context of an imagined scenario: what, he asked, if the Harrier reinforcements had been lost with the *Atlantic Conveyor*, and if the media had been asked to suppress this news because of the damaging operational consequences? He *thought* he would probably have been willing to hold back the information for a couple of days, but no longer, whereas he had been quite willing to suppress the fact that the Argentines were 'being incompetent with their fuses' until given the go-ahead by MoD to publish. Similarly, he held back for several days the news of 5 Infantry Brigade's landing. These were not controversial topics – but had the British forces been left with air support so inadequate as to call into question their ability to discharge their task reasonably safely, that would, he felt, have been a legitimate issue to bring before the public. He went on to say:

> There were certain things that anybody in his right mind would have wanted to conceal because it might have led to the loss of lives. On the other hand, those things we were ready to conceal were on the whole things that were uncontroversial and people's judgement about what was going on would not be affected . . . The whole thing was such an extraordinary success with very few things going wrong that there was never really an occasion when there was any controversy about whether to report or not. My overwhelming worry is that suppose something had gone wrong, there would have been problems for everyone.[13]

In other words, despite the controversy over censorship and disclosure, the crucial issue of how the media should handle news about operations that was *politically* controversial was never raised. In Snow's view, the media were never asked to

conceal anything of major importance and the crisis of
confidence and conscience that such a request would have
caused never arose. In the hypothetical situation where this did
occur, Snow said all his instincts would have been to publish.
The reporting of the Vietnam War and the immediacy of
modern communications had, he believed, changed things so
that while the publication of sensitive material could be delayed
(to save lives, for example) it should not be suppressed. 'There
is a duty on those of us who know to tell people what the
balance of power is, and what's at stake down there.' He
accepted that the situation would be very difficult, but the
expectation of modern audiences was that information would
be open and journalists had a duty to reveal matters 'of
legitimate public discussion'.

Jon Connell of the *Sunday Times* (a paper not noted for its
silence on matters of public controversy) took a different view
and one which came closer to the findings of the HCDC. In the
scenario described by Peter Snow, he would, he said, consult
his editor but in principle he would be entirely willing to
suppress a story if there were clear and obvious operational
penalties in releasing it. He believed that the principle of 'the
public's right to know' could be overemphasised – in many
cases, he was sure the public would prefer not to know, if there
was the least risk of endangering lives. His only hesitation
about holding back on a story lay in a less philosophical, but
understandable, concern for his reputation as a journalist: 'You
would want to be sure that your rivals weren't going to publish
it – if they were, then why should I hang back. Not to publish a
story when other people were would undermine my credibility
as a journalist with my readers.'

All this suggests that, on the whole, the Ministry of Defence
were right to be cautious about the media's attitude
towards operationally sensitive material. The consensus among
journalists seems to be that, if asked to do so, they would
temporarily delay the publication of such information, but that
delay could not be indefinite, nor would they sustain it if they
believed that the material was going to be published elsewhere.
The MoD can, however, carry caution too far, by refusing to
advise reporters on whether material is operationally sensitive.
There is a standard form of words used by MoD in reply to
questions on certain subjects such as the presence of nuclear

weapons in a given location – the 'we can neither confirm nor deny' formula. This may be fair enough when the information involved is of such sensitivity that it is preferable for it to be published as an unconfirmed item rather than for it to be suppressed if that requires even one journalist to be given confirmation of the information. Where it involves material that is of *immediate* operational sensitivity, but which has little or no long-term security information, the value of the practice is questionable. In the case of the Falklands, at least one correspondent believes that it led to the publication of material which, in retrospect, he feels should have been withheld. Christopher Lee referred in this context to the interview on 18 May in which he referred to the likelihood that the 5 Infantry Brigade troops from the *QE2* were cross-decking to other ships.[14] MoD would not comment on the story, nor would they say whether there was any objection to its being published. In the event, Lee broadcast the information, which was accurate, but, as noted earlier (p. 128), he now regards this as a security leak which 'slipped through'. According to the *Financial Times*, the task force commanders were angered by the publication of the material.[15] In that instance, and in any similar situation, there is a good case for suggesting that a reliable and experienced defence correspondent could have been told something along the lines: 'Look, I can't actually confirm this story for you, but it would be of help to us if you would sit on it for a little while because of the risk to the people who could be involved. We'll let you know as soon as it can safely be published.' Defence correspondents are, after all, dependent on the good will of the Ministry of Defence if they are to do their job properly; they are in competition for information with the political and parliamentary lobby reporters and so need to set up and encourage a good flow of information. It should be possible under these circumstances – as has frequently been the case in the past – for the two parties, correspondents and Defence Public Relations, to cooperate with each other.

Where such informal arrangements are impossible, either because of the sensitive nature of the information involved, or because of a lack of reciprocal good will, it would appear that there is little point in the MoD piously hoping that the media will exercise discretion. They may do so, but then only for limited periods of time and it cannot be guaranteed. This was the dilemma which faced Sir Frank Cooper when he unattributably briefed the media prior to the San Carlos landings and specifically denied that D-Day type landings were imminent: he forecast a series of hit and run raids. The media were subsequently furious at what they saw as an attempt not only to mislead them, but also, by using an unattributable briefing, make it seem as though they were the ones who had got it wrong. They felt they had been manipulated. The actual circumstances of the briefing do not support an accusation of cold-blooded, planned deception, but suggest rather opportunism by Sir Frank Cooper. None of the defence correspondents interviewed by the author thought that Sir Frank should have taken them into his confidence; most thought that he should have refused to comment – but accepted ruefully that even a 'no comment' would have been subjected to analysis and interpretation.

THE RETIRED SERVICE OFFICERS

If Christopher Wain could describe the need for discretion as among 'the rules of engagement' for defence correspondents, it must be recognised that for the second group of expert commentators, the retired servicemen, it was engraved on their hearts. They knew only too well the risks which could flow from breaches of security; many of them had family, friends and former colleagues who were involved in Operation Corporate. They also, however, had a very fair idea of the amount of material that was available and of the kind of information that could safely be assumed to be well known to Argentina. In fact, some of the retired officers who appeared in or were quoted by the media also criticised the amount of factual information given out by both MoD and the media. Vice-Admiral Sir John Roxburgh, who appeared on television and radio a number of times, is reported to have said: 'There is too much exposure of everything . . . we should have said nothing about the Exocet attack on the *Sheffield*. They did not say anything and we should have kept quiet . . .'[16] – a not entirely practical suggestion – while Marshal of the Royal Air Force Sir Arthur Harris wrote to the *Daily Express* in response to an article in that paper: 'I have all along criticized the extraordinary amount of detailed information given out by the media which could be of use to a potential enemy . . .'[17] Others were even more critical: Major General Butler wrote:

> Many people with military planning experience will be profoundly worried by . . . examples of the mishandling of news reports which when carefully studied reveal a wealth of information which is not apparent to the layman.[18]

In a sense, of course, this misses the real issue, which is not whether the information was apparent to British laymen, but whether it was so to Argentine intelligence. This raises the question of how efficient Argentine intelligence was. Certainly their surprise at the British reaction to the invasion suggests a misreading of the political situation; information about military intelligence is harder to come by. It appears from the static and concentrated nature of the defence that they mounted in the Falklands, that their intelligence about what was happening on the ground was not particularly good, while the British task force commanders suspected that whatever the quality of the intelligence collected by Argentine headquarters back on the mainland, it was not being utilised to the best advantage in the Falklands themselves.[19] The same might not be true of another enemy in another war.

Many of the former Service officers involved in the media commentary on the Falklands conflict did have what Major General Butler termed 'military planning experience'. Their number included former Chiefs of Staff, commanders of major formations, senior staff college lecturers and an ex-Director of Army Operations. Indeed, most of the senior officers who appeared in the media can be presumed to have had staff experience gained in an operational command or headquarters, since such postings are normal steps in a successful military career.

In general, the commentators were fully aware of the risk that by divulging the wrong material they could give information away to the Argentines. This undoubtedly influenced what they had to say and how they said it.

Several military commentators refused to comment or speculate on particular issues. Sometimes they were quite abrupt: David Bolton told Brian Redhead that it would be 'irresponsible to speculate on detailed consequences or the courses of action that [the task force commander] might have in mind'.[20] Rear Admiral Edward Gueritz was equally adamant after the San Carlos landing: 'Certainly it's not for me to forecast where and when the next problems are going to arise.'[21] Remarks of this kind were not untypical. Many commentators were particularly reluctant to identify difficulties facing the task force and preferred to offer reassurance, however vague: for example, Major General Nigel Gribbon told an ITN interviewer: 'It would be wrong to speculate on tactics . . . The formation commander has at his means all the forces necessary for battle.'[22]

The military commentators do not appear to have been particularly helped by the media in maintaining this discretion. David Bolton recalled one interview when the ground to be covered had been agreed in advance, but as soon as the programme went on the air he was asked to comment on one area they had agreed not to touch on. In the altercation which took place afterwards, the interviewer claimed 'once you're on the air, the adrenalin makes that kind of thing all right' – in other words, he had hoped that Bolton would be pressured by the occasion into blurting out a reply. Derek Lewis of BBC radio saw occasional advantages in using military commentators instead of defence correspondents because sometimes with the former: 'you would get a freer discussion than you could from a defence correspondent. That was one reason why MoD were so jumpy – some old admirals would become extremely forthright.' He cited one example, a retired officer who had been involved in off-loading troops in a number of amphibious operations and who commented on hearing of the losses at Bluff Cove that it was 'a disgrace'. Jonathan Alford, on the other hand, had been in the *Newsnight* studio when that news came in: he realised that something must have gone wrong, but refused to comment because he was not fully aware of the circumstances.

There were thus several ways that military commentators could assist the Argentines or damage the British cause – by giving away hard fact, by criticising the conduct of operations, but above all – and this particularly concerned MoD – by revealing something of the general tenor of British military thinking. On this point, the Ministry commented:

Although an armchair strategist by definition has no access to the decision making process, intelligence sources, etc., and is therefore essentially giving his own opinion, he nevertheless has advantages, particularly if he is an ex-military man with a background in MoD which make his opinions slightly better informed than pure speculation. They are therefore potentially of use to any enemy, particularly Argentina whose forces were in fact ignoring many straightforward precautions which normal commonsense would have demanded.[23]

General Jeremy Moore endorsed this view and set it in a more specific context. The Argentines had, he said, been trained by the United States in amphibious warfare. The American Marine Corps has an attitude and in consequence tactics entirely different from those of the Royal Marines. They rely on numbers, on heavy concentrations of force, rather than on the skill and subtlety which are features of Royal Marine operations. The Argentines had expected attack of the sort favoured by the US Marine Corps; they never overcame that expectation. If the British invasion of the Falklands was to be successful, it was essential that it should contain an element of surprise: 'The geography was very limited, but there were nuances in what you could do, and they might not have anticipated those nuances.' General Moore's concern was that the commentary, by alerting the Argentines to the way British operations might be mounted, would deprive him of that surprise. In fact the Argentines on the Falklands apparently did not believe that the British forces would cross East Falkland by foot to attack Stanley from the west and north; they seem to have ignored or been oblivious to the forecasts by armchair strategists in Britain – but the risk identified by General Moore was a real one, had the opposition devoted more effort to intelligence of that kind.[24]

Some commentators were aware of this problem. Jonathan Alford said:

I was familiar with planning procedures and concepts . . . I was very conscious of the risk that giving away the way you think could give comfort to the enemy . . . My misgivings were not about facts, but about giving away the British military way of thinking about things.[25]

The problem was that that was precisely what the media wanted of the retired Service officers. Peter Snow described the role of the military commentators on *Newsnight*:

> On the whole, we found them useful just to give one a flavour of the sort of attitudes and language and temperament of the people involved in this kind of exercise. Very rarely did we expect any one of them to come out with prophetic information about what they would do: we were looking for knowledge and expertise about the sort of considerations that would be behind judgements taken by people in the South Atlantic.[26]

This role of the military commentators was probably potentially the most dangerous in terms of prejudicing the safety of operations. It was particularly in evidence when retired officers were asked such questions as 'What should the task force commander do now?' or 'Where would you land in the Falklands?' David Nicholas, Editor of Independent Television News (ITN) told the HCDC: 'I think if you are saying "Here is how I would invade" that would be objectionable. I would submit that we never actually did that.'[27]

In fact, that is precisely what some interviewers – for ITN and others – did ask retired officers to say, although no very detailed answers were ever given.[28]

This kind of approach was popular with current affairs programmes in general and particularly with *Weekend World*. In effect, it seeks to put the participants into the position of decision-makers: it involves a degree of role-playing in which we see the television presenter as Chief of Staff *manque*. Jon Connell said of the *Weekend World* programmes in which he participated that they simulated 'the kind of discussion that might have gone on in Cabinet'. Jonathan Alford said of *Newsnight* and of some programmes made for the US network ABC, where maps and models were much in evidence, 'There was a temptation to turn the thing into a briefing room. The media liked the visual impact but they do have a tendency to trivialise things.' This was not the media's objective, but none the less it was a risk they ran, and one that could be compounded by thoughtless or sloppy presentation. This was exemplified in a *Newsnight* programme when Peter Snow was introduced by the words:

. . . Now the military situation on the ground in the Falklands. With the Argentine forces now virtually encircled, here's Peter Snow with the outlook for the final assault on Port Stanley. Peter.[29]

This could just as easily have been introducing the sports commentator for an assessment of the likely outcome of a Cup Final. Whatever their intentions, clearly reporters and editors alike ran the risk of being carried away by the excitement of the story they were covering.

Occasionally, military commentators fell into the same trap, particularly if they were unused to dealing with the media. For that reason, certain programmes generally avoided employing them: we found very few instances, for example, in the BBC's *Nine O'Clock News*. Christopher Wain, the BBC television defence correspondent, described himself as against the use of 'pundits' for several reasons, including the danger that 'if someone got too involved, he might say too much'.

Some of those within the media were reluctant to use retired officers for other reasons. Julian Holland, editor of *Today*, explained that the timing of his programme (early morning) meant that they were better placed to give an up-to-date briefing on the news than to engage in more detailed analysis. He felt that the amount of speculation elsewhere had been unproductive and repetitive and that many of the retired Service officers had little to say. He preferred to make only occasional use of them.[30] *The World at One*, on the other hand, appears before much of the day's news is known, and can therefore devote more time to what were described as 'think-pieces'. This was reflected in their greater use of commentators. By the time *PM* is broadcast, the House of Commons has been sitting for a couple of hours; there are ministerial statements to report and analyse and most of the day's domestic news has happened. Hence, again, there was only limited use of experts and greater emphasis on straightforward reporting.

Others outside broadcasting also expressed doubts about the value of using former Service officers. Some of the military commentators were themselves less than flattering about their former colleagues. One thought that there was 'a dearth of people experienced in dealing with the media . . . retread admirals of twenty years before who were no good at being

interviewed and who gave their military judgements badly'.
Another said he had been amazed at things said by 'people who
should have known better' – including basic errors of fact about
equipment: 'There were comments from Air Marshals about
aircraft performance that were rubbish; Admirals revealed, even
to a layman in maritime operations, that they didn't understand
current procedures.'

Journalists and broadcasters themselves had mixed views
about the value of military commentators' contribution. Defence
correspondents on the whole thought they had added little
except in certain specialised subjects like submarine warfare or
for general background information. Some of the broadcasting
production staff suggested they had provided a livelier and
more authoritative contribution than would otherwise have
been the case. There was, however, quite a widespread feeling
that the retired officers had been used too much. Peter Snow
said that in retrospect, he would have thought more seriously
about the wisdom of making so much use of 'obviously
concerned, committed ex-servicemen instead of more
neutral pundits like those from the IISS and some weapons
experts'.

This question of commitment is an important one. To what
extent can the military commentators, the retired ex-servicemen, be seen as impartial and objective commentators?
Retired Service officers tended consistently to play down the
dangers of operations, or at least to balance them by positive
and up-beat assertions – for example, about the excellence of
British training and expertise. This reflected something of their
loyalties. Although they were not government spokesmen, most
clearly continued to identify closely with the armed forces. This
is not surprising: a number of studies have noted the importance
of group identity as a key to military behaviour and this
identity is not easily shed. The retired Service officers had thus
the habits of a lifetime's loyalty; and with friends and family
serving with the task force, as was often the case, they had an
even greater personal interest than the population at large in
the success of military operations, along with a heightened
consciousness of the importance of morale. Their views, although
given in an individual and not an official capacity, were
therefore often coloured by considerations other than pure
objectivity, and they themselves recognised that they had

identified with the task force and were critical of those in the media who denigrated the Services.

At least one defence correspondent took the view that the public themselves would not see the ex-Service commentator as independent. Christopher Lee argued with some cogency that the public did not necessarily distinguish between retired Service officers as individuals; they would be recognised simply as authoritative voices speaking from a military or quasi-military point of view. This seems a fair point.

Several of the media professionals most closely involved with the retired Service officers were convinced that at least some of the latter were acting under instructions from the MoD, whether formally or informally through old colleagues. The MoD confirm that some retired officers were approached and asked to display caution in their dealings with the media.[31] There were also attempts to bring the commentary more under MoD's control. Sir Henry Leach told the HCDC that as First Sea Lord, he had suggested to Sir Frank Cooper, Permanent Secretary at the MoD,

> that we should get the concurrence of a small number of retired naval officers and we should have them making it clear to the media that they were available for such purposes; that they themselves should be briefed; and therefore they would know a great deal more than they were entitled to by virtue of their retired position, and would be on their guard accordingly to stop the indiscriminate speculation.[32]

Sir Terence Lewin, the former Chief of Defence Staff, told the HCDC that this had been done, but MoD could find no record that this was so and Sir Frank Cooper confessed that, disagreeing with the proposal, he had delayed implementing it.[33]

It is difficult to see how the various interpretations of the role of the 'armchair strategist' can be reconciled. For the Ministry of Defence, he is someone who risks giving away to the enemy information described by Sir Henry Leach as 'potentially, if not actually, highly prejudicial to the success of the operation'.[34] The commentators saw themselves differently, as engaged in 'an attempt to cover dispassionately and accurately an extremely complex military operation'.[35] Peter Snow saw a need 'constantly to question those who have the power to direct events and to question the assumptions and assessments on which they make their decisions'.[36] Jonathan Alford took part in the commentary in order to help inform the public: he wanted to ensure that 'interested people who wanted some sense of the choices and difficulties involved would be helped to understand them'. David Bolton was similarly trying to ensure that informed opinion was enhanced: 'When I was in the Services there was frequently the feeling that the Serviceman's viewpoint went by default. I was trying to give some background to what was going on, using my own experience and knowledge to give a military focus to that background.'

It seems inevitable that the media will continue to analyse and interpret military operations involving British forces. At the same time, the people engaged in planning, controlling and executing those operations will be suspicious and resentful of the media commentary. The MoD say that they would endeavour to discourage speculation if similar circumstances arose again;[37] those in the media and those among the outside experts interviewed all took the view that commentary and speculation could not be avoided. The most that could be done was to ensure that it had a sound factual basis of information that was not sensitive in order to reduce the time and space available for conjecture which could actually prove operationally damaging. Events which followed the Falklands elsewhere in the world were to highlight different ways of dealing with this issue.

NOTES

1. At the start of the conflict all the regular defence correspondents had their passes (which gave them access to the Ministry of Defence) cancelled: it was left open to each newspaper, agency and broadcasting organisation to designate whom they wished to attend the MoD briefings. Some of the publications involved had little record of serious interest in defence issues and the reporters designated to cover the Falklands were in effect novices on this subject.
2. Interview with the author.
3. Interview with the author.
4. Interview with the author.
5. Interview with the author.
6. *The Times*, 17 May 1982.
7. HCDC *Report*, vol. i, para 24.

8. *The Times*, for example, withheld 'any information that had direct operational implications . . . until we were satisfied that the enemy must also know what was afoot' (HCDC *Report*, vol. II, p. 120). Derek Lewis of BBC radio said that 'We didn't make too much [of security]. After all, there was no bipartisan agreement in the Commons not to give away information, and material was coming out of Argentina.'

9. Memorandum by MoD, *HCDC Report*, vol. II, p. 1.

10. Ibid., p. 120.

11. Ibid., Q1153.

12. Ibid. Memorandum by the *Glasgow Herald*, p. 135.

13. Interview with the author.

14. *The World Tonight*.

15. 'Angry Commanders Tighten Curb on News', *Financial Times*, 7 June 1982.

16. Quoted in William Hickey, 'TV Admirals never know the Taste of Defeat', *Daily Express*, 7 May 1982.

17. *Daily Express*, 21 May 1982.

18. Major General H. D. G. Butler, letter to *The Times*, 14 June 1982.

19. Interview with Major General Jeremy Moore.

20. *Today*, 5 May 1982.

21. BBC, *Nine O'Clock News*, 21 May 1982.

22. ITN, *News at One*, 27 May 1982.

23. Letter from MoD (Defence Secretariat 11) to the author, 30 April 1984.

24. Interview with Professor Freedman and the author.

25. Interview with the author.

26. Interview with the author.

27. HCDC *Report*, vol. II, Q270.

28. For example, Peter Sissons, *News at One*, 27 April 1982; Denis Tuohey, *TV Eye*, 29 April 1982; Gordon Clough, *The World at One*, 1 May 1982; Peter Snow, *Newsnight*, 19 May 1982.

29. *Newsnight*, 5 June 1982.

30. Interview with the author.

31. Letter from MoD to the author. One commentator told the author that it was only retired members of the Royal Marines who were approached by MoD; certainly none of those interviewed by the author had been contacted.

32. HCDC *Report*, vol. II, Q1425–6.

33. Interview with Professor Freedman and the author.

34. HCDC *Report*, vol. II, Q1424.

35. Letter to *The Times*, 17 May 1982.

36. Letter to *The Times*, 8 May 1982.

37. Letter from MoD to the author.

11 Into the Future: the Falklands Factor

LEBANON

Even before its conclusion, the Falklands campaign was overtaken in the media interest by the conflict in Lebanon. During June and July of 1982, access to the war in the Lebanon was only possible courtesy of the Israeli Army – a courtesy which appears to have been fully extended to bone fide reporters and observers at that time, although later on access was to be limited in certain respects.[1] An organisation staffed by Army personnel was set up to deal with correspondents: it apparently worked very well – the HCDC were told: 'The most efficient military censorship known to the BBC is the Israeli system which, until recently, has operated in a way which suits both journalists and the requirements of military security.'[2]

Briefings were given to defence correspondents by press officers who were members of the Israeli Intelligence Corps, and therefore fully familiar with both background to and the security implications of their material. On visits to the front, correspondents were accompanied by military conducting officers and given clear instructions about what they were permitted to do. Photographs and scripts were checked by intelligence experts so that information of value to an enemy could be deleted.

This censorship was supposed to be applied exclusively to material affecting the security of the state but ITN told the HCDC: 'In recent weeks . . . there are indications that the censor is applying political values.'[3] The *Daily Mail* described censorship as haphazard and commented, 'It was always worth taking a chance on breaking it'[4] – a view which shows the need for media cooperation if even a formal system of censorship is to be effective.

Although the media may have been reasonably happy with the arrangements, the Israeli government seems to have been less than comfortable about the outcome. Dr David Kimche, Director General of Israel's Foreign Ministry, was quoted as saying that 'distorted coverage' of the Israeli invasion had done 'irreparable damage'. Speaking at an international workshop on the media in war, Dr Kimche disclosed that the government was now asking itself some 'very painful questions', including whether Israel should in future 'act like the British in the Falklands by shutting the place off to journalists and saying, "to hell with democratic values"'.[5]

Dr Kimche's interpretation of what had happened in the Falklands is interesting: journalists were *not* excluded from the Falklands – the Royal Navy took them there. The campaign was extensively reported; the censorship exercised does not appear to have seriously prejudiced the public's access to information. None the less, before a year was out, an international mythology had grown up around the media coverage of the Falklands, that somehow the British government had suppressed the news and got away with it. For example, in an article discussing the media's role in the Vietnam War, Professor Lawrence Lichty of the University of Maryland was quoted as follows:

> ... if one accepts that TV coverage lost America the [Vietnam] war, then a Government like yours can argue in the case of the Falklands that it must have censorship. And indeed the Falklands is discussed a lot by the US military who would keep the press out ...[6]

GRENADA

A few months later, the US military were indeed to have the opportunity to 'keep the press out', while parallels with the Falklands flowed fast and furious.

Early on Tuesday 25 October 1983, forces of the United States invaded Grenada, a small Caribbean island where government and the rule of law had collapsed. The invasion was highly controversial for reasons outside the scope of this study, but there was another aspect to the controversy. The media had no official forewarning of the invasion nor were they permitted to accompany the US forces or to set foot on the island until some forty-eight hours after the first wave of troops had gone ashore. Even then, the number of reporters permitted to land was severely restricted – fifteen on Thursday 27 October, thirty on Friday 28 October and another fifty on Saturday 29 October. The fury of the 400 or so correspondents reduced to reporting their story from neighbouring Barbados can only have been increased by the reported failure of some of the reporters and photographers who went in on the first day to honour their promise to 'pool' information.[7] The restrictions began to be eased on 30 October, however, when a further 163 reporters and photographers were allowed access to Grenada although with no promise of military cooperation.[8]

The media were left in no doubt as to the inspiration for their exclusion. Colonel Robert J. O'Brien, Deputy Director of Defense Information at the Pentagon reportedly told CBS News: 'We learned our lessons from the Falklands War.'[9] There were attempts to question this parallel: *Newsweek* reported journalists' comments that task force correspondents had at least been allowed ashore.[10] Nevertheless, the Falklands campaign has continued to serve as a point of reference for criticisms of the US government's handling of the media during the Grenada operation.[11]

The media coverage of Grenada itself became a media issue and a brief analysis reveals several points of interest. First, the operation was not a 'bolt from the blue' which found the press totally unprepared, nor was media coverage completely suppressed as claimed. Cable News network sent a reporter and crew to Barbados the day before the invasion, after receiving a tip-off from a 'pretty solid' source. The first landings were reported on the early morning television programmes *on the actual day of the invasion*, with film of the US Marines' aircraft leaving Barbados. Voice reports were received from Grenada that day as the operation was actually under way.[12] NBC News had also photographed US military transports on Barbados on Monday 24 October and had questioned a White House foreign policy spokesman about the possibility of an invasion of Grenada, only to be told by another press secretary that the idea was 'preposterous'. (Les Janka, the foreign policy spokesman, subsequently resigned because despite his own good

faith his credibility had been damaged 'perhaps irreparably'.[13])
What the media wanted, it seemed, was to observe and record
not only the news of the invasion, but the operation itself.

Secondly, like the British government, the US government
was accused of misinforming the public when they failed to
disclose the bombing of a mental hospital, inflated the number
of Cuban military personnel on the island and did not announce
several other mishaps.[14] Other sections of the press argued that
the consequences of the invasion were sufficiently beneficial at
least to excuse and even to justify the administration's handling
of media coverage.[15] The controversy led the US government to
carry out its own enquiry – a panel of officers and journalists
was set up to review the news restrictions imposed on the initial
days of the Grenada invasion and to suggest rules for the press
coverage of military actions. This panel concluded that the
media should be allowed access to information about military
operations 'to the maximum degree possible, consistent with
the security of the mission and the safety of troops'.[16]

The debate over Grenada focused on the invasion itself and
the treatment of the media: the actual content of the media
coverage was of less concern. The exclusion of the press from
the actual landings and their relatively straightforward nature
in military terms meant that there was little commentary on
military aspects of the campaign. The reporting of the departure
of the Marines from Barbados did no damage in the event,
since the resistance on Grenada was not of a standard to strain
US military capabilities. The media claimed that had they been
brought into the operation from the start, they would not have
disclosed secret plans. This assertion remains unproven.
Certainly any leak of US intentions would have made it much
more difficult in political terms, and possibly more costly in
military terms, to undertake the invasion.

THE BEACH REPORT

Following the Falklands campaign, the British government also
set up an internal enquiry on information policy – the Study
Group on Censorship, chaired by General Sir Hugh Beach with
members drawn from the media, the Ministry of Defence and
the Foreign Office:

To consider, not least in the light of experience during the Falkland Islands operations, whether any new measures, including the introduction of a system of censorship, are necessary in order to protect military information immediately prior to or during the conduct of operations.[17]

The study group published its report in December 1983. Much of what it had to say relates not only to straightforward reporting of military operations, but also to the analytical and speculative commentary that has been the subject of this study.

In defining the term 'military information', the report recognised that hard and fast rules could not be laid down as to what might or might not help an enemy. It pointed, however, to the risk that

spies may be targetted not only on direct sources of information but also on secondary sources: for instance, newspapers, television bulletins or radio hams. If valuable information is continually disseminated through these sources, then the enemy's task is considerably simplified.[18]

The report identified as relevant such information as operational plans, the state of morale and the capabilities of equipment – all subjects of analysis and commentary during the Falklands operation. At the same time, it recognised that in present circumstances 'A public accustomed to open communications and fast, comprehensive, world-wide coverage is not likely to tolerate for long any unnecessary withholding of news.'[19]

The Beach Report concluded that although many journalists were willing to exercise self-restraint, they could not always identify the information that would be of help to an enemy, and that 'Some form of official censorship in time of conflict is therefore desirable.'[20] Censorship should, however, be limited to 'the untimely disclosure of information which would prejudice our own or Allied operations and assist the enemy'. In particular it noted that:

Well-informed speculation in the media may occasionally give the enemy useful leads. Retired officers and others in receipt of official information should therefore be required to check with MoD before accepting invitations from the media in times of conflict. (Recommendation V)

In a major conventional war, the report recommended a full system of censorship. In a limited conflict such as the Falklands, no formal censorship would apply at home but 'there would be merit in providing an improved advisory service for journalists'. In either event, 'Once information is published outside this country, its publication in the British media must be allowed.'

It is difficult to see how effective the system envisaged would be in controlling speculation and analysis. The suggestion that retired officers should check with MoD before accepting invitations to appear in the media would carry little force unless it was made obligatory, with MoD being prepared to deny requests for permission and to invoke sanctions (for example, withholding pension rights) against those who fail to comply. In theory, Queen's Regulations could already be used for this purpose, but in practice, at least during the Falklands campaign, they do not seem to have been invoked. The offer of briefings to those invited to appear on the media might, if this were envisaged, be helpful – but might also carry the risk that as a consequence the retired officers concerned would have yet more sensitive information at their disposal which, on the odd occasion, might inadvertently be let slip. Otherwise, the most that could be done would be to remind those concerned of the need for caution and perhaps of particular subjects to be avoided.

In any case, as the Falklands conflict showed, civilian defence correspondents can often bring nearly as much detailed knowledge to bear on their analysis and speculation as retired Service officers. Controlling one group without controlling the other would hardly be effective.

There is also the question of the foreign press. In the Falklands War, considerable detailed interpretation and speculation appeared, for example, in the US media: this is clearly beyond the control of the British government. The Beach Report recognised the need in a major war in Europe for consultation within NATO about the type of information to be protected and for firm direction on military information policy; none the less there could be no guarantee that the Alliance partners would all adopt the same measures. In the nebulous area of commentary on military operations, some allies might be particularly reluctant to impose stringent regulations. Experience in the first year of the Korean War, when Britain argued for the censorship which the US were reluctant to impose, certainly suggests that the risk is high.

The approach in the Beach Report to the control of speculation is thus not entirely coherent. It is hard to avoid the suspicion that Recommendation V contains an element of window-dressing – the use of retired officers by the media during the Falklands caused anxiety to the military and to politicians, therefore something had to be said about it. Given, however, that the actions of retired officers cannot be controlled by relying solely on their good will and that British and foreign media cooperation in suppressing or withholding information cannot be guaranteed, it seems likely that MoD will have either to grit their teeth and bear with the detailed media commentary which has now become a feature of war coverage or consider the imposition of formal measures of censorship.

THE MEDIA AND THE PUBLIC

Public reaction to such measures would probably be to accept them, although doubtless with some cynicism as to the truthfulness of the resultant information: the HCDC made some pointed observations on the public's attitude to information in wartime:

> It is easy to argue that to suppress the truth is inherently alien to a democratic society, but even this argument can be given an exaggerated emphasis. In particular it must be remembered that the Government's credibility may appear quite different in the eyes of the media and of the public at large. The two are closely related since public opinion is influenced by media reporting and commentary, but they are not always equal quantities. Many principles, supposedly regarded as sacred and absolute within the media are applied in a less rigid and categorical way by the public as a whole when it is judging its Government's conduct of a war . . .[21]

The Committee recognised the dangers, but concluded that the public was willing to accept being misled *to some extent*, if as a result the enemy were also misled and the prospects of the campaign's success thereby improved. The evidence suggests that the media do not show the same degree of acceptance: for whatever reasons, principled or commercial, they set their own claims higher. A *Times* leader during the Falklands conflict proclaimed that:('The first, indeed, the paramount interest in a democracy must be to inform the public as soon as possible about what is happening on its behalf . . .'[22])Certainly informing the public is an extremely important task, but, as Jon Connell pointed out, the public might well consider that in certain circumstances, its interests would be even better served by a degree of secrecy about the actions undertaken on its behalf.

The question at the heart of this issue is whom do the media represent? In the controversy over the coverage of Grenada, one US journalist, Dan Rather, gave a succinct reply: 'If the press isn't there the people aren't there.' The *Washington Times* went so far as to claim 'The press is the representative of the people just as much as is Congress.'[23] None of the British media suggested that the press has the same claim to represent the people as does Parliament. None the less the notion that the press stands proxy for the people was at times implicit in the British media's view of their rights and their role – for example in the failure to accept it as reasonable that important news should be announced first in Parliament by government ministers before being published by the media.[24] It is noteworthy that to the public at large, the media appear to be less than uniformly and totally credible: in an opinion poll conducted in 1983, only 38 per cent regarded television as 'generally honest'.[25]

There is, of course, a fundamental point of principle here. The role of the media in a democracy is not merely to pass on information for information's sake, but to enable the people to know, understand and *judge* the actions undertaken by their government on their behalf. The media plays a vital role in helping people to decide whether or not they approve of what their government is doing. The way in which the media serve to form and influence public opinion is, however, an extremely contentious issue. Radicals claim that a capitalist press will inevitably present the established order in the best possible light, while the establishment sees the media as insufficiently patriotic and supportive of an elected government in times of crisis and frequently carping and hypercritical at other periods.[26]

If the information published by the media is consistently inaccurate or distorted, then the press in fact undermines the proper functioning of democracy. If the media are to make a proper contribution they must report events objectively and dispassionately. That is not to deny editors the right to comment by expressing opinions, but comment and reporting should be clearly distinguishable from each other. The media need not be impartial as between different political parties or different courses of action but, in order to help the public reach a proper judgement, their handling of facts must be accurate and objective. Unfortunately, the quality of much reporting is questionable. This inevitably raises doubts about the validity of the media's claims to be governed by high principle. Articles about knickers printed with words of support for the task force may have entertained, but could they really be claimed to be upholding the principles of democracy?

There are grounds for thinking that issues of principle dominate the media's day-to-day activities rather less than do the more prosaic – but equally professional – concerns about getting a job done as well as possible – filling columns and programmes, beating rivals with the news and attracting as large an audience as possible. In these circumstances, reporters may forget to identify with the public they serve. This was highlighted when, speaking on *Newsnight* on 2 May, Peter Snow said: 'Until the British are demonstrated either to be deceiving us or to be concealing losses from us, we can only tend to give a lot more credence to the British version of events.' The criticism focused on Snow's supposed questioning of British credibility, but far more significant and revealing was his use of the words 'we' and 'us'. if there is a distinction to be made between 'The British' and 'us', it is fair (if ungrammatical) to ask who is 'us'? When this was put to him in retrospect, Snow suggested that instead of 'The British', he should have referred to 'the British government'; 'we' would then have referred to the British public with whom he was identifying. But that is *not* what he said; we are left rather with the image of the media as the arbitrators of events standing above and outside of them.

This concept of the fourth estate as an independent entity finds its highest expression in the type of reporting which seeks not only to inform about events but also to influence them. This is not the obvious type of pressure brought by, for example, comment in a newspaper editorial, but a more subtle process. It was particularly exemplified during the Falklands crisis in

Weekend World where Brian Walden, the presenter, repeatedly asked his panel of experts such questions as 'How should Britain try to bring the war to a successful conclusion?', 'What should Britain's next move be?', 'What should the government decide to do?' The commentary moves from the analytical and speculative to the prescriptive as the media seek to advise or influence decisions which may be extremely complex, requiring an understanding far deeper than a television or radio panel discussion can provide.

In the course of the HCDC enquiry, some further light was shed on media attitudes to public information. As part of its investigations, the Committee (which is composed entirely of Members of Parliament elected to represent their constituents) asked the Ministry of Defence for the transcripts of a briefing given by Sir Frank Cooper to the press on 20 May. The MoD sought the view of the group of defence correspondents who had attended the briefing and replied to the HCDC that

> A majority of those present took the view that it would be wrong for the Ministry of Defence now to release tapes of briefings which were clearly intended at the time, and as far as they are concerned, still are, unattributable.[27]

The journalists asked that such briefings should no longer be taped and MoD agreed to this, and supplied the Committee with only part of the transcript of the briefing in question. It is difficult to square this denial of information with assertions such as that by the BBC: 'The BBC's function in this crisis was to provide the maximum amount of truthful information to the public'[28] or ITN's claim that 'the public expectation of a full flow of accurate information is an essential part of a democratic society. This proposition should be not just grudgingly accepted, but warmly embraced.'[29] Implicit in the incident was the notion that the media should be empowered to decide what information the public are to receive.

There is other evidence that this may be a view the media takes. Commenting on the Grenada controversy, one American newsman argued that the reporter had the right to information, and *it was his right to get that information wrong*.[30] In other words, what must be guaranteed is the *media*'s access to accurate information: the public will, it seems, have to take what it is given by the media.

In its most acute form, the attitude of the press thus appears to be that it is above government and people alike. In practice, however, the worst excesses consequent on such a view are avoided, partly because of the integrity and good sense of individual journalists and editors and partly because, while they are not accountable to the public in any electoral sense, the media are totally dependent on public approval in a commercial sense. It is more palatable to talk in terms of high principle than in the language of the market place, but it is the latter that in one way or another dictates not only the content but the very existence of the media. Unless they are meeting a public demand, they cannot survive. Commercial sense – the need to market a professional and attractive end-product – is the ultimate driving force behind much of what the media does, and this has its advantages. It ensures that in the last resort the media are not entirely self-serving or inward-looking. In this context, moreover, there is surprisingly little to choose between the different ends of the media spectrum. It would be hard to find two more dissimilar vehicles for the dissemination of information than *Weekend World* and the *News of the World*, but two quotations from a book about the former bear comparison with Derek Jameson's remarks about the selling qualities of war and bingo (quoted in Chapter 9, p. 150). Hugh Pile, editor of *Weekend World*, commented:

> I saw the Falklands conflict from the point of view of the programme as unique. First of all, it was a big story the like of which I as a journalist and *Weekend World* as a programme might never see again. Secondly, it seemed to me something for which *Weekend World* was designed . . .

and the author, Michael Tracey, wrote: 'For a journalist, if not for a soldier, it was a good time to be alive.'[31]

THE MINISTRY – MANIPULATION OR MUDDLE?

If there are inconsistencies in the media's attitude to the task of informing the public, they seem to reflect the even greater confusion that appears to exist not simply within the Ministry of Defence, but in the government as a whole. In Chapter 1, it was suggested that there are discrepancies between the MoD's acknowledgement of a public right to information and its habitual practice on grounds both good and bad of managing the flow of that information. These discrepancies were in many instances reflected in the way the government handled information during the Falklands conflict, and in the inconsistencies in official attitudes to the media commentary, especially to speculation about the likely course of events.

There is little doubt that MoD inadvertently encouraged speculative and interpretative commentary by the very wording of its official on-the-record statements. Their language invited analysis, every word was examined to ensure that no possible significance was overlooked. As Christopher Wain said

> If a briefing said vaguely 'The task force is on course and on time', every single word was pored over. The pressure at this end [i.e. for material to broadcast] was enormous. If there was no information given, the natural result was speculation. Inevitably some of the speculation was very close to the truth.[32]

Some speculation was actually useful to the MoD and was either gratefully noted (as in the case of the HMS *Superb* story) or actively encouraged. MoD noted two incidents which were of the latter kind:

> . . . casualties at Fitzroy (refusal to confirm these led to speculation based on much heavier figures . . . which was helpful in securing the build-up for the final push against Stanley). More generally widespread speculation during the early half of May about our future intentions, encouraged by Sir Frank Cooper's briefing on 20 May, combined to ensure that the location of the initial landings remained unguessed at until the troops were already ashore.[33]

The suggestion that speculation in the first half of May about operations was helpful is particularly interesting given the widespread public and parliamentary criticism of such conjecture. A considerable amount of speculative reporting was prompted by official sources. Defence correspondents continued to receive leaked information from sources outside as well as within MoD, including 'people at a high level who obviously knew what was going on'. Several defence correspondents were actually approached by new sources, and in this context Christopher Lee's broadcast about the impending attack on Goose Green deserves further mention: Lee had worked out for himself that given the size, composition and logistics of the land forces, they were unlikely to remain at San Carlos: Goose Green was on one of the two possible routes out and he believed the Parachute Regiment would be tasked with taking it. After some days of speculation, he was approached by someone, not one of his normal sources, who knew what his 'amateur tactical assessment' was, who told him that the attack was currently in progress and that there was no reason not to announce it. Lee remains adamant that his source was someone sufficiently senior and well-informed to be able to make that judgement on a sensible and responsible basis.[34]

In his evidence to the HCDC, Robert Fox of BBC Radio described the news as having been 'leaked *through Westminster*',[35] while another defence correspondent (not Christopher Lee) suggested that the leak emanated from the then Defence Secretary, John Nott, who, he claimed, had briefed backbench Conservative MPs who then talked to reporters. A BBC editor suggested that the origin of the story lay with 10 Downing Street – a reference perhaps to the unattributable briefing given by Bernard Ingham, the Prime Minister's Chief Press Secretary, the weekend before the attack. Whatever the truth of these two accounts, the overwhelming burden of evidence to the HCDC was that information was frequently given away by ministers and particularly through the parliamentary lobby. The *Daily Mail* cited two instances when events were known about and discussed in the House of Commons before they had been formally announced by MoD or by ministers.[36] ITN said: 'News of developments would frequently gain currency from contacts in defence circles or from disclosures relayed from sources in Parliament.'[37] Similar claims were made by other witnesses.[38]

MoD doubt that 'there were any significant leaks via the Parliamentary lobby',[39] but the evidence suggests that on more than this one occasion information was given to the media by MPs who had received it from government sources. Clearly, information given to MPs cannot automatically be regarded as secure, but the political pressures are such that ministers are bound to wish to continue to keep their own backbenchers informed about events.

With the exception of the three examples cited on p. 185 – HMS *Superb*, the Fitzroy casualties and the San Carlos landings – none of the journalists interviewed for this study identified any other instances when MoD actively encouraged speculation. None the less, it must be recognised that just as undue reticence stimulates the imagination of the press, so the imparting of information can also lead to speculation, whether as a result of official statements, leaks, briefings, or indeed carelessly chosen words noted in other settings – in the UN for example (see p. 105) or in overseas broadcasts.[40] As far as the media commentary on the Falklands campaign was concerned, there is no evidence, apart from the well-known cases cited, of attempts by MoD at manipulation, but there is considerable evidence of confusion and inconsistency.

DID THE COMMENTARY GIVE AWAY INFORMATION?

In retrospect it is unclear that the media commentary prejudiced British operations. The only specific example picked out by the MoD on these grounds was the speculation surrounding the move on Goose Green:

> Argentina almost certainly moved men forward to reinforce Goose Green following these reports (although not necessarily because of them, or exclusively because of them). The task of capturing Goose Green may therefore have been all that much harder.[41]

Clearly this is less than firm proof that the media commentary was damaging. There was controversy over the publicity given to the failure of Argentine bombs to explode. Here, MoD say that: 'There is no evidence that the statements on UXBs (later suppressed by MoD) led the Argentines to improve their success rates in the later attacks.'[42]

It has also been claimed that the task force commanders were concerned about the speculation relating to possible landing sites in the Falklands and Chris Wain was singled out for criticism on these grounds by one of the more prominent military commentators. As MoD's comments on p. 185 show they actually found this speculation helpful. In any case, the conjecture about landing sites was far from conclusive and even though San Carlos was identified more than once, it was by no means a favourite forecast: the Argentines at least do not seem to have been alerted to it. Chris Wain, speaking of his own role, said that it was clear to him that 'there were only about six possible places to land'. He did however make sure that when he was indicating possible landing sites on the map the pointer never stopped moving long enough to suggest one place.[43]

The greatest risk seen by MoD, by the task force commanders and by some commentators themselves was that the commentary might have given the enemy a new insight into British military thinking by alerting them to the kind of tactics which the task force might adopt. It is not clear how familiar the Argentines were with British tactical theory; they had trained primarily with the Americans but none the less, because of defence sales and traditional links with the UK, they had had recent, albeit limited, contact with the British armed forces. The risk that Argentine intelligence could have been assisted by the commentary existed, but in practice it appears that the Argentines did not pay close attention to what was being said or, if they did, did not take account of it in their own tactics.[44]

In the narrow context of the Falklands campaign, it does not therefore appear that this particular concern – that the way our force commanders were thinking would be revealed – was realised. But what of the wider context?

Books and journals dealing with military operations and equipment can be supplemented by the many military memoirs and histories available. A power which saw itself as a potential enemy of this country could be presumed to have studied British tactical and strategic theory from published material and from other intelligence sources either before becoming committed to any conflict or as soon as it threatened – just as British military intelligence studies and analyses the military thinking of other potentially hostile states. It is in any case questionable whether knowledge of an opponent's tactical and strategic thinking would necessarily lead a country to change the broad thrust of its own strategy or tactics, for these may be dictated by other factors – the availability of manpower for example. If Chinese military thinking consistently relies on vast resources of manpower, or that of the US on the value of heavy firepower to neutralise a defence, or that of the Soviet Union on the importance of massed armour, then the knowledge that an enemy places a higher premium on mobility and manoeuvre, or on tactical surprise, will not change the overall concept of operations of China or the US or the Soviet Union. The danger lies rather with the risk that in the great volume of material emanating from the commentators, someone may let slip a specific piece of hard information which could affect the way an enemy conducts a particular operation. The specific is thus more perilous than the general.

There is another reason for concern about commentary and speculation in the media on military operations and that is the effect on the perceptions of the soldiers actually fighting the war. Even if in fact the commentary reveals nothing, it may be perceived by the commanders in the field, and by their men, as giving away vital information. This could have several consequences. It could affect morale, by making the men on the ground feel that the media in their own country do not care what happens to them. It could also affect operational planning if, for example, a commander feared that his intentions had been disclosed and that it was consequently necessary to change his plans – even though such fears were groundless.

CONTROLLING THE COMMENTARY

These concerns – the risk of specific operations being compromised, or of potential damage to morale or of difficulties in operational planning – could be advanced as arguments for controlling the media. Before considering whether this would be acceptable in principle, we have to consider what measures it would entail.

First of all, it should be noted that the main substance of the commentary came not from the retired Service officers, but from the defence correspondents who were, on the whole, more willing to talk in specifics rather than generalities. The importance of the defence correspondents as sources of informed speculation and analysis is such that unless they can be persuaded to exercise restraint, there is little to be gained by seeking to control the commentary provided by retired Service officers. The weaknesses in the Beach Report proposals were noted earlier. The suggestion advanced by Sir Henry Leach, and apparently accepted by his military colleagues, that a panel of retired officers suitably briefed should be made available is probably also not a satisfactory solution. The media would be likely to distrust the members of such a panel on the grounds that they were being used to disseminate the 'official line', without being attributable as official sources. Also, if the members were given information not publicly available, there would arise the risk that they might, under the not inconsiderable pressures of a television or radio appearance, let something slip out. In any case, there would be nothing to prevent retired officers who were not on the panel being used by the media, nor would the creation of such a panel diminish the role and influence of the defence correspondents.

During the Falklands War, the undeclared aim of the Ministry of Defence, tacitly accepted by the War Cabinet, was to reveal as little information as possible. This is in line with normal MoD practice.[45] If the ministry wishes to maintain this attitude when future operations are in progress, it may be feasible – although perhaps not sensible – to do so. What is important is that the government's decisions on the release of information should be consistent and coherent. A broadly defined policy on the release of information should be worked out in peacetime when issues can be thought through to their logical conclusion and when the time can be taken to measure that policy against the likely demands and needs of the media and to ensure that the latter understand it. Within this framework specific rules can be worked out relevant to a particular context when a crisis or conflict occurs.

With regard to the commentary which interprets and speculates upon events, there are three broad approaches open to the government. The first would be that proposed by the Beach Committee in the event of general war – the introduction of censorship.[46] The likely speed of events in any future war and the sophistication and immediacy of modern communications must call into question the practicality of such a step, as the government has recognised in its comments on the Beach Report.[47] One military authority has suggested that the speed of modern armoured warfare is such that in a conventional war, the correspondent would face severe practical constraints on reporting because he simply would not be able to keep abreast of events.[48] Sir Frank Cooper told the HCDC:

> It is highly unlikely we should get anything as simple as the Falklands in a real shooting type war . . . In real life, in a European situation, I think this problem would be of a nature we have barely begun to appreciate seriously in Government or press, let alone with allies.[49]

It is conceivable that the only way the government could effectively limit unauthorised disclosure in these circumstances is by taking physical control of the media. This is implicitly recognised in the government's reply to the Beach Report which states that while, in a general war, the control of information should rest on an 'improved advisory service for journalists . . . circumstances could arise where additional powers need to be taken for the control of information'.[50]

A second option would be to follow more consistently the approach taken in the Falklands campaign, keeping official statements to basic factual reports on operations. This would imply that the government should take all possible steps to avoid stimulating speculation and comment in the media, but they would have to accept that these were none the less inevitable. The third possible approach would be to make available as much information as possible using official and military spokesmen within simple and clearly defined guidelines, such as not giving advance information on operations. This last would be the most expensive in time and manpower; it would be by far the most difficult to get right and much would depend on the calibre of the people responsible for making it work. On the other hand, it would go furthest towards meeting the public's right to information and the media's demands for material while reducing both the quantity of speculative reporting and comment and the undoubted sense of frustration felt by the media.

CONCLUSION: PRINCIPLES AND PRACTICE

It is of course easy for an outsider to propose what appear to be simple and clear-cut solutions to problems which in practice are a mass of loose ends and conflicting interests. The fact is that there are no easy answers to the issues raised by the frequently adversarial relationship between democratic governments and the media, although perhaps the former may take some comfort from the fact that the public seem on the whole marginally more ready to trust politicians than they do the press. It is worth noting that following the US invasion of Grenada, media complaints about misinformation, news management and deception were overtaken by a backlash of anti-media sentiment. The disrepute of the US media in fact saved the government from suffering the worst consequences of its mishandling of the information issue.[51] The Israelis, on the other hand, made considerable efforts to accommodate the requirements of the media but felt that the widespread and detailed reporting on their involvement in the Lebanon was unfair, and that their image and reputation suffered as a result.

These problems reflect the nature of the relationships between governments and the media. The BBC told the Annan Committee in 1977 that

> it was the BBC's responsibility to recognise that, as itself part of the nation, and the constitutional creation of Parliament, it could not pretend it could be impartial between the maintenance and the dissolution of the nation.[52]

The difficulty arises when the existence of the nation is not at stake, when the media do not feel duty bound to support the government. In the circumstances of the Falklands it was possible for Reuters to inform the HCDC, with no expression of regret:

> Reuters has no national role and no national position. We took no more account of any national interest, whether Argentine or British, in this conflict than we do in other conflicts.
>
> We obtained some information which may have had operational implications from sources in countries other than the United Kingdom and Argentina which we published.[53]

The limited nature of the conflict was such that the press could act in this way without fear of the consequences.

The Falklands campaign was unusual in the extent of the control it permitted the government to exercise over the flow of information, but that control was less than total, as was the government's influence over the media. The problems that were raised were not new ones. They have existed since the earliest days of war reporting and they are likely to be repeated in the future.

The difficulty which will face the government, the Ministry of Defence and the commander in the field in any future conflict is reconciling the public's right to know with the requirements of military security. The HCDC described the public's right to know as 'absolute' – not as limited by convenience, or by such concepts as the '*need* to know'. In order for people to exercise in a responsible way their democratic right to judge their government's performance, they *need* the fullest possible information about that performance. The limits which may be applied to the public right to information must be based on criteria which can be generally accepted by the public – although measuring such acceptance is not easy. In broad terms, people are likely to accept limits not only on information which would endanger the survival of the nation, but on a second category which carries lesser perils: putting the lives of citizens or soldiers at risk, gravely imperilling property or undermining the government's ability to conduct negotiations with foreign powers, to give some examples. As already noted, the public may well be willing to accept greater constraints on the publication of information in this second category than are the media – and it is the people who have the right to be the final arbiters in this.

When faced with specific items of hard fact – the location of a particular ship, the design of a new weapon system – the task of deciding whether or not publication is acceptable is relatively clear-cut, although even then government should recognise the considerable amount of information that is already available from open sources. To classify as secret material that is freely available can only bring the system of classification into discredit. When, however, the material in question is analytical or speculative, when it deals with such nebulous areas as possible tactics, or the balance of forces, it is much more difficult to identify the precise degree of damage that disclosure may cause. Setting down guidelines for preventing that damage is correspondingly difficult.

The natural tendency of the military and of officials must be to err on the side of caution, but even a formal system of censorship cannot be relied on to prevent every damaging leak. There is moreover the danger that caution could come to mean an unduly repressive official attitude to the dissemination of information – with such undesirable features as the suppression of bad news for purely political reasons. Even in peacetime, the broad umbrella of the Official Secrets Act permits the government to classify material which, if revealed, would be merely politically embarrassing rather than damaging to the security interests of the country. The greater degree of restriction acceptable in wartime could reinforce this practice.

The best solution, a compromise between these conflicting considerations, may be the most obvious one – to relate the degree of restriction laid down to the extent of the damage which disclosure of information could do to vital national interests. In a limited conflict such as the Falklands, there was little prospect of the media commentary damaging fundamental interests. In a period of more sustained hostilities, particularly where the United Kingdom itself came under attack, or in a general war, the resultant damage to the nation could be greater, and harsher measures might be acceptable to the public, although given modern communications, the steps necessary to enforce censorship would be so draconian that the proper functioning of democracy could be imperilled.

Perhaps a system which has both government and media complaining about the extent of disclosure by the latter and of restrictiveness by the former has something to commend it. Finding the balance between the interests of security and the requirements of democracy cannot be easy; if both sides feel the other is going too far, that balance may have been found. What is certainly apparent is that, in any future conflict, given the accessibility of many potential theatres of war and the immediacy of modern systems of communication, the problems raised by information-handling, and by the speculation and commentary surrounding operations in the South Atlantic in 1982, seem likely to pale into insignificance.

NOTES

1. See for instance 'Israel Attacked over Killing of CBS Crew', *The Times*, 23 March 1985.
2. Memorandum by BBC, HCDC *Report*, vol. II, p. 47.
3. Memorandum by ITN, ibid., p. 72. This particular complaint about the Israeli system was not widespread. Henry Stanhope told the author that during the Yom Kippur War, correspondents were permitted to publish material highly critical of the government, provided no military information was given away.
4. Memorandum, by the *Daily Mail*, ibid., p. 125. The *Daily Mail* was not alone in this attitude: ITN's Memorandum to the HCDC quoted an American media executive who thought that 'few reporters even try to evade censorship' and that 'most times it is not worth getting around'.
5. Christopher Walker, 'A Falkland Factor Israel has taken to Heart', *The Times*, 10 May 1983.
6. Jennifer Selway, 'The Return of the Living Room War', *The Times*, 30 March 1983.
7. 'The Battle over Press Coverage of Fighting', *Washington Times*, 31 October 1983.
8. 'US Eases Restrictions on Coverage', *New York Times*, 31 October 1983.
9. *Washington Times*, 31 October 1983.
10. 'An Off-the-record War', *Newsweek*, 7 November 1983, p. 83.
11. See for example: Roy Gutman, 'Deferring to Military when it Comes to Media', *Long Island Newsday*, 4 November 1983; 'Grenada: Free the Press', *Baltimore Sun*, 2 November 1983; Jessica Catto, 'Publishers Note', *Washington Journalism Review* (December 1983).
12. 'Picturing the Invasion', *Washington Post*, 26 October 1983.
13. *NBC Nightly News*, 31 October 1983.
14. 'In Wake of Invasion, much Official Misinformation by US comes to Light', *New York Times*, 6 November 1983.
15. See for example 'The Bite after the Bark', *Richmond Times–Dispatch*, 5 November 1983.
16. 'Pentagon admits Defeat by Press', *The Times*, 13 February 1984.
17. Beach Report, para 1.
18. Ibid., para 23.
19. Ibid., paras 98–9.
20. The conclusions are set out in para 234.
21. HCDC *Report*, vol. I, para 26.
22. *The Times*, 27 May 1982.
23. *Dan Rather Commentary*, CBS Network, 28 October 1983; 'A Journalist's Perspective', *Washington Times*, 7 November 1983.
24. See HCDC *Report*, vol. I, para 96.
25. Results of poll published – *The Times*, 23 April 1985.
26. Evidence to the HCDC, vol. II, Q1344.
27. HCDC *Report*, vol. II, p. 431.
28. Memorandum by the BBC, HCDC *Report*, vol. II, p. 41.
29. Memorandum by ITN, ibid., p. 79.

30. Bill Plante of CBS, quoted in 'On a Front-line in War for News', *New York News*, 29 October 1983.
31. Michael Tracey, *In the Culture of the Eye*, p. 153.
32. Interview with the author.
33. Letter to the author.
34. Interview with the author. Lee denies that his source was, as stated by Hastings and Jenkins, a senior member of the operations staff.
35. Memorandum, HCDC *Report*, vol. ii, p. 142. A similar 'impression' was reported to the HCDC by Jon Connell of the *Sunday Times*, Q856.
36. Memorandum, ibid., p. 123.
37. Memorandum, ibid., p. 70.
38. For example, the *Daily Express* (p. 98) and the *Sunday Mirror* (p. 108).
39. Letter to the author.
40. Two examples at least have come to light where official sources gave away information. The *Standard* of 14 June 1982 carried an article headlined 'Secret the MoD told Argentina', claiming that Radio Atlantico del Sur, an MoD-sponsored station, broadcast the news of the 'arrival of reinforcements from the QE2' on the night of 1–2 June. This was when the landings were still taking place, and was despite MoD's requests to the press to keep silent on the subject. According to Sir Frank Cooper, Radio Atlantico del Sur only broadcast information already carried in the British media. But even if this was simply a report of speculation, specifically drawing the latter to Argentina's attention seems to have been at variance with MoD's policy. It was also claimed that Rex Hunt, the former Governor of the Falkland Islands, broadcast information about troop movements on the Islands on the BBC World Service (Memorandum by the London Editor, *Daily Star*, HCDC *Report*, vol. ii, p. 113).
41. Letters to the author. As noted in the HCDC evidence, General Jeremy Moore was also cautious about claiming that the Argentine reinforcement of Goose Green was prompted solely by the media speculation.
42. Ibid. See also HCDC *Report*, vol. ii, p. 420ff.
43. Interview with the author.
44. Interview with General Jeremy Moore.
45. So reluctant are the MoD to release information that the author of this study, which was specifically commissioned by and for MoD, was for over a year refused sight of the attributable on-the-record statements made by official MoD spokesmen. Initially the request was ignored, then it was claimed that the statements 'were not available in written form' (letter from MoD, 13 June 1983). Transcripts of some, although not all, the statements were finally provided to the author at the end of April 1984, only two months before the study was due to be completed, with no explanation of how they had suddenly become available.
46. *Beach Report*, Recommendation (xiv), p. 57.
47. *The Protection of Military Information*, Government Response to the Report of the Study Group on Censorship, Cmnd. 9499 (London, April 1985).
48. General Martin Farndale when Commander I BR Corps, in a press conference on 28 October 1983.
49. HCDC *Report*, vol. ii, Q1858.
50. Cmnd. 9499, para 8.

51. See for example Alice Widener, 'The Mass Media: Our Over-privileged Elite', *USA* (October/November 1983). Harry Martin, 'You Can't Fool All of the People All of the Time', *Defense Systems Review* (November 1983): 'Grenada Casualty', *Chicago Tribune*, 27 November 1983: 'What the Media would have Done', *Washington Inquirer*, 2 December 1983.
52. *Annan Report*, p. 268.
53. Memorandum HCDC *Report*, vol. ii, p. 130.

Annex A: Sources

NEWSPAPERS AND PERIODICALS

Aviation Week and Space Technology
Daily Express
Daily Mail
Daily Mirror
Daily Telegraph
Financial Times
Flight International
Economist
Guardian
New York Times
New Scientist
Observer
Scotsman
Standard
Sun
Sunday Telegraph
Sunday Times
The Times
Washington Post

BBC RADIO

'PM'
Today
The World at One
The World This Weekend
The World Tonight

BBC TELEVISION

The Nine O'Clock News
Newsnight
Panorama

GRANADA TELEVISION

The World in Action

INDEPENDENT TELEVISION NEWS

The News at One
The News at 5.45
The News at Ten

LONDON WEEKEND TELEVISION

Weekend World

THAMES TELEVISION

TV Eye

INTERVIEWS (* with Professor Freedman)

Colonel J. Alford
Geoffrey Archer
Group Captain D. Bolton
*Sir Frank Cooper
Rear Admiral E. Gueritz
Julian Holland
Christopher Lee
Derek Lewis
Derek McAllister
*Major General Sir Jeremy Moore
*Sir Michael Palliser
*Hugh Pile
Henry Stanhope
*Neville Taylor
Andrew Tausig
Christopher Wain

Charles Lawrence (*Daily Telegraph* correspondent with the task force) also spoke to the author by telephone about his experience of war reporting.

Annex B: List of Main Commentators on Military Aspects of the Falklands Campaign

(with details of appearances identified)

RETIRED SERVICE OFFICERS

(* details taken from *Who's Who*)

Colonel Jonathan ALFORD, Deputy Director, International Institute for Strategic Studies since 1978; retired Army 1976. Appeared: *Weekend World*, ITN, Radio 4, *Newsnight*, and was widely quoted in the press.

*Air Marshal Sir Alfred BALL, Vice Chairman (Air) Council of TAVRAs; Military Affairs consultant, ICL; retired RAF 1979, former Deputy CinC RAF Strike Command. Appeared *Newsnight*, *Panorama*.

*Vice-Admiral Sir Lancelot BELL-DAVIES, retired RN 1981; former Commandant NATO Defence College; staff of SACLANT. Appeared: *Newsnight*, Radio 4.

*Group Captain David BOLTON, Director, Royal United Services Institute for Defence Studies; retired RAF 1980. Appeared: *Weekend World*, Radio 4, consulted by the press.

*Field Marshal Lord CARVER, Chief of Defence Staff, 1973–6. Appeared: Radio 4.

Admiral Sir Andrew CUNNINGHAM, British naval commander, Mediterranean, Second World War. Quoted in *New York Times*.

Colonel Gerald DRAPER, Professor of International Law, University of Sussex. Appeared: Radio 4, *Newsnight*.

Major Bob ELLIOT, International Institute for Strategic Studies. Appeared: Radio 4, quoted in the press.

Colonel Robin EVELEIGH, former Director, Army Operations; retired Army 1977. Appeared: *Newsnight*.

Air Chief Marshal Sir Christopher FOXLEY-NORRIS, former Chief of Personnel and Logistics; retired RAF 1974. Appeared: *Newsnight*, *Weekend World*, ITN, Radio 4.

Air Commodore Brian FROWE. Appeared: Radio 4.

Major General Nigel GRIBBON, retired Army 1972; former Assistant Chief of Staff (Intelligence) SHAPE. Appeared: ITN.

Rear Admiral Teddy GUERITZ, defence consultant, writer and broadcaster; retired RN 1973; former Director Royal United Services Institute for Defence Studies. Appeared: BBC TV News, *Weekend World*, ITN, Radio 4, consulted by press.

Admiral of the Fleet, Lord HILL-NORTON, former Chief of Defence Staff; Chairman NATO Military Committee 1974–7. Appeared: Radio 4; widely quoted in the press.

Air Vice-Marshal Norman HOAD, retired RAF 1978; former Commander UK Joint Airborne Task Force; Staff of Royal College of Defence Studies. Appeared: Radio 4, *Newsnight*.

Brigadier Ken HUNT, defence specialist and writer; former Director British Atlantic Committee; has held various academic positions. Appeared: *Weekend World*, Radio 4, *Newsnight*.

Major General Bob LOUDON, RM, retired Royal Marines 1975; former Major General RM Training Group. Appeared: Radio 4, *Newsnight*.

Vice-Admiral Sir Ian McGEOGH, Editorial Director, *Naval Forces*; author; retired RN 1970; former Flag Officer Submarines; Flag Officer Scotland and Northern Ireland. Appeared: Radio 4, *Newsnight*.

Colonel Neil MAUDE, RM. Appeared: *Weekend World*.

Air Vice-Marshal Stewart (Paddy) MENAUL, Defence Consultant; retired RAF 1967; former Director Royal United Services Institute for Defence Studies. Appeared: ITN, Radio 4, *TV Eye*.

Lieutenant-Colonel Colin MITCHELL, Chairman, Garrison Ltd; retired Army 1968. Appeared: *TV Eye*.

Captain J. E. MOORE, RN, Editor, *Jane's Fighting Ships*; retired RN 1972. Appeared: Radio 4.

Rear Admiral John NUNN, Editor, *The Naval Review*; Bursar and Fellow, Exeter College Oxford; retired RN 1980. Appeared: Radio 4.

Major General John OWEN RM, retired RM 1973; last post: Major General Commando Forces RM Plymouth. Appeared ITN, *Newsnight*, Radio 4.

Admiral of the Fleet Sir Michael POLLOCK, former First Sea Lord; retired 1974. Appeared: Radio 4.

Brigadier Dick PURVES, Director General, Defence Manufacturer's Association; retired Army 1975. Appeared: Radio 4.

*Vice-Admiral Sir John ROXBURGH, retired RN 1972; last post Flag Officer Submarines. Appeared: Radio 4, *Newsnight*, *Panorama*.

Air Chief Marshal Sir Alastair STEEDMAN, retired RAF 1980 previous posts: UK Military Representative to NATO; Air Member for Supply and Organisation. Appeared: *Weekend World*, Radio 4 *Newsnight*.

Captain Peter STEWART, RN, Former Naval Attaché, Buenos Aires Appeared: Radio 4, quoted in the press.

Captain Roger VILLAR, RN, naval consultant to Defence Manufacturers' Association; Editor, *Jane's Weapon Systems*. Appeared Radio 4.

*Major General Sir Walter WALKER, retired 1972; former Commander-in-Chief Allied Forces N. Europe. Appeared: Radio 4.

Rear Admiral Martin WEMYSS, retired RN 1981; former Assistant Chief of Naval Staff (Operations). Appeared: *Panorama*, ITN, quoted in the press.

General Sir Peter WHITELEY, Lieutenant Governor, Jersey; retired RM 1979; former Commandant General Royal Marines, CinC Allied Forces, N. Europe. Appeared: Radio 4.

JOURNALISTS

R. W. APPLE, Jr, London correspondent, *New York Times*

Geoffrey ARCHER, defence correspondent, ITN

Bridget BLOOM, defence correspondent, *Financial Times*

Charles CAWDREY, editor, *Baltimore Sun* (also appeared on Radio 4)

Jon CONNELL, defence correspondent, *Sunday Times* (also appeared on *Weekend World*)

Air Cdre G. S. COOPER, air correspondent, *Daily Telegraph*

Jackson DIEHL, staff reporter, *Washington Post*

Leonard DOWNIE, staff reporter, *Washington Post*

Harvey ELIOT, defence correspondent, *Daily Mail*

Michael EVANS, defence correspondent, *Daily Express*

David FAIRHALL, defence correspondent, *Guardian*

Maj Gen C. FURSDON, defence correspondent, *Daily Telegraph* (also appeared on Radio 4)

Michael GETLER, staff reporter, *Washington Post*

Keith GRAVES, diplomatic correspondent, BBC TV News

R. H. GREENFIELD, defence correspondent, *Sunday Telegraph*

Harold JACKSON, Washington correspondent, *Guardian*

Christopher LEE, defence correspondent, BBC Radio

Drew MIDDLETON, military correspondent, *New York Times* (also appeared on *Newsnight*)

Chris MULLINGER, *Scotsman*

Ellis PLAICE, defence correspondent, *Daily Mirror*

Doug RICHARDSON, *New Scientist*

Jay ROSS, staff reporter, *Washington Post*

Hugh O'SHAUNESSY, Latin America correspondent, *Financial Times*

Peter SNOW, presenter, *Newsnight*

Henry STANHOPE, defence correspondent, *Times* (also appeared on Radio 4)

Andrew THOMPSON, editor, *Latin American Newsletter* (also appeared on *Weekend World, Panorama*)

Christopher WAIN, defence correspondent, BBC TV News

Brian WALDEN, presenter, *Weekend World*

Desmond WETTERN, naval correspondent, *Daily Telegraph*

Andrew WHITELY, former Buenos Aires correspondent, *Financial Times* (also appeared on *Weekend World*)

Andrew WILSON, *Observer*

George C. WILSON, staff reporter, *Washington Post*

Nicholas WITCHELL, staff reporter, BBC TV News

ACADEMICS AND OTHERS

Patrick BERNSTEIN, Falkland Islander (knowledgeable about Stanley airfield). Appeared: ITN.

Harold BLAKEMORE, Institute of Latin American Studies. Appeared: *Weekend World*, Radio 4.

Admiral Robert FALLS, US Navy Chairman NATO Military Committee. Quoted in the press.

Professor Lawrence FREEDMAN, Professor of War Studies, King's College London. Appeared: *TV Eye*.

Bill GUNSTON, writer; consultant to *Jane's All the World's Aircraft*. Appeared: *World in Action*, Radio 4, widely quoted in and wrote for the press.

Professor Michael HOWARD, Chichele Professor of History, Oxford. Appeared: Radio 4, quoted in and wrote for the press.

Admiral I. C. KIDD, United States Navy. Quoted in the press.

John LEHMAN, United States Secretary for the Navy. Widely quoted in the press.

Guillermo MAKIN, Argentine academic writer. Appeared: *Weekend World*.

Kenneth MUNSON, deputy editor, *Jane's All the World's Aircraft*. Quoted in the press.

Norman POLMAR, American naval analyst. Appeared: *Newsnight*.

Anthony PRESTON, naval analyst; editor, *Navy International*. Appeared:
BBC TV News, ITN, Radio 4, widely quoted in, and wrote for, the
press.

Mike RENDALL, former Sergeant, Royal Marines (familiar with
terrain and conditions in the Falklands). Appeared: *Newsnight*.

Adam ROBERTS, Fellow in International Law, All Souls' Oxford.
Appeared: Radio 4.

Dr Paul ROGERS, Department of Peace Studies, Bradford. Appeared:
Newsnight.

Norman ROUTLEDGE, former quartermaster, 45 Commando, Royal
Marines. Appeared: Radio 4.

Manfred SHOMFELD, columnist, *La Prensa* (Argentine newspaper).
Appeared: *Panorama*, Radio 4.

Jim SHORT, writer on Special Forces. Appeared: *Newsnight*.

Dr William TAYLOR, Director of Political/Military Studies,
Georgetown Centre for Strategic and International Studies. Quoted
in the press.

Admiral Stansfield TURNER, US Navy; former Head of CIA. Quoted
in the press.

David WATT, Director of Royal Institute of International Affairs.
Appeared: *Newsnight*.

Ian WHITE, former pilot, Falklands Islands Government Air Service.
Appeared: Radio 4.

Philip WINDSOR, Reader in International Relations, London School
of Economics. Appeared: *Weekend World*, Radio 4.

Admiral Elmo ZUMWALT, US Navy. Widely quoted in the press.

Annex C: The Falklands Campaign (Operation Corporate): A Chronology

APRIL

Thurs 1   Intelligence indicates Argentine invasion of the Falklands likely by 2 April. Various diplomatic steps. Decision taken by Prime Minister, Foreign and Defence Secretaries to put troops on immediate notice for deployment to South Atlantic. Argentine landings begin at night.

Fri 2   Argentine forces seize Port Stanley. Royal Marines surrender after three-hour battle and are flown out the same evening, with the Governor. Formation of the task force announced.

Sat 3   UN Security Council Resolution 502 passed. Britain breaks off diplomatic relations with Argentina. Emergency Commons debate: Prime Minister announces that some ships are already at sea. Grytviken, South Georgia, captured by Argentines under observation by helicopter from HMS *Endurance*. Argentine corvette *Guerrico* damaged by Royal Marines.

Mon 5   Rear Admiral J. F. Woodward appointed to command the task force. Requisitioning and chartering of merchant vessels, including SS *Canberra*, announced to Commons. 3 Commando Brigade embark and task force (including HMS *Invincible*, HMS *Hermes* and HMS *Fearless*) sails.

Wed 7   Second Commons debate: Setting up of Maritime Exclusion Zone (MEZ) with effect from 12 April announced, also leadership and command of British forces. It is also announced that the task force will include HMS *Fearless* and five landing ships.

Thurs 8   Haig 'peace shuttle' begins. PM announces enquiry into events leading up to crisis. Requisitioning of merchant vessels *Elk*, *Salvagemen*, *Irishman*, *Yorkshireman* announced. 3

Parachute Battalion (the Spearhead Battalion) embark on
SS *Canberra*.

Fri 9   SS *Canberra* sails.

Sat 10   MoD describe task force as twenty-one ships including
support vessels.

Mon 12   Mr Haig flies to London from Buenos Aires. 200-mile
MEZ takes effect for Argentine vessels.

Tues 13   British press claim submarines have arrived off Argentine
coast.

Wed 14   Mr Haig in Washington. Argentine government complain
that British are violating Treaty of Tlatelolco by sending
SSNs to South Atlantic. Third Commons debate:
Composition of task force described as two carriers, five
guided missile destroyers, seven frigates, one assault ship
with five landing vessels and supporting vessels (including
SS *Uganda* as a hospital ship). It is also announced that
Nimrod aircraft are patrolling South Atlantic and additional
Harriers to be sent, 'nearly doubling' size of Harrier force.

Thurs 15 Mr Haig returns to Buenos Aires.

Fri 16   Media correspondents embarked with task force are refused
permission to land on Ascension Island.

Sat 17   Statement by Soviet Ministry of Foreign Affairs. British C
in C Fleet visits Ascension Island.

Sun 18   Main task force sails from Ascension Island (although
some elements, including HMS *Invincible* are subsequently
reported to have left earlier).

Mon 19   Mr Haig leaves Buenos Aires. Embarkation of 2nd
Battalion Parachute Regiment and supporting elements of
5 Infantry Brigade announced. SS *Uganda* sails from
Gibraltar.

Tues 20   Mr Haig in Washington. HMG told of latest Argentine
proposals. Dockers' strike at Hull delays sailing of SS
Norland.

Wed 21   Sea Harrier intercepts Argentine Boeing 707 on
reconnaissance near task force. SAS landings on South
Georgia.

Thurs 22 Foreign Secretary arrives in Washington to consult Mr
Haig. Publication of Statement on Defence Estimates (the
White Paper) postponed. Two helicopters crash while
lifting SAS of Fortuna Glacier South Georgia: all safely
rescued.

Fri 23   Defence zone around task force announced – Argentine
government warned in evening not to let its forces approach
the task force. Sea King ditched.

Sat 24   Foreign Secretary returns to UK.

verhinder

Sun 25	Mr Haig says retaking of South Georgia would not prevent settlement. Imposition of Air Exclusion Zone announced. Argentine submarine *Sante Fe* hit and driven ashore by helicopter attack: announcement made by MoD two hours later. British forces recapture Grytviken and Stromness, South Georgia, without suffering casualties. 180 prisoners taken.
Mon 26	PM's statement to Commons – omits mention of aborted SAS landing on South Georgia. Formal Argentine surrender of Leith on South Georgia. Argentine prisoner on South Georgia shot dead due to confusion about his intentions; inquiry set up.
Tues 27	Meeting of Organisation of American States (OAS) opens. Diversion of RFA *Tidepool* (about to be sold to Chile) to Operation Corporate announced.
Wed 28	MoD announce Total Exclusion Zone to take effect from 30 April.
Thurs 29	Fourth Commons debate, which includes some argument about tactics. PM announces that thirty-four merchant ships have been taken up. RAF Vulcans arrive on Ascension Island. Bad weather delays task force.
Fri 30	US openly sides with Britain, indicating failure of Mr Haig's mediation attempts. Total Exclusion Zone takes effect. Argentine announce their own exclusion zone. MoD confirms that HMS *Exeter* (which Argentines claim to have sunk) is still in Caribbean. Main task group reaches area around Falklands. Sea Harrier reinforcements arrive in Ascension Island having flown via Gambia.

MAY

Sat 1	Vulcan refuelled in flight from Ascension Island drops 21 × 1000 lb bombs across Stanley airfield, inflicting one 'hit' on the runways. Harriers follow later and also attack Goose Green airfield. Argentine aircraft on ground damaged. Naval bombardment begins, led by HMS *Glamorgan*. Warships are attacked by Argentine aircraft; two Mirages and one Canberra shot down, one Canberra damaged and one Mirage believed to be Argentine 'own goal'. HMS *Arrow* superficially damaged. Frigates and helicopters hunt for Argentine submarine believed to be in the area. Major General J. Moore appointed land deputy to C in C Fleet. First Special Forces patrols 'inserted' into Falklands Islands.

Sun 2   Foreign Secretary in Washington. Argentine cruiser *General Belgrano* sunk by Mk 8 torpedoes from HMS *Conqueror*. At the time of the sinking, the cruiser was escorted by two destroyers, outside but near to the exclusion zone. 360 believed dead.

Mon 3   Foreign Secretary meets President of the UN Security Council and UN Secretary General before returning to London with first Peruvian proposals. Attack on *General Belgrano* (but not sinking) made public in morning news. MoD learn of her loss. Two Argentine patrol vessels fire on Sea King helicopter. One (the *Sommellero*) claimed sunk, but now known to have survived; one (*Sobral*) damaged by Sea Skua missiles fired from Lynx helicopter[s].

Tues 4   PM's questions: reference to task force's defensive zone. Statements by Mr Nott in Commons on sinking of *General Belgrano* and loss of HMS *Sheffield*. HMS *Sheffield* abandoned after being hit by one of two AM-39 Exocet missiles fired from Super Etendard aircraft; twenty-one dead, twenty-four injured. One Sea Harrier shot down over Goose Green; pilot dead. Further unsuccessful Vulcan attack on Stanley airfield.

Wed 5   Statement by Mr Nott on loss of HMS *Sheffield*: in reply to questions, he hoped to give more details on the sinking of the *General Belgrano* – which was within the rules of engagement. Agreement on priority for Sea Wolf. Statement by Mr Pym on diplomatic measures. RAF Harriers arrive on Ascension Island.

Thurs 6   Peruvian proposals ('Belaunde–Terry proposals') formally presented to the UN: Argentina disagrees. PM's questions: media criticised. France stops delivery of Super Etendards to Argentina. Two Sea Harriers collide; both pilots killed.

Fri 7   Peruvian initiative collapses. Foreign Secretary makes Commons statement on diplomatic measures. Extension of Total Exclusion Zone to twelve miles off Argentine coast announced. 3 Commando Brigade sail from Ascension Island with HMS *Fearless*. SS *Atlantic Conveyor* sails from the UK. Deployment of Nimrod aircraft to Ascension Island announced.

Sat 8   Extended Total Exclusion Zone comes into effect. Mirage attack on carrier group driven off by Sea Harriers. Long-range air drops from Ascension Island to the task force begin. Media correspondents embarked with the task force reported to be unhappy at restrictions on their reporting of the 6 May Sea Harrier losses, subsequently made public by MoD in the UK.

Sun 9   Sea Harriers turn back Argentine transport aircraft and attack Stanley airfield. HMS *Coventry* shoots down two Skyhawks. Argentine fishing vessel *Narwal*, allegedly being used for surveillance, is attacked by Sea Harriers and then captured by helicopter. Sea Dart missile shoots down Puma helicopter. Naval bombardment of Stanley airfield. HMS *Sheffield* sinks.

Mon 10   UN Secretary General's statement on his mediation attempt. Peruvian President lobbies for ending of EEC sanctions. The *Narwal* sinks.

Tues 11   UN Secretary General seeks diplomatic compromise. Argentina complains to IAEA about presence of SSNs in South Atlantic. PM's questions – clashes over the media. Daily attacks on Stanley airfield continue.

Wed 12   *QE2* sails from Southampton with 5 Infantry Brigade, HMS *Alacrity* sinks Argentine supply vessel, *Isle de los Estados*, in Falkland Sound. Three Argentine Skyhawks shot down by Sea Wolf missiles from HMS *Brilliant*, and a fourth Skyhawk lost to Argentine anti-aircraft fire over Goose Green. HMS *Glasgow* hit by UXB [not announced at the time].

Thurs 13   UN Secretary General continues negotiations. Fifth Commons debate: chartering of a further nineteen ships announced. Defence Secretary winds up with account of *Belgrano* sinking. One Sea Harrier lost as a result of enemy action. BBC given permission to establish TV link from Ascension Island to the UK on a daily basis, but no permission for filming.

Fri 14   British ambassadors to USA and UN return to UK for consultations. Task force placed on active service.

Fri/Sat   Special Forces night raid on Pebble Island: eleven
14/15   Argentine aircraft destroyed.

Sun 16   Naval Gunfire Support party and SBS land at San Carlos. Sea Harrier attacks on Argentine supply ships in Falkland Sound.

Mon 17   British ambassadors to USA and UN return to USA. UN ambassador meets UN Secretary General. EEC Finance Ministers agree to extend sanctions for one week.

Tues 18   HMS *Invincible* sails on special task (according to a later report). Amphibious Group rendezvous with Carrier Group outside TEZ and begins transfer of men and material. Decision taken to set up Radio Atlantico del Sur.

Wed 19   Sea King crash: twenty-one dead, including eighteen SAS. Radio Atlantico del Sur begins to transmit. (According to a later report) HMS *Hermes* sails on a special task, and launches a Sea King helicopter.

Thurs 20   HMG announce that, since Argentine government has rejected 'all reasonable proposals', all the concessions advanced by the UK are withdrawn. Sixth Commons debate: mainly on diplomatic measures. RAF Harriers attack Fox Bay. Two Sea King helicopters lost. A further Sea King helicopter is found burnt out, near Punta Arenas, in Chile. Argentine newsflash claims invasion of Falklands under way.

Thurs/Fri 20/21   Naval bombardment of Goose Green and Stanley airfields and installations around Stanley. Diversionary attack on Darwin by SAS. San Carlos landings take place.

Fri 21   UN Security Council meets for UN Secretary General's report. Peruvian efforts to find a compromise continue. Seventy-two Argentine aircraft from mainland, and a small number of those based in the Falklands, attack British forces. Sea Harriers bring down nine and possibly ten Argentine aircraft. Total Argentine losses: three helicopters, five Skyhawks, four Dagger and one Pucara. British losses: five damaged, of which HMS *Ardent* sinks with twenty-two dead, seventeen injured, three helicopters (one on *Ardent*), one Harrier GR3 brought down by anti-aircraft fire, pilot taken prisoner. HMS *Antrim* and *Argonaut* hit by UXB.

Sun 23   UN Security Council still in session. Further Argentine air attacks on British forces. Argentine losses: four Argentine helicopters and one Skyhawk and one Dagger (five as a result of Harrier operations), one transport ship, the *Monsunnen* beached. British losses: HMS *Antelope* severely damaged by UXB which exploded later that night, killing two and wounding seven. One Sea Harrier lost in accident, pilot killed.

Mon 24   UN Security Council still in session. Mr Nott makes statement to Commons reporting San Carlos landings. Six Sea Harriers attack Stanley airfield. Argentine air attacks on task force. Argentine losses: three Daggers, one Skyhawk. British losses: three RFAs hit by UXBs, suffer slight to moderate damage. Order to attack Goose Green given and then rescinded [following intelligence of Argentine reinforcements].

Tues 25   Argentina's National Day. UN Security Council Debate ends. Mr Tam Dalyell MP is refused a debate on SAS operations in South America. Argentine air attacks. Argentine losses: three Skyhawks. British losses: HMS *Coventry* hit by several bombs and sank with twenty dead and twenty injured. SS *Atlantic Conveyor* hit by Exocet missile and abandoned, with four dead. HMS *Broadsword* hit by UXB, but no casualties and remains operational.

Wed 26   UN Security Council Resolution 505 adopted. Mr Nott makes statement to Commons on action so far and details of task force: over 100 ships, 25 000 personnel of whom about 5000 have landed. 3000 men of 5 Infantry Brigade following as reinforcements. Harrier has achieved dominance in air, combat. Attack on Argentine air bases not feasible. No evidence that Super Etendards have been refuelled in flight. Frigate and destroyers reinforcements join Battle Group. 2 Para begin to advance before first light. 3 Para and 45 Cdo advance on foot. Sea King crew fly out of Chile.

Thurs 27   Meeting of Rio Treaty states. PM's Questions: details of loss of HMS *Coventry* and SS *Atlantic Conveyor*. PM criticises public discussion about timing and details of operations. SS *Canberra*, MV *Norland* and *QE2* rendezvous at South Georgia. Argentine air attack on Base Maintenance Area at Ajax Bay. BBC Overseas Service refers to advance by 2 Para on Goose Green. One Argentine Skyhawk shot down.

Fri 28   British UN Ambassador meets UN Secretary General. MoD announce prematurely the capture of Goose Green. 2 Para with RM, RA and RE units, retake Darwin.

Sat 29   2 Para and supporting units recapture Goose Green: 17 British, 250 Argentine dead, 1400 Argentine prisoners. 45 Cdo and 3 Para secure Teal and Douglas. 5 Infantry Brigade leave South Georgia aboard SS *Canberra* and MV *Norland*. Argentine air attacks. Argentines begin using high-level attacks with Canberras. Tanker *British Wye* attacked. *Atlantic Conveyor* sinks while under tow. SS *Uganda* ordered in to Grantham Sound to evacuate casualties.

Sat/Sun 29/30   Eight Harriers arrive at Ascension Island from the UK.

Sun 30   Argentine air attacks on task force with Exocet missile (which missed) involving two Super Etendards and four Skyhawks. Two Skyhawks shot down. Major General Jeremy Moore arrives in the Falklands. D. Sqn SAS occupy Mt Kent.

Mon 31   Meeting of Neutral and Non-aligned states (NNA) begins in Havana. UN Secretary General presents new five-point peace plan. RAF Vulcan attack on Stanley airfield. Elements of RA and 42 Cdo move by helicopter to Mt Kent. 45 Cdo move to Teal with Blues and Royals. 3 Para move to Malo Bridge. Advance parties of HQ 5 Inf Bde land.

JUNE

Tues 1 Two Harriers shot down while attacking Stanley airfield: pilots rescued. Harriers destroy an Argentine C-130 Hercules believed to have parachuted special forces into East Falkland. HQ 5 Inf Bde lands at San Carlos. RFA *Sir Percival* moves to Teal Inlet. Accident involving exploding ammunition leads to casualties among Argentine POWs.

Wed 2 RM units capture survivors of Argentine special forces. Leaflet raids on Port Stanley urging surrender. Remainder of 5 Inf Bde begins landing. UK TV and press comment on UXB on *British Wye* despite agreement to refrain.

Thurs 3 RAF Vulcan lands in Brazil after difficulties in refuelling. Off-loading 5 Inf Bde continues. 5 Inf Bde HQ moves to Darwin. 2 Para take Bluff Cove.

Fri 4 Britain vetoes Argentine UN call for ceasefire. 5 Inf Bde continue to off-load. 3 Para in position on Mt Longdon, 42 Cdo on Mt Kent.

Sat/Sun 5/6 2SG embark for Pleasant Bay (Bluff Cove) on RFA *Sir Tristram*.

Sun 6 MoD announces 5 Inf Bde's arrival on Falklands. 2SG land at Fitzroy and 1WG embark at San Carlos for the same destination on HMS *Fearless*, but they fail to rendezvous.

Mon 7 UN Secretary General puts forward new ceasefire plan. Argentines claim in Security Council that Britain has offered the US naval and air facilities in Falkland Islands. Argentine troops on Lafonia surrender to 4 Gurkhas.

Tues 8 Two Harriers fly in from Ascension Island; one crashes on San Carlos air strip, putting it out of action at the same time as Argentine air attacks on the RFAs *Sir Galahad* and *Sir Tristram* at Bluff Cove. British casualties (not announced at the time): fifty-one dead, forty-six injured. Argentine air attacks on landing craft, six dead. HMS *Plymouth* damaged by UXBs, five injured. Argentine losses: three Skyhawks shot down by Sea Harriers. Most British infantry and artillery units deployed in forward positions around Stanley.

Wed 9 Loss of *Sir Galahad* announced, no casualties given. 5 Inf Bde regroup at Fitzroy. Argentines attack neutral tanker, the *Hercules*, in two separate attacks. ICRC observers land at San Carlos.

Thurs 10 Commons statement by Defence Secretary, giving details of action since 29 May. US protest at bombing of *Hercules*.

Fri 11 Mt Longdon, Two Sisters, Mt Harriet, Goat Ridge taken.

	Sea Harriers attack Stanley airfield. Mine-sweeping operations begin in Beukely Sound.
Fri/Sat 11/12	British troops advance to within five miles of Stanley; at midnight, battle for Stanley begins.
Sat 12	HMS *Glamorgan* hit by land-based Exocet, thirteen dead, ship still operational. SS *Norland* arrives in Montevideo with more than 1000 prisoners of war. Neutral zone established around cathedral in Stanley.
Sun/Mon 13/14	5 Inf Bde move into position: 2 Para retake Wireless Ridge, 2 SG retake Tumbledown Mt. 1/7 Gkas retake Mt William.
Mon 14	Ceasefire established. Surrender of Argentines on Falklands to Major General Moore.

Select Bibliography

HMSO PUBLICATIONS

Report of the Committee on the Future of Broadcasting, Cmnd. 6753, 1977 (The Annan Report).

House of Commons Defence Committee First Report 1982–3, *The Handling of Press and Public Information during the Falklands Conflict*, vols I & II, 1982 (The HCDC Report).

The Falklands Campaign: The Lessons, Cmnd. 8758, 1982 (The White Paper).

Falkland Islands Review, Report of a Committee of Privy Counsellors, Cmnd. 8787, 1983 (The Franks Report).

K. S. Morgan (ed.), *The Falklands Campaign – A Digest of Debates in the House of Commons 2 April to 15 June 1982* (1982).

The Falklands Islands: The Facts, Foreign & Commonwealth Office, May 1982.

Report of the Study Group on Censorship, Cmnd. 9112, 1983 (The Beach Report).

The Protection of Military Information, Cmnd. 9499, 1985.

OTHER BOOKS

Jonathan Alford (ed.), *Sea Power and Influence*, Adelphi Library 2 (London: 1155, 1980).

Edward Behr, *Anyone Here been Raped and Speaks English?* (London: Hamish Hamilton, 1981).

Shelford Bidwell, *Modern Warfare* (London: Allen Lane, 1973).

Patrick Bishop and John Witherow, *The Winter War: The Falklands* (London: Quartet Books, 1982).

Peter Braestrup, *Big Story* (Boulder Colorado: Westview Press, 1977).

Asa Briggs, *The History of Broadcasting in the United Kingdom*, vol. III: *The War of Words* (London: Oxford University Press, 1970).

Philip Caputo, *Rumor of War* (New York: Holt, Rinehart & Winston, 1977).

Michael Carver, *War Since 1945* (London: Weidenfeld & Nicholson, 1980).

Anthony Cave Brown, *Bodyguard of Lies* (London: W. H. Allen, 1977).

Winston Churchill, *The Second World War*, vols III & IV (London: Cassell, 1950).

Tam Dalyell, *One Man's Falklands* (London: Cecil Woolf, 1982).

John Ellis, *The Sharp End of War* (Newton Abbot: David & Charles, 1980).

Jeffrey Ethell and Alfred Price, *Air War South Atlantic* (London: Sidgwick & Jackson, 1983).

Captain A. Farrar-Hockley, *The Edge of the Sword* (London: The Companion Book Club, 1955).

S. E. Finer, *The Man on Horseback* (London: Pall Mall Press, 1962).

Robert Fox, *Eyewitness Falklands* (London: Methuen, 1982).

Benson P. Fraser, *The Broadcast Coverage of the Korean War* (Michigan: Microfilms International, 1983).

Maj. Gen. John Frost, *2 PARA Falklands* (London: Buchan & Enright, 1983).

Roy Fullick and Geoffrey Powell, *Suez, The Double War* (London: Hamish Hamilton, 1979).

Rupert Furneaux, *News of War*, (London: Max Parrish, 1964).

The Glasgow University Media Group, *Bad News* (London: Routledge & Kegan Paul, 1976).

Graham Greene, *The Quiet American* (Harmondsworth: Penguin, 1977).

Brian Hanrahan and Robert Fox, *I Counted them All Out and I Counted them All Back Again* (London: BBC, 1982).

Robert Harris, *Gotcha!* (London: Faber & Faber, 1983).

Max Hastings and Simon Jenkins, *Battle for the Falklands* (London: Michael Joseph, 1983).

Francis H. Heller (ed.), *The Korean War: A 25-year Perspective* (The Regent's Press of Kansas, 1977).

R. A. Hooper, *The Military and The Media* (Aldershot: Gower, 1982).

International Institute for Strategic Studies (1155), *The Military Balance* (London: 1155, 1981–2).

Harold James and Denis Sheil-Small, *The Undeclared War* (London: Leo Cooper, 1971).

Philip Knightley, *The First Casualty* (London: Andre Deutsch, 1975).

Daniel Kon, *Los Chicos de la Guerra* (London: New English Library, 1983).

James D. Ladd, *Royal Marine Commando* (London: Hamlyn Group, 1982).

Brian Lapping, *The Bounds of Freedom* (London: Constable, 1980).

Latin America Bureau, *Falklands/Malvinas: Whose Crisis?* (London: LAB, 1982).

Mary McCarthy, *Vietnam* (New York: Harcourt Brace and World, 1967).

Captain J. Moore (ed.), *Jane's Fighting Ships, 1981–2* (London: Jane's, 1981).

Chapman Pincher, *Inside Story* (London: Sidgwick & Jackson, 1978).

J. C. W. Reith, *Into the Wind* (London: Hodder & Stoughton, 1949).

Anthony Sampson, *The Anatomy of Britain* (London: Hodder & Stoughton, 1962).

William Shawcross, *Sideshow* (London: Andre Deutsch, 1979).

SIPRI, *Tactical and Strategic Anti-Submarine Warfare* (Cambridge, Mass. London, England: MIT Press, 1974).

The Sunday Times Insight Team, *The Falklands War* (London: Sphere Books, 1982).

John W. R. Taylor (ed.), *Jane's All the World's Aircraft, 1980–81* (London: Jane's, 1980).

Hugh Thomas, *The Suez Affair* (London: Weidenfeld & Nicholson, 1966–7).

David Tinker, *A Message from the Falklands* (Harmondsworth: Penguin Books, 1983).

Michael Tracey, *In the Culture of the Eye: Ten Years of Weekend World* (London: Hutchinson, 1983).

Jeremy Tunstall, *The Media in Britain* (London: Constable, 1983).

Captain Roger Villar (ed.), *Jane's Weapon Systems, 1981–82* (London: Jane's, 1981).

Evelyn Waugh, *Scoop* (London: Chapman & Hall, 1934).

ESSAYS AND ARTICLES

(Excluding newspaper articles identified in the main text and footnotes.)

'Argentina: Facts and Figures on National Defense', *MILTECH*, 7 (1979).

Major J. Bailey, 'Training for War: The Falklands 1982', *British Army Review* (April 1983).

Colonel A. Barker, 'Propaganda', *Army Quarterly* (October 1963).

Virgilio Rafael Beltrán, 'The Army in the 20th-century Argentina' in J. van Doorn (ed.), *Armed Forces and Society* (The Hague: Mouton, 1968).

David Chipp, 'Where Does Patriotism Begin and End?', *Jane's Defence Weekly* (3 March 1984).

Gregory R. Copley, 'How Argentina's Air Force Fought in the South Atlantic War', *Defense and Foreign Affairs* (October 1982).

Major P. J. Fitzpatrick, 'News Media and Military Operations – Democracy in the Balance', *Defence Force Journal* (Jan/Feb 1983).

Professor L. Freedman, 'The Falklands War: Exception or Rule', Paper presented to British International Defence Studies Association, December 1982.

——, 'The War of the Falklands 1982', *Foreign Affairs* (Fall 1982).

Globe and Laurel (Journal of the Royal Marines) (July/August, September/October, Christmas, 1982) passim.

Lt Col B. I. D. Gourlay, 'Struggle in Sarawak', *Marine Corps Gazette* (December 1965).

Stuart Hall, 'A World at One with Itself', *New Society* (18 June 1970), reprinted in S. Cohen and J. Young, *The Manufacture of News: Deviance, Social Problems and the Mass Media* (London: Constable, 1983).

Anthony Harrigan, 'Borneo Center of Crisis', *Military Review* (February 1964).

——, 'The Indonesian Threat', *General Military Review* (November 1963).

Michael Herr, 'The War Correspondent: A Reappraisal', *Esquire* (April 1970).

C. Richard Hoffstetter and David W. Moore, 'Watching TV News and Supporting the Military', *Armed Forces and Society*, vol. 5, no. 2 (February 1979).

Colonel W. V. Kennedy, 'It Takes More than Talent to Cover a War', *Army* (July 1978).

Guenter Lewy, 'Can Democracy keep Secrets?', *Policy Review* (Fall 1983).

Michael Mandelbaum, 'Vietnam: The Television War', *Daedalus* (Fall 1982).

General T. R. Milton, 'A Blessed and Troubled Land', *Air Force Magazine* (April 1982).

Major General Sir J. Moore and Rear Admiral Sir J. Woodward, 'The Falklands Experience' (Lecture, printed in *The RUSI Journal*).

Major General V. L. Moulton, 'A Brush-fire Operation – Brunei December 1962', *Brassey's Annual, 1963* (London: William Clowes, 1963).

Dr Juan Carlos Murguizur, 'The South Atlantic Conflict: an Argentinian Point of View', *International Defense Review*, 2 (1983).

Major Edgar O'Ballance, 'Revolt in Borneo', *Army Quarterly* (October 1963).

——, 'The Other Falklands Campaign', *Military Review* (January 1983).

Royal Institute for International Affairs, 'The Falkland Islands Dispute: International Dimensions' (London, April 1982).

Royal United Services Institute, 'The Falkland Islands Aide Memoire' (London, 1982).

Dr R. L. Scheina, 'The Argentine Navy Today', *Naval Forces* (April 1981).

——, 'The Malvinas Campaign', *Proceedings of the US Naval Institute/Naval Review* (1983).

Major E. W. Sheppard, 'The Military Correspondent', *Army Quarterly* (January 1952).

Colonel J. M. Strawson, 'Operations in Malaya and Borneo', *International Defence Review*, 12 (1965).

A. E. Sullivan, 'Getting the Story: Some Facts about War Correspondents', *Army Quarterly* (January 1961).

Robert O. Tilman, 'The Sarawak Political Scene', *Pacific Affairs* (Winter 1964/65).

Time Magazine, 'The Press', in editions 24 and 31 July, 14, 21 and 28 August 1950.

Christopher Wain, 'Television Reporting of Military Operations – a Personal View', *RUSI Journal* (December 1974).

——, 'Espionage – the Lasting Damage', *The Listener*, 16 December 1982.

——, 'How the Press Swallowed "a Whopper"', *The Listener*, 27 May 1982.

——, 'Mr Nott's Defence Policy', *The Listener*, 19 August 1982.

——, 'The Falklands – Britain's Albatross?', *The Listener*, 17 June 1982.

Gen. Sir Walter Walker, 'How Borneo was Won', *The Round Table* (January 1969).

Rear Admiral M. La T. Wemyss, 'Submarines and Anti-submarine Operations for the Uninitiated', *RUSI Journal* (September 1981).

Index